TRENDS TOWARD THE FUTURE IN PHYSICAL EDUCATION

John D. Massengale, EdD
University of Nevada–Las Vegas
Editor

Human Kinetics Publishers, Inc.
Champaign, Illinois

Library of Congress Cataloging-in-Publication Data

Trends toward the future in physical education.

Bibliography: p.
Includes index.
1. Physical education and training. 2. Physical
education and training—Forecasting. I. Massengale,
John D.   II. Title.
GV343.T72   1987   613.7'07   86-34282
ISBN 0-87322-103-6

Managing Editor: Peg Goyette
Production Director: Ernie Noa
Typesetter: Angela Snyder
Cover Design: Jack Davis
Printed By: Braun-Brumfield, Inc.

ISBN 0-87322-103-6

Printed in the United States of America

10 9 8 7 6 5 4 3 2 1

Human Kinetics Publishers, Inc.
Box 5076, Champaign, IL 61820

About the Contributing Authors

Elizabeth S. Bressan is in the Department of Physical Education at the University of Oregon. She holds a PhD from the University of Southern California and has completed postdoctoral studies at UCLA. Professor Bressan is an experienced teacher and coach at all levels, is a Fellow in AAHPERD's Research Consortium, has been elected to office in AAHPERD, and is a recognized scholar in the areas of motor development, pedagogy, and philosophical foundations.

John J. Burt is Professor of Health Education and Dean of the College of Physical Education, Recreation and Health at the University of Maryland. He holds an earned doctorate from the University of Oregon and has completed postdoctoral study at the University of North Carolina Medical School. Professor Burt is well published in the areas of health education and physical education, and is the recipient of several prestigious scholarly awards.

Michael J. Ellis is Professor and Head of the Department of Physical Education at the University of Oregon. He received his PhD from the University of Illinois and has worked extensively in the areas of elementary physical education pedagogy, motor performance, play, and leisure studies. A former Olympic athlete for Great Britain, Professor Ellis has held many leadership positions in professional organizations in both the United States and Canada. He is a Fellow in the American Academy of Physical Education and a Fellow in the American Academy of Leisure Sciences.

Donald R. Hellison is Professor of Physical Education at Portland State University. He received his PhD from The Ohio State University and is a recognized scholar in the area of pedagogy. As an editor, writer, and lecturer, Don has used his well-known humanistic perspective to enhance the quality of professional service and leadership that he has provided for NASPE, AAHPERD, and NAPEHE.

Shirl J. Hoffman is Professor and Head of the Department of Physical Education at the University of North Carolina at Greensboro. Shirl earned his EdD from Teacher's College at Columbia University. As an established scholar in the areas of motor learning, motor control, and pedagogical kinesiology, Professor Hoffman has been actively influential in the evaluation and administration of graduate programs in physical education.

John D. Massengale is Professor of Physical Education and Director of the School of Health, Physical Education, Recreation, and Dance at the University of Nevada, Las Vegas. He holds an earned doctorate from the University of New Mexico, with emphasis in social and behavioral science aspects of physical education and sport. Professor Massengale is a former college football coach, a past officer of AAHPERD, a Fellow in the Research Consortium of AAHPERD, and has served as editor of *Quest*. In 1982 he was a co-recipient of AAHPERD's Research Writing Award.

Alexander W. McNeill is Head of the Department of Health, Physical Education, and Recreation at Montana State University. He holds certificates and diplomas from institutions in his native Great Britain, as well as undergraduate and graduate degrees from the University of Oregon. As a scholar, Professor McNeill has earned the respect of his colleagues because of his analytical, clinical, and practical applications of exercise science, sports medicine, total fitness, and the general concept of wellness.

Margaret J. Safrit is the Henry-Bascom Professor in the Department of Physical Education and Dance at the University of Wisconsin, Madison. She received her PhD at the University of Wisconsin and is a former Department Chair at her alma mater. Jo Safrit's main professional responsibilities are in the area of assessment, measurement, evaluation, and research design in physical education. She is a former editor of the *Research Quarterly for Exercise and Sport*, has been selected as an Amy Morris Homans Lecturer, and has been elected President of the American Academy of Physical Education.

George H. Sage is Professor of Physical Education at the University of Northern Colorado. He completed his doctoral studies at UCLA where he specialized in the social foundations of physical education. He is a former college basketball coach, a former college administrator, and the recipient of the University of Northern Colorado's highest professorial award. Professor Sage has published several important textbooks, served as President of NAPEHE, and President of the North American Society for the Sociology of Sport. In 1985 he was chosen AAHPERD's Alliance Scholar.

Betty van der Smissen is Professor and Director of the School of Health, Physical Education and Recreation at Bowling Green State University. As a professor in the field of recreation, she has assumed an active leadership role as an officer in several professional associations. Professor van der Smissen is a true pioneer in the development and implementation of Sport Management degree programs. In addition, she has helped create the North American Society for Sport Management.

Thomas J. Templin is Associate Professor and Chair of Physical Education in the Department of Physical Education, Health and Recreation Studies at Purdue University. He holds a PhD from the University of Michigan and is a nationally recognized scholar in the areas of teacher preparation and teacher effectiveness. In addition, Tom has been instrumental in establishing and developing quality research and literature regarding the professional socialization of physical education teachers and coaches.

Contents

Preface

In 1983 the National Association for Physical Education in Higher Education (NAPEHE) decided to sponsor a special project. The NAPEHE Board of Directors, with the leadership of President Hally B.W. Poindexter, explored several directions, considered many ideas, and generally searched for a special project that would be timely and important and have the potential to make a significant contribution to physical education in higher education. Finally it was decided that the special project should take the form of a publication—a publication that would examine, describe, and analyze *real* trends, *real* movements, and the *real* future in the field of physical education. This anthology is the product of those efforts.

As an integral part of education, contemporary physical education continually attempts to renew its significance for a modern society that finds itself in a continual process of change and uncertainty. Modern times appear to be more and more complex, and a clear and accurate perception of the present often becomes elusive. In addition, any serious attempt at predicting real direction becomes even more elusive. Although change is always present in any complex society, the accelerated rate of this change is clearly becoming a misunderstood and disruptive force. Concern for this situation, which is reflected in all of our institutions including the whole realm of American education, is receiving increasing attention.

In the field of physical education there is growing concern that our acknowledged leaders know very little about the future and yet tend to explain too much. For years physical education has lacked the ability to predict, control, or determine its own destiny; it has been manipulated by people from all sectors of American society whenever a fad appeared on the scene. The field of physical education has been reshaped by the women's movement, expelled by educators during economic depression, ignored by educational reformers during their zeal for excellence, abused by television, and exploited by glamorous entertainers. It has also become a required course through the insistence of the military establishment, served as an arena for social unrest, and allowed health and fitness movements to be waged by unqualified entrepreneurs. This process of development has been whim, fad, and circumstance, little of it related to any planned direction or future.

I hope this anthology will counter the process of development through whim, fad, and incidental circumstance by presenting an accurate understanding of the present and then identifying and anticipating *real* trends, *real* movements, and the *real* future. The contributors to this text have attempted to keep the same frame of reference, an accurate and objective perception of the state of contemporary physical education—the way it is, not the way it could be or necessarily the way it should be. This frame of reference, then, served as a foundation for presenting the trends toward the future of physical education. The contributors have carefully considered authoritative consensus, examined probable as well as possible social consequences, suggested professionally controlled agenda, and attempted to structure alternative futures and contingencies.

Given that forecasting the future has evolved into a systematic intellectual endeavor, practiced by professionals from many different disciplines, the contributors have attempted to limit their suggestions to the most relevant and timely issues in contemporary physical education, especially those relating to professionalism, careers, and scholarly development. Trends and movements were examined with special consideration given to those that promised to provide a lasting influence, regardless of whether such an influence was perceived to be positive or negative.

Finally, this book was prepared from the perspective of *alternative* futures and rejects the very notion of a single *inevitable* future for physical education. The physical education of tomorrow can be created, or at least greatly influenced. Alternative futures can be created and then selectively chosen, which in effect becomes part of the dynamic process of altering tomorrow. Leaders in physical education can create alternative futures, select the appropriate one—which is really predicting the future— and then proceed to make their prediction come true. Such a process will never be easy, but in many ways it is better than having little power, legitimate authority, or control over the destiny of one's chosen field. Indeed, the very need for this type of self-actualization, self-determination, and professional destiny has fostered the ideas that have culminated in this anthology.

John D. Massengale

Considering the Future of Physical Education

John D. Massengale
University of Nevada–Las Vegas

It appears that futures research is here to stay and that physical education as a discipline is unprepared. Many institutions in American society have made futures research a priority item. This has resulted in a growing number of think tanks, institutes, and commissions such as the RAND Corporation, the Institute for the Future, the Hudson Institute, and various working groups whose titles associate them with the year 2000. But where is physical education in this process?

Physical education has no futures institutes, no think tanks, no futures commissions, no funded task forces that are specifically addressing the future. No one is attempting to forecast the future for physical education on a regular basis, nor is there a method for determining who could do this forecasting or how they should be selected. Occasionally an aspiring futurist or an organization of futurists will venture into the general area of physical education, typically through a limited consideration of health promotion, wellness, or leisure studies. Some of these forecasts are appropriate for education, sociology, recreation, or general wellness, but they are usually far from adequate for the general area of physical education.

This situation is further complicated by three factors. First, physical education as a discipline has done nothing to prepare professionals who might be interested or competent in forecasting the future, and for their part, very few physical education professionals have developed a serious appreciation for futures research as a bona fide scholarly area of study. Second, physical education as a discipline has been unable to distinguish between a real trend and a passing fancy, and there is little evidence that this will change in the future. Third, physical education as a discipline suffers from institutionalized helplessness, continually displaying its inability to accurately predict, control, or determine the professional destiny of its own members, which in turn greatly affects the quality and extent of services its members are able to provide society.

The Physical Education Futurist

What is needed, and being proposed, is a group of professionals associated with the general field of physical education who have the ability to conduct advanced research with some creativity. This calls for development of a group of professionals who can demonstrate an appreciation for the study of the future while continually displaying sound judgment. Such a task will not be easy for a field of study that has yet to determine whether it really is an academic discipline and still has trouble distinguishing between research and scholarship, while also perpetuating hierarchies and stereotypes that have no basis other than one's affiliation with hard or soft sciences. Professional physical educators have yet to be identified who, for purposes of futures research, might be able to fill this void in the current practice and procedure of physical education research.

A productive futurist in our field could be a professional physical educator with the desire and ability to upgrade the quality of forecasting, at the same time recognizing fads, bandwagon effects, and unrealistic expectations for what they are. The field of physical education has witnessed too many hula hoops, too many parachutes, too many movement movements, too many behavioral objectives, and most recently too many people from too many fields who proclaim themselves experts in health promotion. Futurists in physical education must emerge from the profession's leadership; they must be capable of reinforcing the scholarly acceptability of forecasting. Futurism in physical education must be established and strengthened as a scholarly enterprise, eliminating the type of ridicule that relates it to science fiction, astrology, palm readers, crystal balls, or the adventures of Buck Rogers. If futures studies are not perceived as a scholarly endeavor, then physical education will continue to be vulnerable to one fad after another.

Working futurists in the area of physical education could be employed at colleges or universities, or could arrange sabbatical leave projects with AAHPERD. They could also organize and structure a national physical education futures research data retrieval system that serves professional organizations.

Systems that would allow physical educators to select the most attractive alternative future could be established, since the study of alternative futures has been deemed one of the best methods of futures research in all areas of general education (Organization for Economic Cooperation and Development, 1972). People can establish some control over their professional destiny, although the extent of this control is most often associated with appropriate judgment, not necessarily with fact. According to one of America's most prominent futurists (Gordon, 1972), judgment is the most important ingredient in making forecasts, regardless of the method of futures research employed. Therefore, the selection of forecasters in physical education should consider the forecaster's judgment, which has yet to be done by the discipline or any of its professional organizations. We have tended to judge our professional leaders by their popularity and/or their professional competence, but not by their judgment capabilities.

As physical educators we have seen priorities change as our society has changed, and we have been unprepared. The result has been the evolution of a typical physical education/athletics management style that goes from crisis to crisis. As physical educators we have often been excluded from long-range planning and futures research, have had to adjust or react to the planning and decision-making of others, have had to negotiate in crisis situations that we did not create, and have been forced to survive in an environment over which we have little control. By establishing acceptable priorities, futurists in physical education could do much to alleviate this problem.

Any aspiring futurist with an earned doctorate in physical education will already have an area of specialization that could serve as a foundation for some method of futures research. In addition, expertise in at least one, and preferably more than one, area of futures research methods could be developed. For instance, historians and philosophers might specialize in trend extrapolation, sport sociologists and sport psychologists might specialize in research using consensus models or game simulation methods, measurement people could specialize in the use of input-output matrices or other mathematical models involving computer science; the discipline's most creative individuals might adapt their imagination to the art of scenario writing.

Regardless of specialization, any aspiring futurist must be able to critically examine and evaluate the past, or it will be impossible to learn enough from it to shape or change the future. An understanding of the past includes the ability to identify pertinent issues, events, and variables that are likely to have an influence on the future. A thorough understanding of past experience is one of the most valuable tools for forecasting the future. However, experience is only functional when a person uses this knowledge of the past as raw material from which to make estimates of the future (de Jouvenel, 1967).

Any futurist must be capable of using past experience without being influenced by personal prejudice, opinion, or intuition. Judgment of this quality also requires the ability to recognize which factors establish the most accurate forecasts. The integrity of any profession will require extraordinary judgment from its futurists. According to Hirsch (1967), when alternative futures are established and analyzed, futurists often guide the future while trying to predict it.

To be considered a futurist, one would normally be regarded as an expert by his or her peers in their chosen field. He or she would also be expected to demonstrate the ability to use consensus methods of research when gathering expert opinion. After all, expert opinion is admissable research data when the area of inquiry has no laws of causality, since it is often correct about likely results in inexact areas of study (Gordon, 1972). The use of expert consensus research methods in education has rapidly gained acceptance, especially the method that came to be known as the Delphi Technique (Dalkey, 1969).

The design, organization, and self-participation in game simulation types of futures research would be a desirable function of all physical education futurists, regardless of their personal interests or specializations. Game simulation can expose the real issues concerning a forecast, reveal the interaction of important variables, include human emotions that can affect variables, and improve the communication involving real issues. Game simulation can also be combined with mathematical models for prediction purposes.

Any forecast in physical education might also include a scenario, a narrative detailed description of potential developments and a type of future history. It might resemble science fiction but be based on events that resulted from systematic forecasting methods. According to Kahn and Weiner (1967), scenarios can call attention to alternative futures, force the forecaster to deal with often neglected details, consider the element of human interaction, and establish valuable, if artificial, case histories.

Higher Education's Future in a Changing Environment

Any concern for the future of physical education must be within the context of higher education, which itself is always influenced by an ever changing environment. Today, as in years past, there is a growing concern about whether academic communities will accurately perceive the changes and recruit and retain those faculty members necessary for the immediate future as well as the long-term future.

University faculties are a very select group of leaders in our society, who willingly assume the responsibility of influencing approximately half of our youth. It is the university faculties who educate our leaders, as well as those who teach others in our society. Faculties conduct most of our scientific research, advance our understanding of human behavior, serve as principal scholars of philosophy and religion, and preserve our cultural heritage through literature, art, and history. They help establish governments, analyze public policy, and teach the value of social criticism. Faculties form academic communities that provide social, recreational, and intellectual life for those being educated, and they must assume ultimate responsibility for the foundation of our culture (Bowen & Schuster, 1986).

With this tremendous responsibility should come a legitimate concern for the future, especially since our future is so closely tied to a continually changing environment. It is difficult to find a group more qualified to predict the future than members of the academic community, regardless of area of specialization. Faculties tend to be interested in youth (who, after all, are the future), have high levels of social responsibility, are usually highly intelligent and possessed of vigorous, inquiring minds, have broad-based educations, and are often easily motivated. Generally speaking, faculties are creative and possess exceptional ability.

Although faculties are probably the most qualified to conduct futures studies and share a growing concern about the future, there are characteristics of a changing environment in higher education that make futures research difficult. These concern the work environment of faculties and suggest an uncertain future. In other words, the condition of contemporary faculties is declining and the quality of their replacements is questionable, therefore the quality of futures research development is also questionable. There are various reasons for this. After considerable research and thought, Bowen and Schuster (1986) have documented many of the contributing factors and concluded that the rewards of an academic career are simply not what they used to be and that the quality of faculty replacement has become a paramount issue.

During the past 15 years academic salaries have declined 16.5% while other occupational groups have gained about 3%. Granted, money is not the only reward that is important to faculty; however, many traditional intrinsic rewards have also deteriorated. Faculty cite examples such as obsolete equipment, reduced government funding, reduced library budgets, reduced travel to professional conferences, a lack of involvement in professional organizations, and more stringent policies concerning sabbatical and other leaves. Faculty participation in shared governance has declined, and professional administrators have replaced academicians in many educational bureaucracies. Faculties are being diluted by a growing number of part-time instructors, who are teaching a growing number of part-time students. Faculty mobility has decreased during the past 15 years but the rate of faculty turnover has doubled.

Yet, even the most pessimistic demographic data are not nearly as critical to the future as the current outlook of uncertainty. The uncertainty surrounding the changing environment in higher education must be removed before any serious improvement can be made at studying trends and futures. Academic careers must once again project a clear focus as a worthwhile endeavor in order to attract the caliber of people needed to study the future. The academic community today has both a growing recruitment problem and a visible competitive weakness.

The removal of uncertainty will probably best be accomplished by reaffirming the traditional values found in the academic profession, while reversing the current trend that shifts institutional risk to faculty members. This trend, often attempted under the guise of expediency, is clearly in danger of becoming institutionalized (Bowen & Schuster, 1986). Not only does it affect the future of higher education, but it also affects the ability of higher education to predict and determine the future. To seriously address the future, higher education must firmly establish its ability to recruit, encourage, and develop the talent necessary to enhance the academic community.

If our society is to heed the warning signals and look for forecasts that are encouraging, then higher education, and physical education within it, must flourish in new ways in the decades ahead. Persistence must prevail, and it must become more accountable for essential resources as well as in the area of educational performance and excellence.

The Future Starts Now

Although organizations conducting futures research tend not to consider the general area of physical education, there has been some movement in the field from a few interested professionals. New courses and workshops have been designed, some existing courses have been altered. Curriculum interests have become more sensitive to the future, especially in the wake of Toffler's book *Future Shock* (1970). After the concern and excitement created by Toffler reached the field of education, a representative book entitled *The Educational Significance of the Future* (Shane, 1973) was published and futures research in the field of education appeared to be on its way to legitimacy. In the field of physical education, two professional organizations jointly sponsored a special thematic issue of the journal *Quest*, which was edited by Spears (1974) and subtitled *Quest for Tomorrow*, and Welsh (1977) published a timely anthology entitled *Physical Education: A View Toward the Future*.

Then, about as suddenly as it appeared, interest in futures research in physical education seemed to disappear. It simply died. Physical education had witnessed the emergence of one more fad, one more time.

Then, *Megatrends* by Naisbitt (1982) hit the market and spent 60 weeks on the best seller list, eventually becoming the nation's number one best seller. Interest in the future and futures research in American society was rekindled, and consequently, rekindled interest is again surfacing in physical education and sport. It seems that concern over the future is suddenly becoming more important due to the pressure caused by limited resources in physical education/athletics and to a renewed national concern for excellence in education.

The chapters that follow are partly the result of this renewed interest in the future and were certainly prepared from a timely perspective. The subject of each chapter, as well as the author chosen to write it, were selected with two of Naisbitt's (1982) major contentions in mind. They are, "trends, like horses, are easier to ride in the direction they are already going" (p. xxxii), and "the most reliable way to anticipate the future is by understanding the present" (p. xxiii).

One trend already has direction—the largest and only real peacetime fitness/activity movement that our country has ever witnessed. This trend is so strong that it is restructuring professional organizations, adding new dimensions to concepts of professionalism, and challenging accepted definitions of scholarship in physical education. This trend has been greatly influenced by the women's movement, which was ignited by subtle as well as overt acts of discrimination. In view of this trend, physical education has the potential to greatly affect the real working world of the typical teacher/coach by altering professional preparation, by questioning certification procedures, and by careful use of strategic political posturing.

Modern physical education is being influenced by trends that seem to suggest that the business of physical education is business; these are sometimes presented to the public under the facade of educational and social well-being by groups who are least qualified to make those decisions. This business movement has had far-reaching economic effects on many facets of American society such as the media, advertising, clothing styles, and discretionary spending patterns. In addition, corporate attitudes have become so acceptable to educators that the field of sports management has gained a considerable foothold in many graduate schools. Combined with the ever-present altruism of American education, this trend is suddenly giving new meaning and priority to the leisure revolution and has gained support from business, industry, the financial community, government, and religious organizations as well as assorted opportunists. At the same time, this business trend seems to be gaining support from para-medical constituencies that are normally associated with exercise science, wellness movements, health promotion, and holistic health.

The current trend is indeed an easy horse to ride, but rather difficult to guide correctly. It can only be done by professionals who have a thorough, accurate understanding of the present and who have continually displayed good judgment as described earlier. The authors of the following chapters are such professionals. They are not futurists, but they are all highly respected for their accurate understanding of the present, as well as for their judgment. Since physical education has no futurists, the authors will attempt to fill a void in the professional literature with their own brand of intellect, insight, creativity, and bravado.

The Future
and the Profession of Physical Education

George H. Sage
University of Northern Colorado

The desire to know what will happen next year, next decade, next century seems insatiable. Business leaders look for predictions about population trends and shifts in consumer preferences, young adults seek information about trends in occupations in hopes that the career for which they prepare will be a gateway to opportunity, and everyone seems fascinated with outer space and the mysteries it holds for the future. Some of the most popular books have been futuristic in theme (Huxley, 1932; Orwell, 1961; Toffler, 1970, 1980), and the past few years have produced a flurry of books peering into the 21st century (Asimov, 1981; Cetron & O'Toole, 1982; Kahn, 1982; Naisbitt, 1982). Groups of social forecasters have also been busy with futuristic studies under the auspices of private foundations and governmental agencies. Some of the best known are the Commission on the Year 2000, Forecasting International, The Hudson Institute, and The Futures Group. Finally, the publication of periodicals on futurism such as *The Futurist* and *Omni* indicates that people like to read speculation about the 21st century.

Physical educators, like other people, are curious about trends and developments that will affect them and their profession. Physical education is located in three sectors of American organizational life: elementary and secondary education, higher education, and private companies. The largest number of physical education professionals teach in the elementary and secondary schools. Physical educators in higher education, the second largest group, provide instructional physical activities for the general student and professional preparation programs for aspiring physical educators. A small but growing group of physical educators work in the private sector—in corporate fitness programs, health and conditioning spas, and sport clubs—helping clients enhance and maintain health and fitness. This paper will focus on trends and the future of physical education in higher education.

Demographic Trends and Higher Education

Higher education does not function in a vacuum; indeed it is extremely sensitive to various demographic factors. It seems useful, therefore, to review some of the most salient demographic trends and projections that will affect the future of college and university physical education.

It is estimated that by the year 2000 the population of the United States will increase from its present 237 million to some 268 million, and then to 306 million by 2036, a 32% increase in the next 50 years (Kahn, 1982; *Statistical Abstracts,* 1985). As important as the total number is, the composition of the population is equally important to higher education. The United States has had a young population in the 20th century because of the high birth rate for an increasing number of people of child-bearing age. This condition is changing rapidly, and the long-term trends for birth and death rates are expected to decline. Thus, the proportion of young people will diminish as the proportion of older people increases (Powell, 1985). The average age in the U.S. will rise dramatically from 31 in 1986 to about 41.1 in 2036. An increase of 3 years in life expectancy—to 80 years—between now and 2036 will cause the American elderly population to grow to more than one fifth of the population. Persons 65 and over presently number about 31.5 million; they will increase to about 39 million at the turn of the century and to 71 million in 2035 (Powell, 1985). Not only will there be many more older persons, but they will be healthier and more active than ever before ("What the Next 50 Years Will Bring," 1983; "10 Forces," 1984). Said one researcher, "People who are 70 will look as if they are 35 and people who are 100 will only look 50" ("What the Next 50 Years," 1983, p. A10).

While the so-called birth dearth will result in a decrease in the *proportion* of school-age population over the next 50 years, their actual numbers will not decrease. A report on school enrollments by the National Center for Education Statistics projects that enrollments will gradually increase in elementary and secondary schools beginning in 1985 and will continue throughout the 1990s, resulting in enrollment increases that by the turn of the century may surpass the peak years of the early 1970s. This enrollment growth, combined with a declining number of teacher education graduates, could produce a significant teacher shortage (Razor, 1983).

In the post-World War II era, the golden age of growth in higher education was between 1955 and 1974 as the percentage of 18- to 24-year-olds enrolled in college rose from 18% to 33.5%. Between 1975 and 1985 the number of bachelor's degrees awarded increased by less than 1% (*NEA Almanac,* 1985). Forecasts of future overall enrollment in higher education vary widely. The 1985 National Education Association (NEA) *Almanac of Higher Education* (1985) predicts that the number of college students is expected to decline about 10% by the 1990s; this decline is expected to apply to undergraduate as well as graduate students. But a projected increase in the enrollment of women and older and part-time students is expected to offset about half the decline of full-time students.

Some regions are likely to be more favored in enrollments than others in the next 20 years. The migration of people and industry has created decline in some regions and growth in others. Public institutions of higher education are adversely affected in regions of population stabilization, eroding tax bases, increased energy costs, and high unemployment, all of which lead to out-migration and decreased government spending. On the other hand, regions benefit where there is population growth, economic expansion, and relatively low energy costs. The shift in population from the north to the southwest and Florida will gain momentum during the next two decades, thus college enrollments will increase in those states. Naisbitt (1982) predicts that Florida, Texas, and California will see the largest population increases.

Physical Education Programs, Trends and Future

The Basic Instruction Program

The basic instruction program (i.e., the "service program," the "general activity program") is the program for which physical education was originally admitted to a place in higher education. The first college physical educator with faculty status, Edward Hitchcock, was hired at Amherst College in 1861 to establish a basic instruction program of physical education for all students. By the turn of the century many colleges and universities had initiated a basic instruction program, and over the next 50 years physical education increasingly became a requirement for graduation. By the late 1950s basic instruction had become a high visibility program in higher education; it had the support of college faculty, administration, and students, and was required in almost 90% of all colleges and universities (Oxendine, 1961). Then came a movement throughout higher education to reduce required courses. The physical education requirement came under attack and was abolished on many campuses. By the late 1970s it was required in less than 57% of the institutions, and on some campuses its very legitimacy was being questioned (Oxendine & Roberts, 1978). Some colleges completely eliminated it in favor of an informal campus recreation program, while others delegated the responsibility for it to a branch of student services.

In the past few years the basic instruction program has seen a revival, due largely to societal trends emphasizing health and fitness (Oxendine, 1985; Trimble & Hensley, 1984). The 1970s began with personal physical fitness being nearly inconsequential to most Americans and finished with fitness as a goal of recreational activities, employee health programs, personal lifestyles, and a focus of media interest; all of this has continued through the 1980s. Indeed there has been a revolution in personal fitness. The recent *Miller Lite Report on American Attitudes Toward Sports* reported that "almost half (44%) of all Americans say they engage in at least one athletic activity every day or almost every day, and 71 percent say they engage in a sport or physical exercise at least once a week" (*The Miller Lite Report*, 1983, p. 29).

A special report in *U.S. News and World Report* noted, "Richer and with more leisure time than ever, the U.S. has truly become a sport-crazy nation. In every age group, in every region, in every walk of life, a passion for athletics is blossoming" (Maloney, 1984, p. 23). More than 3 million men and women belong to fitness centers and health spas that emphasize physical conditioning. Consumer sales of exercise equipment topped $1 billion in 1985—more than double 1982 sales—and this is expected to hit $2.5 billion by 1990 (Carroll, 1984).

There is consensus among futurists that the fitness boom is more than just another fad. As one executive for a company marketing health programs noted, "I think wellness is in its infancy. There's a growing realization that wellness programs are the key to containing health costs" (Carroll, 1984, p. 3B). It is likely that interest in fitness, combined with the growth in outdoor physical activities of all kinds, will produce an enthusiasm on the part of college students for the basic instruction program in the future. Team sports activities will be overshadowed by individual sports, aerobic activities, water sports, weight training, self-defense, and wilderness activities such as backpacking, rock climbing, orienteering, and hiking (Trimble & Hensley, 1985).

Although commercial conditioning spas and corporate fitness programs will undoubtedly continue to expand in the future, the basic instruction program will have an important role. Promotion of lifetime fitness and wellness attitudes will become the main thrust for basic instruction. New methodologies and organizational arrangements will be explored. Independent study programs in physical education basic instruction will become more accepted as a way to wean students away from dependence on close teacher supervision and toward self-directed patterns of behavior. The move from teacher-controlled physical education experiences toward student-managed learning experiences will be accompanied by self-paced learning, designed to give students optimum flexibility to participate in physical activities of their own choosing.

The opportunities for educating, motivating, and directing students toward positive, healthful lifestyles through the basic instruction program appear unlimited. Jack Razor, executive vice president of AAHPERD, has articulately described the challenge to college physical educators:

If [the basic instruction program] is to be a viable, beneficial, and exciting part of the education offerings in higher education, it must receive increased attention and support from department chairpersons and college deans. The existence of these programs is directly related to the type and quality of leadership provided. The major challenge in the basic instruction program is getting the department, schools, divisions, and colleges of physical education to make a sincere commitment to the program and to identify creative, skilled, and committed leadership for the program. (Razor, 1983, p. 73)

If colleges and universities do not fund this program, students will likely demand it even if they have to pay for the classes. Indeed, a more recent trend is to offer basic instruction courses through a fee-based system (Brassie, Trimble, & Hensley, 1985), a form of funding that will probably increase throughout higher education.

Professional Preparation

Professional preparation in physical education began in the latter part of the 19th century, but it was not until the 1920s that the demand for physical educators became acute. By 1930, 36 states had legislation requiring physical education in the public schools. Meanwhile, the public system of secondary education was expanding rapidly. These two forces combined to create a need for thousands of physical educators. The supply had hardly caught up with the demand when World War II began (Snyder & Scott, 1954). After the War, renewed demands for physical educators necessitated the expansion of college physical education departments. By the mid-1960s supply had caught up with demand, and since then there has actually been an oversupply of physical education teachers.

According to Brassie (1980), more than 700 institutions offer the baccalaureate degree in physical education in the United States, 275 offer master's degrees, and 60 offer a doctorate. Until rather recently, professional preparation in physical education meant preparation for teaching in the schools. But during the past 10 years preservice programs have expanded to include nonschool and nonteaching specializations, or options, in sports medicine, sport management, athletic training, exercise and fitness, sport communication, and so forth. Indeed, this expansion of physical education into nonteaching areas has become a major trend in physical education.

Although it is never easy to account for all the forces at work in the changing contours of a field of study, three factors have been salient in the trend toward diversification in physical education. First, some physical educators in the mid-1960s began to conceptualize physical education as an academic discipline with the same overall goals as other disciplines (Henry, 1964), namely, scholarly study for understanding and advancing knowledge about the discipline. The role of college and university departments, according to this view, was to provide general education experiences for every student's personal-social enrichment and liberal education, professional preparation for persons who wished to apply the subject matter to occupational tasks, and an environment where professors may study and do research.

The second trend was related to student enrollment. By the early 1970s the massive expansion of public schools ended as the baby boom generation completed its formal education. Demand for teachers decreased, resulting in an oversupply. The number of physical education majors decreased as the job market for teachers dropped, creating enrollment and employment problems in departments of physical education.

The third factor that has had an impact on physical education has been the enormous expansion of health, fitness, and sport occupations over the past 20 years. This has created a demand for trained personnel in enterprises outside of education.

The disciplinary thrust, decline in employment opportunities in education, and new markets for persons in health, fitness, and sports occupations combined to recontour professional and scholarly directions in departments of physical education. One outcome of this trend is described by Ray Welsh (1983):

> In many physical education departments it is becoming increasingly difficult to find any physical educators. More typically, college and university departments seem to be staffed by sport psychologists, sport sociologists, exercise physiologists, kinesiologists, curriculum specialists, or some other disciplinary titled individual. At times it seems that our profession is overrun with individuals who are basically alienated from their own profession. (pp. 14-15)

Diversification in physical education has been debated furiously. Some claim that physical education has an identity problem, that it is "lost in the shuffle due to the very nature of [its] organization. Basically it is an organization without a function, leading to a proliferation of interests" (VanderZwaag, 1983, p. 68). Others call diversification a splintering or fragmenting of the physical education field (Hellison, 1985). Ginny Studer (1977) summarizes how many feel about it:

> At present [physical education] reflects the principles of separatism, specialization, and hierarchy. As a result, the field is fraught with dichotomies, fragmentations, and duplications. We have sports sociologists and dance historians, kinesiologists and philosophers, men

and women, amateurs and professionals, coaches and teachers, performance teachers and theory teachers, researchers and scholars, and so on. (p. 29)

What will be the future of professional preparation? It could be argued that this tendency of physical education to be something other than teacher preparation is the sign of a professional group that has lost sight of its common purpose and is in the early stages of its own dissolution (Hoffman, 1985; VanderZwaag, 1983). Or, it could be argued that the disciplinary aspects of physical education are valid, its diversification of professional preparation an appropriate response to changing social and economic conditions (Thomas, 1985). The second argument seems more in tune with the future, as it is unlikely that professional preparation in physical education will ever again mean only teacher preparation. The subdisciplines have matured to the point that several have spawned new occupational outlets for majors, and social and economic conditions call for professionals to fill a variety of roles in sport, fitness, and health occupations.

The notion of a single, central mission for physical education—teacher preparation—has been abandoned, and for the next 20 years programs will likely become more compartmentalized, both in the organization of academic subject matter and in the development of varied preservice options. In the face of this specialization and diversification, future college physical education faculties will be challenged to find ways of interpreting and synthesizing the subject matter of the subdisciplines and physical education practices as expressed through exercise, sport, and dance (Shea, 1985).

It is still uncertain how many jobs there will be in the private sector and whether physical education departments will have the expertise and resources to deliver what may be needed. The possibility also exists that other departments will claim jurisdiction in the preservice training of people in health, fitness, and sport occupations. Projections of lifestyles into the 21st century point to a need for more research and scholarship on wellness and fitness, disease prevention, and other health related activities; a byproduct will be the expansion of varied occupations. New careers in health promotion and leisure businesses will emerge, and with them the need for trained professionals.

The projected changing composition of student populations in higher education suggests that regardless of the types of programs offered in physical education, the curricula and delivery systems will have to be adapted to older and part-time students. As noted, enrollment trends indicate a projected decline in the "traditional" 18- to 24-year-old student, while older and part-time student enrollment is expected to increase (*NEA*

Almanac, 1985). Keller (1983) observed, "By 1990 . . . more than half of all students will be learning part-time, including some of the most gifted. Campuses will need to redesign their delivery of educational services, as some are already beginning to do, to adapt to . . . changes in the nature and attendance patterns of their clientele" (pp. 14-15).

John Naisbitt (1982), author of the best seller *Megatrends*, emphasizes that every organization must regularly assess its role when faced with changing conditions. According to Naisbitt, professionals who are not sensitive and responsible to change will find others filling their roles as they themselves become obsolete and unemployed. The same idea was expressed many centuries ago by Confucius, who said, "Only the supremely wise and the abysmally ignorant do not change." If physical education is to maintain its viability, it will have to be responsive and adaptive to the rapidly changing world of the future.

Any discussion of the future of physical education is incomplete without noting the unresolved question about the appropriate title for the disciplinary and applied aspects of the field. Some have called for abolishing the term *physical education* and substituting a title reflecting a field of study such as kinesiology, or professional and applied concerns such as sport management (Abernathy & Waltz, 1964; Husman & Kelley, 1978; Kroll, 1971; Sheehan, 1968; VanderZwaag, 1983). This topic has been debated vigorously for 15 years. As long as the disciplinary and professional preparation aspects of the study of human movement are termed physical education, the confusion about identity will be inevitable. The term physical education replaced the term *physical training* in the early 20th century in recognition of a modern philosophy and methods of education. Now, however, the term physical education is inappropriate for a number of the new exercise and sport disciplines and the diverse nonteaching preservice options.

Already a trend is well under way to use more appropriate terminology for the academic study and professional preparation programs being offered. By the year 2000, the term physical education will be limited to the basic instruction program and the teacher education preservice program. Several other terms will be deemed more appropriate, with kinesiology, exercise science, human kinetics, and sport management being among the most popular.

The Physical Education Professor

Physical Educator/Coaches

Departments of physical education in higher education are organized in either of two ways: The first and most common is a joint physical education–intercollegiate athletics department (Marshall, 1969; Sage, 1980).

Faculty in departments of this type usually coach athletic teams as well as teach basic instruction courses and, if a professional preparation program exists, they may teach in this program as well. The second type of departmental organization is one that separates physical education from athletics, hence the physical education faculty do not coach. Their role focuses on basic instruction and professional preparation. In some departments of major research universities, a few faculty will have graduate program responsibilities only.

It has been estimated that some 70% of college coaches—both men and women—teach physical education in addition to coaching (Sage, 1980). Most have their academic training in physical education. We will not examine here the connection between college physical education and intercollegiate athletics (for reviews of this historical connection, see Berryman, 1976; Lewis, 1969; Sage, 1976). Suffice it to say that the majority of college physical educators also coach.

Several trends are making it increasingly difficult to sustain the dual role of physical educator/coach. Specialization in all sports is increasingly eliminating the "sport season" concept. Athletes are choosing (or are being forced) to specialize in one sport early, and they train and compete in that sport year-round. Concomitantly, coaches are specializing in one sport and coaching it year-round. The consequence is that it has become almost impossible for physical educator/coaches to maintain interest or competency in physical education because they are increasingly pulled toward year-round coaching.

The proliferation of collegiate sports is making it difficult for colleges to employ full-time faculty members, assigned to the physical education department, to coach all of the institution's teams. Consequently, colleges are increasingly employing part-time coaches. Typically these are persons who make their living in other occupations; coaching is a second job for them.

Related to these two tendencies is the view on many campuses that the intercollegiate athletic program should be used primarily for public relations purposes. When this view prevails, pressure is put on athletic departments to step up in competition and have a winning team. There are two outcomes to this, the first being that the role of physical educator becomes more marginal as the coaching role becomes more salient. The second is that the departments of physical education and intercollegiate athletics are separated, making coaching a full-time job and severing it completely from physical education. Indeed, this has been the trend for the past 20 years (Marshall, 1969; Sage, 1980).

Another trend that makes it more difficult to maintain the dual role of physical educator/coach is that the body of knowledge in physical education is becoming more specialized, complex, and sophisticated. In order to remain current and competent, the physical educator must keep abreast of current research developments. This is virtually a full-time, year-round job, so the physical educator/coach who wishes to remain in physical education is often forced to quit coaching.

College physical educator/coaches tend to pursue career mobility patterns based on their coaching achievements, not their achievements as physical educators. This means that a winning coach will have opportunities to improve his/her job status, moving perhaps from a small college to a larger one, or at least a more prestigious one. For the very successful coach, who may aspire to coach at a major university, promotion to such a position will mean the separation from a career in physical education. Although many small college physical educator/coaches have this aspiration, relatively few ascend from small college coaching to a major university coaching position (Loy & Sage, 1978).

The future for college physical educator/coaches does not appear to be promising. As noted, there has been a long-term trend to separate physical education and intercollegiate athletics in institutions of higher education. In the first half of this century many physical education departments were established primarily to provide employment for coaches and classes for athletes (Berryman, 1976; Lewis, 1969; Savage, Bentley, McGovern, & Smiley, 1929). Between 1950 and 1975 enrollments grew and college sports prospered. The past 10 years have seen stabilization and retrenchment (Mingle, 1981). Keller (1983) has predicted that 10 to 30% of today's colleges and universities will no longer exist by the year 2000. Undoubtedly, most of these will be small colleges, where the physical educator/coach pattern is most prominent.

There are other factors that may reduce the number of physical education faculty during the next 25 years: first, a growing awareness that professional preparation programs in physical education are not being adequately served by national and regional accrediting agencies. Many people feel that these agencies for professional education programs have done very little monitoring to maintain high standards; many undergraduate and graduate programs are believed to be of low quality. There is increasing sentiment that professional associations, such as the American Alliance for Health, Physical Education, Recreation, and Dance (AAHPERD), need to develop accreditation standards that physical education departments must meet in order to continue offering undergraduate and graduate degrees in physical education. Within the past few years AAHPERD has sponsored several task forces to study the accreditation process, make recommendations for accreditation standards, devise ways for conducting departmental evaluations, and develop recommendations on department accreditation. If accreditation standards are formulated and a means for enforcing them is developed, it is likely that some departments will not meet those standards and will be terminated (Mood, 1983), thus reducing faculty positions.

Second, because colleges have found they can field athletic teams with part-time coaches, the physical educator/coach position is definitely in peril. Moreover, decreasing enrollments in physical education, combined with reorganization and more stringent accreditation standards, will likely eliminate some of the smaller departments of physical education.

Physical Educators in Major Universities

In departments of physical education that are autonomous units, faculty are able to focus on basic instruction, professional preparation, and research. There are approximately 150 universities of this kind, some 60 of which have doctorate programs. After several decades of growth and prosperity, the past 10 years have been rather dismal for physical educators in these institutions. The prolonged recession of the 1970s, decreasing state and federal support for higher education, enrollment declines, and internal departmental disputes about the mission of the physical education department have combined to create turmoil and despair in many departments. Some departments have been terminated (e.g., University of Washington) and others have been threatened with termination.

Prior to 1970 most physical education professors viewed themselves as teachers of basic instruction physical education classes and instructors to aspiring physical educators. They tended to be generalists, sometimes teaching three or four different courses. To be sure, each department had faculty who specialized in human anatomy, exercise physiology, or kinesiology (the forerunner to biomechanics); however, these faculty did not perceive their academic affinities with the parent disciplines but instead solely as the preservice training of physical education teachers. Beginning with the disciplinary movement in the mid-1960s, graduate programs in physical education became increasingly specialized and the graduates of these programs emerged calling themselves exercise physiologists, sport psychologists, biomechanicians, sport sociologists, and so forth. Because many of them had taken courses in the parent discipline of their specialization, they had been exposed to, and in some cases internalized, the goals of that discipline, namely that the main thrust of scholars of a discipline is understanding, explanation, and prediction and that these tasks are best carried out through research and publication.

As young physical education professors with this background were employed in departments of physical education, they brought with them a disciplinary orientation. The discipline-profession conflict and the diversification of programs discussed above were two of the outcomes. Since these issues will be discussed in more detail in other chapters in this volume, they will not be examined further here.

Some physical education faculty and their departments have actually prospered from the new diversification. They have reorganized their programs, typically offering traditional teacher preparation programs but also adding new nonteaching programs. A new vigor and optimism among faculty in these departments promises to position them as leaders into the 21st century. The key ingredient will be multifaceted programs that are relevant to the needs of an information society in which health and fitness considerations are prominent throughout the life cycle. In a recent analysis of future employment in higher education, Bowen and Schuster (1986) indicate that higher education will provide openings for new faculty sufficient to have a steady infusion of "new blood" in the next two decades. Indeed, they predict,

> The number of openings for new appointments to the nation's faculties is likely to be greater than is usually assumed. Our studies lead to the conclusion that attrition might average 4 percent in the years ahead to the late 1990's and might even reach 6 percent by the beginning of the 21st century. . . . At an annual rate of 4 percent, over ten years about 32 percent of all faculty positions would become vacant through attrition, and over twenty-five years 70 percent would become vacant. (p. 186)

Part-time faculty will likely replace some of the current full-time faculty in physical education. One of the most significant trends of the past decade has been the increase in part-time faculty, a 50% increase since 1975. About one third of postsecondary faculty are now part-time (Gangstead & Esplin-Swensen, 1982; NEA Almanac, 1985). Gangstead and Esplin-Swensen (1982) have predicted,

> If physical education part-time employment patterns continue to follow the trend established in academia at large, the part-time instructor will become more qualified in terms of education and training. As the supply of instructors continues to be favorable and the job market reasonably restricted, unemployed physical educators will be more eager to accept part-time employment arrangements in the hope that these temporary positions will develop into full-time jobs. (p. 111)

Career Mobility.   Career mobility among college physical education professors has followed patterns similar to those for professors in other fields. Without the doctorate degree, mobility is severely restricted. It is almost impossible to secure a tenured position; the highest rank one can hope for is assistant professor, and salary increments are minimal. The doctoral degree is the minimum for one who wishes to have a successful career in college physical education at the larger universities.

The choice of a department from which to obtain the doctorate is important to career mobility. Approximately 60 universities confer the doctorate in physical education, and they are hierarchically ordered on the basis of perceived quality or prestige (Massengale & Sage, 1982). Prestige based on doctoral origin is a powerful predictor of a faculty member's likelihood of being employed in one of the top departments. The lower the prestige of the doctoral degree department, the more likely its graduates are to obtain positions in lower prestige departments or in departments that do not have a doctoral program (Massengale & Sage, 1982). Thus, physical education faculty are essentially bound to the same career status attainment system as other faculties in higher education (Crane, 1970; Gross, 1970, 1971; Hurlburt, 1976; Long, 1978; Shichor, 1970). Career mobility is closely linked to the status attainment process throughout higher education. Over the next 25 years, prestige ranking of graduate physical education programs will change as departments experience new hirings and retirement; however, graduates of high prestige departments will still have the best chance of securing positions in the elite group.

Professor Income and Working Conditions. A chronic issue in higher education is the low salaries paid professors vis-à-vis salaries of other professionals with comparable educational credentials. Although most persons who choose a career in education do not expect to become wealthy from this occupation, nevertheless they would like to receive an income fitting a professional. Unfortunately, governing agencies (i.e., state legislatures, boards of trustees) have typically provided only modest salaries for faculty in higher education. Worse, over the past 15 years there has actually been a 20% decline in real income (Bowen & Schuster, 1986; Shaw, 1985), and working conditions in higher education have deteriorated considerably, especially in terms of routinization of academic tasks and the loss of faculty autonomy.

The future does not hold much promise of faculty in higher education raising their real income to any great extent. State legislatures are faced with increasing demands for money, while educational institutions must keep a careful balance between paying salaries, maintaining equipment and facilities, and being realistic about what parents can pay for their children's education. Therefore, political and economic conditions will not favor large increases in appropriations for higher education. The rewards of the academic profession have always been largely intrinsic, and that will continue (Bowen & Schuster, 1986).

In a thorough analysis of changing working conditions in higher education, Bowen and Schuster (1986) say,

> From our study of working conditions including our field visits, we conclude with considerable confidence that in many respects the conditions of faculty work have been slowly deteriorating. . . . with the deteriorating of working conditions combined with the slow ero-

sion of faculty pay and with the uncertainty of the future, faculty morale has sagged. (p. 135)

In order to redress grievances about income and governance, faculty in higher education have increasingly turned to collective bargaining. The National Center for the Study of Collective Bargaining in Higher Education and the Professions reported that bargaining agents in colleges and universities expanded from 277 in 1974 to 427 in 1980 (Douglas & DeBona, 1984). Shipka (1985) noted,

> During the last two decades, more than a third of all faculty and staff on U.S. campuses have turned to collective bargaining. This trend includes individuals from every imaginable type of institution—public and private, research and teaching, liberal arts and technical, single campus and multi-campus. That so many within such a self-reliant constituency have organized so quickly represents a truly remarkable achievement in the history of both the American labor movement and American higher education. (p. 3)

Although the number of institutions having collective bargaining agreements in the early 1980s has declined somewhat, some futurists suggest this was just a brief reorganization phase before another expansion occurs that will continue throughout the next decade. One factor that seems destined to increase the collective bargaining movement in higher education is the fact that faculty who bargain collectively receive higher salaries than their nonbargaining colleagues (*NEA Almanac,* 1985). The future of working conditions in higher education remains unclear; in summarizing their vision of future working conditions for college and university faculty, Bowen and Schuster (1986) see it "as being neither bleak nor bountiful" (p. 161). Much will depend on the national commitment to higher education.

Summary

The fascination with trends and the future is reflected in literature, the media and movies, and the popularity of organizations whose role is predicting the future. Physical educators are as curious about the future as anyone else because their careers will be affected by it.

Demographic trends will have dramatic effects on physical education. As the proportion of young people declines and the proportion of older people increases over the next generation, there will be fewer college-age students in higher education but more older students, part-time students, minorities, and women. Population shifts to the sun-belt states seems destined to continue, causing retrenchment in and even the closing of some colleges and universities in northern states.

After steady growth for almost 100 years, basic instruction programs suffered serious declines in the 1960s and 1970s, but growth has reoccurred more recently, due largely to a nationwide enthusiasm for health and fitness. Basic instruction programs show promise of being viable physical education components in higher education into the 21st century.

Diversification of programs in physical education has been one of the most salient trends of the past decade. The single-purpose department of physical education—the preparation of teachers—appears to be a remnant of the past. Subdisciplines within physical education are advancing the body of knowledge about human movement and, indirectly, they have spawned new professional preparation programs that are unrelated to teaching and coaching.

Changes both in athletic coaching and in the field of physical education have jeopardized the physical educator/coach position. Although some 70% of college physical education faculty also coach athletic teams, the year-round nature of most sports and the increased specialization of physical education suggests that by the turn of the century fewer professionals will be involved in the dual role of physical educator/coach.

Physical education faculty in major universities have had a tumultuous time since 1970. Decreasing support from their own universities, decreasing government and private funding, enrollment declines, and internal dissension over the disciplinary-profession issue have combined to weaken many departments. In spite of this, however, some departments have reorganized and rebounded with new vigor and optimism.

Career mobility patterns among college physical education faculty are similar to those of faculty in other disciplines. There tends to be a circulation of elites among the doctorate-granting departments. Persons who earn doctorates from one of the most prestigious departments tend to be employed in one of these departments. Few persons who earn doctorates from low prestige departments secure employment at a top university.

Low salaries, routinization of academic tasks, and reduction of faculty autonomy over the past 20 years have resulted in a growing interest in collective bargaining in higher education. Physical education faculty, like faculty throughout higher education, appear willing to organize to secure better salaries and improved working conditions.

The Future of Scholarship
in Physical Education

Elizabeth S. Bressan
University of Oregon

The best thing for being sad . . . is to learn something. Learn why
the world wags and what wags it. That is the only thing the mind
can never exhaust, never alienate, never be tortured by, never fear
or distrust, and never dream of regretting. Learning . . . is the thing
for you.
(Merlin's advice to a despondent young Arthur in T.H. White's
The Once and Future King)

Scholarship is at once the process and the product associated with
the activity of scholars. Scholars are individuals with naturally inquiring
minds; learning is a kind of expressive imperative for them. It is no casual
literary vehicle that finds images such as "thirst" or "hunger" for knowledge and understanding associated as descriptors for scholarly activity.
Scholars "need" to be engaged in the process of learning. Inquiry is their
passion. Discovery gives them their energy.

The relationship between scholarship and the two related processes
of inquiry (research and theorizing) is a delicate one. It is also a relationship that has not been defined with care and, as a result, has allowed
all three terms to be employed with progressively deteriorating clarity.
Scholarship is the most sophisticated form of inquiry. It entails rigorous
examination of and communication about the fundamental patterns that
underlie the premises upon which a body of knowledge is structured.
In other words, it deals with issues about the effectiveness of the paradigm
that serves to define and organize inquiry within a discipline. Scholarship establishes that paradigm, elaborates upon it, elucidates it, challenges
it, and may even put forth rationale for reconceiving it. In this fashion,
scholarship is central to the intellectual "health" of a discipline, because
it sustains dialogue about the nature of inquiry in relation to a discipline's
phenomena of interest.

Research, per se, is conducted *within* a paradigm. It accepts disciplinary premises, definitions, and ways of organizing inquiry. The results of research *may* be out of sync with the anticipated results predicted by the accepted paradigm, and thus suggest a possible paradigmatic problem. But because researchers have been educated in rigid traditions within that paradigm, they are not in a position to interpret what might be an anomalie and what might be a true problem. Of course, if a researcher has matured to the level of a scholar, the issue of paradigmatic inadequacies could indeed be addressed as a scholarly extension of a line of research. Most researchers, however, are not educated to be scholars as well.

Theorists, for their part, engage in theorizing, a process of inquiry characterized by speculation, deliberation, logic, and imagination. Theorists conjure up ideas about the structure of a discipline and prepare multiple possibilities for changing or adjusting that structure. They strive to suggest new perspectives on the discipline's phenomena of interest. Their education is more liberal or broad than the education of researchers because it is their function within a discipline to challenge the traditional paradigm with alternative interpretations about what should be studied and how it should be studied. Because theorists have concentrated on acquiring the skills of "idea-getting" rather than research into the credibility of ideas, they are not in a position to test or verify their ideas. If a theorist has matured to the level of a scholar, the support for a new interpretation or proposal for a paradigm could indeed be addressed as research to support and document a theoretical position. Most theorists, however, are not educated to be scholars as well.

Scholars integrate the functions of researchers and theorists, and in so doing create within a discipline a "whole" that is indeed greater than the sum of its parts. The presence of scholarship within a discipline marks its level of sophistication and maturity, for it denotes a community of individuals with active inquiring minds, who are ready to wrestle with the fundamental metaphysical and epistemological concerns that challenge all serious individuals as they attempt to understand the how's and why's of selected phenomena of interest.

The relationship between scholarship and the study of physical education is problematic. While the status of physical education as a discipline is itself a sticky question, even the disregard of that issue leaves two critical dimensions that must be regarded carefully prior to making any predictions about the future of scholarly activity in a subject field that has been identified historically as physical education, and now more commonly as "human movement studies." The first dimension is descriptive, and demands an assessment of the status quo in scholarly activity. Since the future is necessarily preceded by the present, positive and negative indicators about the future of scholarship may be evident in current patterns. These patterns could suggest the prospects for development. The second dimension is speculative. Because the future is to some extent created or at least influenced profoundly by choices, the question must be posed, "Who, if anyone, will choose to pursue scholarship in physical education in the future?"

The Status Quo—Scholarship in General

Naisbitt (1982) identified a current trend toward demystification of our knowledge bases as the industrial age gives way to the information age. Demystification is manifested as a reduction in jargon and a capacity for linking knowledge gained in one area of inquiry to knowledge gained in another. Through carefully designed systems for storing and retrieving information, productive interfaces are becoming possible among scholars as well as practitioners or even interested citizens. Access to these interfacing information sytems is becoming commonplace. There is a shift away from the "exclusive" nature of access to specialized information that has characterized scholarly activity in the past, a condition that has created an aura of aloofness, mystery, and even elitism around scholarly endeavors.

The trend toward demystification of knowledge bases suggests real progress will be forthcoming in addressing the problem of fragmentation that has plagued scientific forms of scholarship over the past few centuries. The advantage of scientific approaches is centered upon techniques for isolating parts or aspects of phenomena for investigation. With careful controls and a narrow focus, bits of information can be gathered. Theoretical activity then is pursued to assemble the bits into coherent descriptive or predictive statements about the phenomena. As productive as this approach has been, it has displayed a recurring weakness. Theoretical activity seldom has been able to capture the intricacy, the comprehensiveness, the "prior to fragmentation wholeness" of the original phenomena selected for study.

The problem of reversing the effects of the academic technique of fragmentation is seen by many scholars as an attainable goal in the coming decades. Bohm (1980) has suggested there are fundamental changes at work in the way we conceive the world. Mind and matter are no longer distinguished as separate entities. We are developing the capacity to look at the world as an undivided whole, in a state of universal flux where some elements are stable while others are unstable—a world in which a focus on certain fragments of experience is seen as useful in only limited contexts.

As scholars' natural fascination with conceiving and re-conceiving structures to facilitate understanding is sustained, patterns of interaction and interdependence among currently distinct knowledge bases will emerge. There is what Bohm called an "implicate order" within all phenomena, there to be discovered, and as scholars' capacity for sophisticated thinking expands, motion toward the discovery of that order becomes increasingly likely.

The level of sophistication and the accompanying global perspective on inquiry currently apparent among scholars from mature disciplines has been raised over the past 20 years by a field of activity entitled the philosophy of science. Inquiry within this field has been focused on questions about the nature of discovery, revolutions in theoretical conceptions of reality, the relationship among the different modes of scientific and philosophical methods, and an evaluation of the role of inquiry in human existence. Philosophy of science is a kind of self-study undertaken by scholars on the processes of inquiry that influence the doing of scholarship. From this self-study, an understanding about how human knowledge and understanding develops has emerged which will provide a texture conducive to the continued evolution of scholarship.

This texture may best be summarized as a recognition and acceptance of what Kuhn (1977) called "the essential tension," a condition that must be present in all sustained, productive scholarly pursuits. This tension is created through individuals within a discipline engaging in both convergent and divergent thinking. Convergent thinking entails the acceptance of a paradigm or theoretical framework to structure inquiry. From this acceptance or consensus about how phenomena should be conceived for study, approved methods of inquiry are applied to produce evidence and insights congruent with the initial paradigm or framework. It is as a result of rigorous convergent thinking that progress is made in the elaboration and refinement of theories. Research, and all of the progress it brings in our store of knowledge, is a function of convergent thinking.

Divergent thinking entails the ability to generate new paradigms or frameworks to explain or describe phenomena once the traditionally accepted designs have been found inadequate. Theorizing is a function of divergent thinking. The irony of the relationship is that only through convergent thinking (research) can inadequacy be discovered, and only through divergent thinking (theorizing) can it be resolved. While these two thought processes are fundamentally different, both are prerequisites to the development of a sound body of knowledge. A scholar not only must respect both processes and understand when each is called for, but must also have mastered engaging in *both* of them.

It is with this recognition of the scholar's intellectual flexibility and maturity that an important distinction may be made. Researchers have mastered convergent thinking. They are committed to a traditional paradigm and approaches to data gathering and verification. Their commitment is a product of their formal preparation—a rigid education/training program within the tradition they have come to embrace. Theoreticians have mastered divergent thinking. They have a propensity for re-conceiving designs, and for taking new perspectives in proposing paradigms to describe and explain phenomena. They have a commitment to produce change as a result of their formal preparation—a liberal, broad background in a variety of paradigms focused on a variety of phenomena.

Scholars have mastered both convergent and divergent thinking, suggesting that not only are they conceptually flexible individuals, but also that they are probably older. It takes a substantial amount of time to have participated in both a rigid education and a liberalizing one. "Wonderkinds" are researchers or theoreticians, not scholars. Concep-tual maturity is also the hallmark of scholars. Knowing when to sustain work within a traditional paradigm and when to break with tradition is a question of judgment, the capacity to recognize whether the source of failure within a line of inquiry is in the traditional paradigm or within some other aspect of the process.

Mature disciplines organized to study identifiable phenomena of in-terest recognize researchers, theoreticians, *and* scholars among their mem-bers. Cultivation of all three roles is a way of cultivating the "essential tension" that drives sound and productive inquiry. The formal study of the philosophy of science has revealed this pattern, and less mature dis-ciplines are now able to use it as an exemplar to guide their own develop-ment. This recognition of progressive levels of development within the processes of inquiry suggest that newer disciplines can choose a pattern of interaction among members that will lead toward a future of accelerat-ed maturity.

There are several other current signs of change within disciplined inquiry in general that support the notion that the future will be a more sophisticated one, and consequently a more productive one. Kuhn (1977) once again made an observation that is helpful. He noted there is evi-dence within the personnel practices of universities that suggests more and more scholars are receiving appointments and recognition. This differs from the pattern of the previous decades when researchers were the primary recipients of attention. Such a one-sided interpretation served to reduce tension in disciplines, thus adversely affecting disciplinary de-velopment.

Kuhn (1977) also contended that previously ignored aspects of phenomena are becoming acceptable foci for inquiry, a circumstance that suggests an intellectual climate in which discrepancies and differences are valued signals for guiding future inquiry, rather than annoying anoma-lies to be discounted as unmanageable or irrelevant. Such a receptive cli-mate is compatible with the doing of scholarship.

In general terms, then, the future for scholarship looks bright. Demystification, the recognition of wholeness and an implicate order, an understanding of the developmental levels experienced within the evolution of disciplines, and tangible signs of a pro-scholarship environment in universities brightens prospects for the present and the future. But that brightness is for the future of scholarship in general—for the majority of disciplines. What about scholarship in physical education?

The Status Quo—Physical Education

The advances in the systematization information processing, storage, and retrieval systems that are projected to contribute to demystification in the knowledge bases of many disciplines certainly will be available to those who study physical education. The question is whether physical educators will be able to mobilize themselves to employ those advantages. Physical educators have yet to define who they are and what they study. Is physical education a professional field in which prescriptive theories and practices are developed to deliver "educationally sound" sport, dance, and exercise programs to school-age children? Is physical education a developing academic discipline that studies human movement phenomena, regardless of the context of the performance? Or is physical education somewhere in between these two extremes?

Without an identity, demystification is out of the question; there is no coherent focus around which to organize demystification. Part of the historical difficulty surrounding the lack of definition for physical education can be found in efforts to embrace both the academic study of human movement *and* the design and delivery of professional services within the same disciplinary structure. Academic or propositional knowledge is of a different type than professional or procedural knowledge. While there are disciplinary patterns that can accommodate this diversity, physical educators have not yet sought them out. Instead, they have tried to adopt patterns evident in either purely academic disciplines *or* in purely professional fields.

The outcome of this identity crisis has been the firm establishment of a fragmented assemblage of areas for study rather than a coherent structure for scholarship. This state is referred to as the preconsensus stage in the development of disciplines. The blind allegiance with which fragmentation is embraced is worrisome to individuals concerned with the future of physical education. The theoretical quagmire that is the disciplinary status of physical education will persist only as long as economic and political conditions allow it to do so. If any established or mature discipline were to reconceive of its theoretical structure so that human movement performance became a part of its focus, the academic efforts now housed within physical education would be absorbed quickly into that discipline. If any currently functional profession were to choose to include the educative, therapeutic, or recreative purposes of sport, dance, or exercise within its realm of practice, all professional concerns and activities now maintained by physical education would disappear in a similar fashion. The current demeanor among physical educators seems to be a careless one, individuals sitting within their own cliques . . . waiting for Godot.

The decision to wait for the future may be attributed to several complicated disciplinary issues. The first involves the complexity of human movement phenomena and the traditional conceptual difficulties wrought by subsequent introduction of the intentionally created forms of sport, dance, and exercise. Every dimension of human "being"—physical, social, emotional, existential, is an integral feature within the performance of sport, dance, and exercise forms. Added to this multidimensional recognition is the notion that involvement in sport, dance, and exercise forms can be facilitated somehow; in fact, if the process of facilitation is carefully organized, individual performers come away with experiences that have a profoundly positive impact on their development as persons.

Whether the act of moving is studied (academic knowledge) or the process of facilitating the moving is studied (professional knowledge), the complexity of moving as a disciplinary focus is apparent. The study of complex wholes is something scholars in mature disciplines are just beginning to resolve. Because physical education is so immature as a field of inquiry (it is bold to refer to it as a discipline), its members have yet to confront the complexity issue. Its members usually identify themselves with single roles as either practitioners or academicians. Academicians identify themselves as researchers or theoreticians. Few if any scholars are evident. The future of scholarship is based upon the structure of a discipline. The nature of that structure is a challenge that demands the intellectual flexibility of scholars. Without scholars, the future bodes perpetual disciplinary immaturity or disciplinary disappearance for physical education.

Disciplinary immaturity is a natural stage in development, so it is to be recognized and dealt with rather than denied and ignored. To date there seems to be little serious recognition of this issue among physical educators, much less any attempts to deal with it. Within universities, researchers seem to receive support, practitioners are tolerated, and theoreticians are scarce or nonexistent. In graduate programs, where one would hope future scholars are receiving their preparation, philosophy of science is not studied and the speculative theoretical activity associated with divergent thinking often is ignored entirely. Study within a single dimension of human movement phenomena, such as the physiological or social psychological dimension, is encouraged early in students' careers. Convergent thinking is not just prized, but it is put forth to students as the only recognized way to approach problem-solving.

Some cracks are beginning to appear in this facade of comfort with convergent approaches. Individuals studying the physiological parameters of moving are increasingly interested in the psychological states that influence performance. Individuals who focus on self-concept from the social psychological perspective show a marked interest in metaphysical questions surrounding the mind–body relationship—long a concern of individuals who study from the philosophical perspective. Biomechanists are expanding their studies toward questions about professional procedures for coaching and teaching.

However, there are also some discouraging signs. Individuals studying the professional practice of teaching physical education are just beginning to pursue fragmentation in earnest. They have identified something called teacher behavior, isolated it from the content being taught, the performers being helped, and the identified educative purposes of a physical education experience. Under the rubric of pedagogy, research is conducted on small aspects of the actions associated with teaching. This means that the body of knowledge being generated is without context. This immature stage of development is normal, but once again it is worrisome to physical educators concerned with understanding teaching, learning, and physical education.

But, at least there are flares of interest, and although these flares promoting a more integrated view of moving are not evidence of truly divergent thinking, they do suggest an intellectual restlessness with the current paradigm that divides the study of human moving into neat and narrow categories for research. Physical education is in a preconsensus developmental stage (the "neat" categories are not fully agreed upon and the relationship among them has yet to be determined substantively). The frustrations encountered by conscientious and capable researchers may lead them ultimately to engage in divergent thinking. It is only through divergent thinking that a new paradigm for regarding physical education and human moving can be created. It is only through such a creation, followed by a new generation of convergent thinking, that the preconsensus stage can be left behind.

Future Possibilities Within Physical Education

If physical educators will choose to develop the manner in which they engage in inquiry in concert with the patterns of development that are reflected in other disciplines, there is every reason to expect that a holistic theoretical paradigm for physical education will emerge. It will emerge because, in choosing to develop rather than simply exist, physical educators will have chosen to encourage and reward scholarship—*real scholarship*—sophisticated strides forward in a body of knowledge that reflects a facile employment of convergent and divergent thinking—researching and theorizing. If the scholarship is sophisticated, it also will incorporate the practical concerns of professional practice in the paradigm, *if* physical educators will make the choice.

If physical educators will allow themselves to grow beyond an antiquated mind–body dualism that is evident in traditional Western cultural conceptions, the holistic view of mind and moving found in other cultures may provide the leverage necessary to break the fragmented research oriented hysteria that dominates current thinking. The sharp mechanistic distinctions that have made the industrial age "work" will be abandoned in the future in favor of the integrated systems view that will help transform our culture to the information age. Current scholarship on cognitive and neurophysiological involvement in motor performance suggests a mechanistic conception of the body is productive, but a mechanistic conception of "moving" is too limiting (Gardner, 1983). As the holistic and integrated nature of moving is increasingly accepted, strides in understanding physical education will become possible, *if* physical educators will make the choice.

The pivotal question upon which hinges the future of scholarship in physical education is, who will make the choices and what kinds of choices will they make? The current disciplinary status of physical education discourages scholarship, thus inhibiting the development of scholars. Polanyi (1946) drew an interesting profile of a scholarly community. He contended that such a community practiced free discussion and that its members were devoted to the proposition that

1. Truth exists;
2. All members of the community love it;
3. They all feel obliged to pursue it; and
4. They all are, in fact, capable of pursuing it.

In terms of the historical development of physical education, there may have been a time when there was almost a community of scholars involved in studying it. Certainly individuals the caliber of Hetherington, Abernathy, and Metheny meet the first three criteria suggested by Polanyi. Indeed, many of their contemporaries would meet those criteria as well. Between 1920 and 1960 there was at least a "consensus of conscience" about what physical education was all about. This consensus produced a body of literature that explored vigorously the purposes and processes of physical education.

Unfortunately, the capability to pursue truth is tied to a level of sophistication in theorizing (which these individuals were able to manifest) *and* a level of rigor in research. It is in the area of research that the pursuit of truth about human moving always has broken down. The realization in the 1960s that lack of research expertise was killing any chances of disciplinary development for physical education contributed to the violent shift away from the theorizing of professional leaders toward the fragmented research efforts of disassociated individuals evident today. The new body of research, however, has not been compatible with the old theorizing, so physical education simply has fragmented and become a disjointed assemblage of individuals rather than a community of scholars.

There appear to be few if any scholars within physical education today. It probably will fall to the researchers to determine whether physical education will move forward. There are a few theoreticians in physical education. They, too, could provide leadership. The manner in which researchers or theorists could effect positive change would appear initially in their personal commitment to cultivate the "essential tension" between convergent and divergent thinking within their own work. It would also appear in an emerging respect between researchers and theoreticians for the contributions each can make to a body of knowledge. The differential reward system that favors convergent research over divergent theorizing would have to be abandoned.

Scholarship could be nourished in such a climate of respect. At this point in the history of physical education, potential scholars are more likely to come from the ranks of researchers than theoreticians. By neglecting the process of theorizing in the education of physical educators in the past 20 years, there is an impoverished tradition of divergent thinking about human moving. As a result, even though current research efforts tend to be narrow, mechanistic, and fragmented, they do represent a decent quality of thinking in their type (convergent). The rigor and precision that must accompany all types of clear thinking is more commonplace in the process of physical education research than in the neglected process of theorizing. This situation would suggest that individuals from research traditions as a group would possess more disciplined and sophisticated habits of thinking. Discipline and sophistication are prerequisites for aspiring scholars.

Another factor that might favor the development of researchers as scholars is the interesting pattern of personal motivation that has been evident among researchers in other disciplines. Kuhn (1977) observed that some researchers, as they gain more experience within the paradigm in which they received their initial training, seem to pass through several stages. During the first stage in their career they focus on collecting information that serves to substantiate the traditional paradigm. During the second stage they strive to make adjustments in the paradigm to account for apparent discrepancies between what had been predicted to occur and what was observed to occur. During the final stage they seek to extend and elaborate their paradigm to deal with areas it theoretically could explain or describe, but for which no research evidence had ever been compiled.

This progression within the careers of researchers suggests motion toward a more creative, more flexible approach to the traditional paradigms. If this progression were to be pursued further, perhaps researchers, frustrated when no amount of paradigm extension and elaboration would suffice to explain their phenomena of interest, would participate in a reconceptualizing process—a kind of scientific revolution. Driven to engage in divergent thinking in order to continue their work, they could mature into scholars and help physical education move to a theoretical consensus based upon reconceived paradigms for structuring inquiry. Researchers, then, would have to become theoreticians as well, thus lifting the sophistication of their work from the level of research to the level of scholarship.

Conversely, a theoretician would have to settle on one of the paradigms he or she proposed, then learn how to do research within that paradigm so that it could be substantiated or refuted. This would require a tremendous expenditure of time and energy since carefully delineated research methods exist only within traditional paradigms, not within newly created ones. This would mean that the theoretician would have to become an expert in a broad range of research strategies before appropriate designs and methods could be established that were compatible with the new paradigm. A possible solution to enable scholarship to be produced under such difficult circumstances would be that of putting together a team of theoreticians and researchers who together could produce scholarship, even if independently none was capable of reaching the level of scholar.

Summary

The status quo in physical education suggests that research on isolated academic dimensions of human movement performance or on professional practices will continue. This research will continue under the broad heading of physical education or human movement studies, or something similar, only as long as other more established disciplines or professions ignore "moving" as a subject to be studied. The preconsensus status of physical education leaves it so theoretically infirmed that it probably will disappear as an area of inquiry if any other discipline or profession decides to subsume all or part of it.

This theoretical crisis can only be resolved by scholars doing the business of scholarship. There is a pathetic sense of comfort and confidence among many current physical educators that somehow "doing research" is scholarship. It is pathetic because it gives many researchers the notion that they have reached some ultimate in disciplined inquiry. Since scholars are more likely to emerge from the ranks of researchers, this attitude is subversive in terms of the development of both theory and practice in physical education.

The future of scholarship in physical education is dependent upon the occurrence of a "disciplinary episode." Such an episode would be marked by an abandonment of the traditional way in which physical educators have regarded the academic study of human movement, sport, dance, and exercise as well as professional practice. It would be marked by an abandonment of the traditional way in which physical educators have regarded the process of inquiry and the structuring of a body of knowledge. Such an episode would be a transformation for physical education—a transformation from a field of interest in which research and some theorizing is "done," to a productive discipline in which scholarship is pursued. Such an episode would bring the development of physical education in line with the development of scholarly inquiry in general.

Who will promote this episode? Will it be researchers and teams of theoreticians and researchers who aspire toward the sophistication that is evident in sound scholarship . . . who aspire to become scholars? Scholars are not trained, they are educated. As Aristotle noted in *Nichomachean Ethics*, "It is the mark of an educated mind to expect that amount of exactness in each kind of which each kind permits." The inherent inexactness of moving and the facilitating of moving is so poorly understood because there are so few "educated" individuals pursuing inquiry in physical education. This situation can change. For individuals who aspire to be scholars, the flexibility and capacity to deal with complexity at appropriate levels of detail can become a natural direction for their inquiring minds. Whether there are (or ever will be) enough physical educators with inquiring minds to produce scholarship is problematic. As with all questions about the future, there are critical choices to be made. And when it comes to the future, not making choices can be as profound as making them.

The Future of University Women in Physical Education

Margaret J. Safrit
University of Wisconsin–Madison

A discussion of the future is by nature inexact, since no one knows what will occur in the years to come. Although any prediction will be somewhat arbitrary, it will be viewed more credibly if based upon relevant facts. For example, at the Naisbitt Institute, predictions are made after reviewing hundreds of newspapers from around the world (Naisbitt, 1982). The amount of space given to a topic often signals its importance for the future, and this information is used to forecast the issue. Forecasting in and of itself has no special significance. Its fundamental value is to guide current decisions to achieve a more desirable future. As an example of forecasting, Renfro and Morrison (1982) described an exercise in which a group was asked to apply two methods of studying the future, using a hypothetical issue in education. The issue they chose was the declining enrollment in liberal arts courses. Based on a chart of enrollments in past years, the group observed a downward trend and projected that it would continue unless an intervention was successfully implemented. First, they began with a justification for increasing enrollments, then proposed steps for preventing further decline in enrollment and initiating an upward trend. Thus, forecasting can represent a proactive rather than a reactive stance.

A treatise on the future of women in physical education is certain to be met with mixed reactions, both within and outside the field. For some, this type of analysis must of necessity focus on gender differences in the treatment of male and female faculty and can lead to an artificial separation of the sexes. This view highlights an interesting paradox. The ultimate goal of the women's movement is to ensure that women and men are treated equally in the workplace. Yet, to determine whether equality is actually occurring, the status of men and women must be compared. Although necessary, this analysis centers the spotlight on differences in treatment rather than job performance regardless of gender. No one would question that job competency is the most important criterion to use in judging a faculty member. One would hope that some day affirmative action will no longer be a major issue. However, at present there is evidence that male and female faculty have received differential treatment on some campuses, treatment that may be unrelated to job performance. Until these historical inequities have been satisfactorily addressed, women and minorities should monitor affirmative action activities in the society at large.

In another context, a review of this sort could provide support for the view held by some physical educators that women in physical education have received inequitable treatment since the recent merger of men's and women's departments. Herein lies another paradox. It has been documented that women faculty in many types of departments have been treated differentially with regard to salary, rank, and so forth. At the same time, questions have been raised about the willingness of some women faculty to establish and maintain productive careers as scholars. These are complex issues that cannot be adequately addressed here. The purpose of this chapter is to discuss the future of women in physical education in higher education. This issue is only partially related to affirmative action issues. Actually, many of the issues raised in this chapter will affect male as well as female physical educators in the future.

To complicate matters further, this chapter has a futuristic element in that the future of women in physical education is its primary focus. This topic is tied somewhat to the future of physical education in general. What will be the primary characteristics of the field in the next century? The future of physical education, in turn, depends partly on the future of education and certain sciences such as sociology, psychology, physiology, biology, chemistry, biochemistry, and neurophysiology. These disciplinary areas will be influenced by the nature of the college and university where they are located. And of course, all institutions of higher learning are affected by the society that encompasses them. Thus, in the best of all possible worlds, this exposition would analyze the future of each of these areas. While each will be dealt with briefly here, a thorough treatise is not possible within the confines of a single chapter, nor could it be accomplished without the expertise of specialists such as an economist, a political scientist, a sociologist, and a social psychologist.

The first section of this chapter deals with society in general—its present characteristics and projected future characteristics. Next, the university and its future are analyzed, followed by an examination of women faculty in the university setting. The focus of the chapter then shifts to education and subsequently to physical education. The last portion of the chapter analyzes the present and future status of women in physical education.

Society

In considering future projections, whether in or outside of education, it is helpful first to examine the society in which the system exists. Following is a brief overview of the present economic climate and the social and political environment in the United States.

Naisbitt (1982) and many others have described our modern society as an information society. Vast amounts of knowledge are being generated daily and this knowledge can, within minutes, be transmitted anywhere in the world via communication satellites. The shift from an industrial society to an information society has had a tremendous impact on the job market in the United States. Many industrial workers have lost their jobs due to automation or obsolescence. Yet, new kinds of jobs have been generated. For example, 4 million new jobs were created in 1984 alone (Willard & Lawler, 1985). It has been suggested that in the future, workers' jobs will change every 5 to 10 years, necessitating reeducation and retraining (Cetron, Soriano, & Gayle, 1985). Many of these jobs will deal with information—generating it, finding it, summarizing it, analyzing it, and publicizing it.

The social and political climate in the U.S. has changed since the late 1970s. The Republican administration, as expected, has adopted a more conservative stance, leading to reduced federal support for a variety of social issues including women's equity. Certainly this climate has blunted the thrust for women's equity (Robin & Robin, 1983). The nation as a whole seems to have responded positively to this conservatism, and various political observers have predicted that the Republican party will retain the leadership in our country well beyond the Reagan administration. If so, federal support of equitable treatment for women and minorities may continue to decline. Although the political pendulum may be suspended to the right at the present time, it will undoubtedly swing to the left, though it is difficult to say when this will occur. The possibility of significant federal intervention in support of women's equity in the next decade seems bleak.

The University

There are many views about the future of the university. In one sense the information explosion is not as earth-shaking on a university campus as it is in society at large, given that the university professor has always had to deal with information. However, there are two differences. First, the amount of information that was produced annually in the past is minute compared to the amount currently being produced and that will be generated in the future. Second, the speed with which this information can be transmitted is immensely greater today. In fact, it can now be transmitted instantaneously. Thus, university faculty must learn how to deal with massive amounts of data. In his book, *Megatrends*, Naisbitt (1982) noted that between 6,000 and 7,000 scientific articles were being written each day and that scientific and technical information would double every 5 years. With new and more powerful information systems, and an increasing population of scientists, however, these data will double every 20 months. According to Naisbitt's prediction, by 1985 the volume of information was expected to be from four to seven times what it had been only a few years earlier. "Scientists who are overwhelmed with technical data complain of information pollution and charge that it takes less time to do an experiment than to find out whether or not it has already been done" (Naisbitt, 1982, p. 17). To cope with this information expansion, both faculty and administrators must be computer literate, able to seek and transmit information through the computer.

Universities have already moved into an era of university-industry cooperation. This has created a new concept of the university, once viewed primarily as a cloistered institution where professors worked in a so-called ivory tower. Earlier in this century, universities became involved with social issues that were viewed as critical by society at large. Now many universities are focusing on biotechnology and telecommunications. Yet, this high-tech emphasis should be balanced with efforts to reinforce the importance of arts and literature on campus.

In line with the political orientation of the country, there is growing conservatism on college campuses (Willard & Lawler, 1985) and generally a trend toward individualism. Thus, social issues such as equal opportunity for women and minority faculty and staff will likely remain in the background.

The traditional university will no longer have a monopoly on higher education. Formal educational programs have been implemented in many businesses and industries. Dunn (1983) suggests that the university of tomorrow will differ considerably from the present one. The role of the professor and organization of the curriculum will be more like that of a medieval university, in that students will undertake more independent work and consult with the professor when problems and questions arise. However, the nature of the independent study will be vastly different due to the electronic media. New information and communications technologies will transform the classroom, and learning will be viewed as a lifetime venture because of the rapid flow of new information. Therefore the student body will comprise a much higher percentage of older adults. Dunn predicts that businesses will become an even stronger competitor in providing full-scale educational programs.

Dunn also proposes that faculty in the university of the future will perform the same roles (teaching, research, and service) but in a different way. They will need more time to keep up with their discipline and changing teaching technologies. The university's reputation will continue to rest with the faculty; thus it will be essential that they work at the forefront of their area of research. To function adequately as a teacher, the faculty member must manage a mini-educational system involving staff support, hardware, and courseware. Since the professor must invest a great deal of time to remain current in his or her area of specialization, staff will be needed to implement support services for teaching. There will be fewer formal lectures to large groups of students, given that individualization of instruction is already more feasible with the use of computers. One difference between yesterday's university and tomorrow's will be the availability of a much more sophisticated system to diagnose weaknesses in learning and prescribe new approaches.

Women Faculty in the University

The future of women in higher education must be considered in light of the changing university and the status of women. The following paragraphs will present an overview of factors affecting women faculty.

The status of women faculty in the university varies across institutions; therefore it is inappropriate to generalize across all universities. However, it is possible to obtain indicators of their status by reviewing recent research on university women. Some of this research was synthesized by Safrit (1984). Differences in hiring practices and continuing salary differentials between men and women were documented. Men's and women's roles on college campuses often differed, with more men conducting research and more women serving on committees. Women's credentials, experience, and performance were evaluated more stringently by employees and supervisors. Women administrators were often perceived differently in academe, and women assumed few high-level administrative positions.

There is evidence that a salary differential continues to exist (Equity Action Committee, 1985; Robin & Robin, 1983). In a large midwestern institution the salaries were monitored over a 3-year period (Robin & Robin, 1983). Between the second and third year a union-negotiated salary equity adjustment took place. During the first 2 years, women had been receiving lower salaries than the average at all ranks, even after statistical adjustments were made for rank, race, college, highest degree, and years in rank. After the equity adjustments were made, however, only women full professors were actually equalized in salary. In another midwestern university, an Equity Action Committee report (1985) documented salary differentials between male and female faculty: For example, the average salary of female full professors was $33,713, while the average for male full professors was $38,315. Of the total tenure track faculty, 24.4% were women, while 66% of the lecturers were women.

The lack of productivity by many female faculty was discussed by Safrit (1984). More recent evidence shows that male and female faculty are equally productive for at least 2 years after completing their doctoral degree; then they gradually diverge, with women faculty becoming less productive. This differential productivity might be explained in several ways. It might be attributed to differences in training in graduate school, the orientation toward teaching by some women, or the service orientation of some women. Since this difference occurs so soon after completion of a doctoral degree, this may suggest an inability to establish an independent line of research. There also may be fewer opportunities to engage in collaborative research.

There is continuing documentation of a differential evaluation of the product of work, such as a scholarly article. Men are seen as more competent than women for the same work (Paludi & Strayer, 1985). Yet, gender does not seem to be a major factor in job burnout; in fact, women fare slightly better. Futhermore, being married and having children does not seem to be a detrimental factor for career women, as was perceived in the past. Women, especially married women, are projected to enter the work force at a faster rate than any other population group (Cetron et al., 1985). Although this has not been documented in education, greater career achievement in the business world was evidenced by women classified as having masculine traits (Wong, Kettlewell, & Sproule, 1985). The term "masculine traits" has been used to refer to the traits of successful men in the business world—assertiveness, competitiveness, dominance, and standing up well under pressure.

Although some women faculty are faring very well in academe, this does not appear to be true for all. The same can be said for women administrators in higher education. Few women are being appointed to the most influential academic posts in institutions of higher learning (Bowker & Dickerson, 1983). Yet, there is evidence that both men and women aspire to the top administrative levels. The reasons for these aspirations are the same for both sexes. The primary reason given was the challenge of decision-making aspects of an administrative position. Both men and women also felt that as administrators they would be better able to help more people reach their educational goals. In addition, they felt they could be more effective than many current administrators.

Hyer (1985) noted that affirmative action policies have fallen short of their intended impact on higher education. A primary role of the government is to pass laws and see that the appropriate institutions implement them. Continual follow-up by the government typically does not occur except on a case-by-case basis; the impact of the federal government becomes minimal after the initial impetus. Furthermore, the political party in power can modify this impact. It is interesting to note that a study of rank equity in the 1960s found greater rank equity in institutions located in counties where most voters voted for the Democratic party (Szafran, 1984). Of course, this period of time preceded the enactment of federal legislation on affirmative action.

Hyer (1985) studied three institutions that had increased the proportion of women on campus, the number of female full professors, and the number of tenured women, and analyzed the factors underlying their success. Clearly, the pivotal link in each case was the top administrator on campus: Campus leadership is a significant factor in affirmative action implementation. The campus head (president, chancellor, or provost) was personally committed to affirmative action and gave it high visibility in public speeches and informal gatherings, treating it as an important institutional priority. Furthermore, the leader also selected and used staff effectively to implement these policies. Hiring decisions were closely monitored and decision-makers were held accountable. There was effective two-way communication on these campuses.

In addition to full commitment of the campus leader, Hyer's study documented the importance of coalition group activity on behalf of women. These were primarily women's groups who dealt directly with key administrators on campus. Two or three senior women on campus provided credible leadership, which reemphasizes the importance of women providing support for women.

Education

The problems facing schools and departments of education in colleges and universities are many. Since one of their primary functions is to train teachers for the public schools, educational problems in the schools are often attributed in part to the training of teachers in higher education.

Several major reports on education in the United States have charged that schools are turning out increasingly inferior students (Hart, 1983; Naisbitt, 1982). Relative to the major Western nations, the U.S. ranks 15th out of 20th in science and math. Some have said we must reconceptualize our educational system in order for it to survive (Willard & Lawler, 1985), while others recommend a stronger emphasis on the traditional basics of reading, writing, and arithmetic plus computer literacy and information management (Gingrich, 1985). Currently there is a lack of computer education programs, resulting in an impending computer-training shortfall among high school graduates (World Trends and Forecasts: Education, 1984). References to computer phobia among female students are becoming as common as references to math phobia.

All too often teacher training is viewed as a last resort for students failing in other areas (Hart, 1983). The shortage of science and math teachers in the U.S. has been well documented. As more businesses develop their own educational programs, the drain on public school teachers will increase in other areas as well as science and math. A group of key educational administrators, known as the Holmes Group, is currently attempting to spearhead a more progressive and demanding curriculum for teacher education programs in the U.S. as well as a more desirable reward system for master teachers in the schools.

There is general agreement that the primary focus must be on education for change and the need for lifetime learning. Educators must learn to forecast public issues. This can be accomplished by discussing emerging issues—those not yet on the public agenda—and examining them by some method (Zentner, 1984). In this way, educators can attempt to predict likely occurrences.

Physical Education

Since there seems to be considerable confusion and disagreement about the scope of physical education, the term will be used here to encompass the educational and/or scientific aspects of sport and physical activity, in this case in institutions of higher learning. This description includes departments of kinesiology and exercise science.

The field of physical education has already changed a great deal in the past 25 to 30 years. During this period, the focus shifted from a predominantly singular mission—teaching—to a more complex mission involving research in subdisciplines as well as teaching. Considering that the information society is viewed by Naisbitt and others as beginning in the 1950s, it is not surprising that physical educators were forced to move along divergent paths during the 1960s. It was no longer possible to be an expert in every aspect of the field. The early giants in physical education, the Renaissance people, not only mastered the existing knowledge in the field but were instrumental in forging the way to generate new knowledge.

Although some of the leading spokespersons in the field have argued against splintering it into subdisciplines, this was a natural consequence of the explosion of knowledge. As the work within a subdiscipline became more and more complex, greater in-depth training was needed in the subdiscipline as well as in other closely related disciplines. This led to less communication between scholars within the field broadly defined as physical education. In fact, today many scholars know very little about the work being done in other areas within physical education, and they have only a general knowledge of the theoretical frameworks being studied in many of these areas. It probably can be said that some of these scholars no longer consider themselves physical educators, even though they may be employed by physical education departments.

Furthermore, some of these departments now have names other than physical education that they feel are more in keeping with their major focus.

Bok (1982), President of Harvard University, has questioned whether doctoral programs in physical education require those special qualities that set research universities apart, or whether other organizations could handle this task equally well. Some educators view physical education as a doubtful enterprise in this respect.

Two levels of teaching take place in many departments of physical education: teaching in the professional physical education program, and teaching in the service program for the general student. Professional physical education programs have undergone changes in recent years. Since their inception these programs were designed to prepare future physical education teachers. Meanwhile, the emphasis on health and well-being led to the opening of fitness centers and sports clubs around the country. Corporations began investing money in corporate fitness centers and health and fitness programs for employees. This of course created a need for trained employees, and physical education majors were considered viable candidates. However, it soon became apparent that the training provided for a future teacher was not adequate for an exercise specialist. On another level, there was substantial growth in collegiate sports, creating a need for more athletic trainers. Again, physical education students were often hired, but again their training was inadequate. Thus, professional programs began to develop several curricular routes such as exercise specialist, athletic training, sports management, and exercise science for students planning to pursue graduate studies.

The service program for the general student also changed to reflect the interest in health, fitness, and individual sports as aerobics and weight-training courses were added to these curricula. Innovative programs involving concentrated courses on weekends or over a period of several weeks offered new activities for students.

These three diverse thrusts—research and scholarship, professional physical education, and service programs in physical education—can conflict with each other because each has a different emphasis. To comprehend these within-department conflicts, many outside observers rank physical education at the bottom of the totem pole in academe because of its historical interest in sports. Thus the field as a whole is striving for increased respectability. One solution would be to operate the service program as an independent unit, merge the faculty who have primary responsibilities in the teacher education program with the education faculty, and retain the nonschool program options and the research programs as a unit.

If a three-way split within physical education seems too drastic, perhaps a separation of the service program from the professional component would be a wise move. Although some physical educators still believe every faculty member should teach a course or two in the service program on a regular basis, this is unrealistic. Considering the time and money invested in specializing in a subdiscipline of physical education, the appointment of a scholar/researcher to teach sport classes is not a wise use of personnel. The physical educator who primarily teaches in the service program will find it increasingly difficult to obtain tenure, especially in a major research university. Such programs can be more efficiently run by a sport management person with a staff of specialists in various activities. This would separate the sport/game courses that serve as electives for students from the professional courses and the research programs, and the separation would clarify the primary purpose of each program.

Although changing the name of a physical education department is a sensitive issue with many physical educators, this could be a good move if the department is part of a major research university. Considering the typical question asked of physical education scholars, "What sport is your specialty?" such a separation would allow faculty and staff to focus on improving the professional program rather than spending considerable time dealing with a sometimes cumbersome service program.

The problems described above may be less severe in smaller colleges where the scope of the program is not as large, and where research and scholarship are not a major emphasis. In these programs the faculty might focus on developing model programs that deal with the knowledge explosion by becoming computer literate and by teaching their students to work with the computer. Regardless of the institution's size, however, of primary emphasis is the avoidance of information lag, since new information will be available almost daily in the future. Physical educators in professional programs must develop and maintain a close working relationship with the education faculty on campus; they must continually be aware of advances in education and take an active role in improving the quality of education. The colleges and universities, for their part, must help physical education teachers learn how to handle new information by providing retraining or continuing education programs.

Researchers will be expected to find answers much faster, as new ideas will be implemented more quickly than ever. In the past it was not unusual to have a 10-year lag before a new idea was implemented. For example, in 1947 Alexander published an article in *Psychometrika* on the estimation of reliability when several trials were available. In the article, he described the intraclass correlation coefficient. Later that year he published an article with Brozek in the *Research Quarterly* on this topic (Brozek & Alexander, 1947). Not until over 10 years had elapsed did the first article to mention using this approach appear in the research literature (Feldt & McKee, 1958). And not until the 1960s were several articles published by physical educators on this topic. The technique was used in the 1970s to estimate the reliability of several newly developed skills tests in our field, but even now some physical educators are aware only of the Pearson product-moment coefficient to estimate reliability. As information becomes more readily accessible, it will be transmitted much more quickly, eventually instantaneously.

Administrators in physical education must also focus on computer literacy. In some ways their job is the most difficult, since they must ensure that students will be properly prepared to obtain and utilize the knowledge they need. Administrators must also ensure that faculty have direct access to information systems, which eventually will necessitate placing a computer terminal in each faculty office. It also will require use of a mail network to enable faculty to communicate with colleagues around the world. When possible, a computer specialist should be available to assist faculty in using the computer to improve instruction.

Many physical educators tend to be conservative in nature and adopt a reactive stance in dealing with issues. For instance, a department may have observed a change in the career options chosen by physical education majors. The change might have been gradual at first; perhaps only a few students chose careers other than teaching physical education to K-12 students. Still, these students were required to obtain teacher certification because that was standard procedure for all. After a few more students indicated they did not wish to teach upon graduation, the curriculum might have been adjusted to allow them to waive certain requirements and graduate with a special degree. Finally, when the number of students choosing nontraditional careers began to outnumber those planning to teach in a school setting, the department might have added new degree programs to include these options. In an attempt to keep up, this department was simply reacting to events that had already occurred.

Another department might have predicted this trend in the early stages of the fitness boom, as new fitness centers and sports clubs began to surface. The growth of these organizations could have been monitored and their needs assessed. Then the curriculum could be adjusted to include new degree programs that would prepare students to meet these projected needs. Students might even have been recruited for the various career options. The reactive nature of many physical education departments is probably a function of several factors, such as conservatism, multiple functions, and historical ties to the competitive sport culture.

Women in Physical Education

As described in the beginning of this chapter, the future of women in higher education in physical education is dependent on the future of society, the university, education, and physical education. Given the current political climate in the United States, it is unlikely the federal government will be a strong advocate for affirmative action. However, universities located in areas that are Democratic strongholds may be more consistent supporters of the rights of women and minorities. Although the status of women faculty has not improved greatly in recent years, this is not true in all universities. The top administrators at some are firmly committed to hiring and granting tenure to qualified women; at those institutions, a few reputable senior women faculty are openly committed to supporting other qualified women, and hiring and tenure decisions are closely monitored.

Recent evidence suggests that women in physical education who obtain their doctorates from prestigious universities have career mobility patterns similar to those of men (Massengale & Sage, 1982). That is, prestigious universities employ graduates (both men and women) from prestigious universities. However, there is a salary differential for men and women administrators in physical education (Douglas & Massengale, 1985). Of the administrators who responded to a survey, 33% were women. The average salary for women was $34,100, while the average for men was $37,900. Differences existed at the Dean's level, Division Chair's level, and the Department Chair's level.

To cope with future demands, the best step a woman can take is to carefully select the university from which she will obtain her doctorate. She must be certain she is enrolling in an area of graduate study staffed by faculty who are active researchers/scholars. She must become computer literate enough to have immediate access to information systems around the world. Upon completing a doctoral degree, careful planning should go into the job search, including an analysis of career goals and commitment to research and teaching. If her commitment to being a productive scholar is weak, she should avoid research universities. Although research and scholarship may hold special prestige, the rewards are often greater for teaching and service on a smaller, teaching-oriented campus. If she has several options, a woman may wish to give strong consideration to an area where most of the voters are Democrats. When interviewing for a position, she should ask the highest level administrator outside the department about his or her commitment to affirmative action.

Computer literacy is an asset for anyone, of course, but it is perhaps more critical for women because computer phobia has been associated with women in particular. To the extent that this exists, the gap can only widen for those who do not develop the computer skills they will need for transmitting and receiving knowledge. Some faculty resist learning more about computers because they feel that computers are strictly for analyzing and storing data and that other specialists can handle such tasks for them. This line of thinking, fairly common 10 years ago, is shortsighted in that it ignores the vastly increased communication network and information pool now available. Computer-aided instruction and simulation procedures will also become more commonplace. Physical educators should not be expected to become computer experts, of course, but they should learn to use the computer to enhance their own work.

Once a woman becomes a tenured professor, in particular a full professor, she should be supportive of other women on campus and in the community. Evidence is clear that such a support group is important in maintaining a positive emphasis on affirmative action. Furthermore, as more competent women become visible on campus, it creates an aura of acceptance for other competent women who are not yet established. Women administrators must be prepared to help graduate students and faculty achieve these goals. Administrators with good research credentials are more likely to be successful in this respect.

Conclusions

Many changes are in store for university women in higher education. Unless they are within 5 years of retirement, women cannot afford to ignore the effect these changes will have on the field of physical education. Affirmative action programs will make little progress, given the current political scene, but women can consider academic positions in institutions and in parts of the country that are more receptive to women's equity. Nevertheless, affirmative action must not be viewed as a free ticket to a job; the most critical component is job performance. Both men and women should strive to eliminate artificial differentiation between the sexes, judging faculty roles on the basis of job competency. It is equally important to note that changes in the future encompass far more than affirmative action issues. These changes are tied to the future of our society, the university, education, and physical education. Finally, it is not merely the forecasting of these changes that is important but also the proposing of viable strategies for guiding desirable changes and defusing undesirable ones.

Some Considerations for Teaching Physical Education in the Future

Thomas J. Templin
Purdue University

It's been 12 years since I left public school teaching and coaching. Since that time, it appears that the difficulties facing schools and teachers have multiplied. In fact, the problems confronting public school educators seem so great that those of us who have been engaged in teaching are compelled to ask, would we become teachers again? My response for now is not an immediate "yes" but instead, "it all depends."

Upon what does it depend? First, it depends on an examination of the ever changing demographics of American society. Second, it depends on the relationship of these demographics to the future of public school education in our society, the future role of the teacher and the future conditions under which teachers must work. Finally, it depends on some soul-searching of my present values and commitments to this troubled occupation.

This chapter, which is primarily atheoretical, will attempt to address these concerns and will do so in relation to two basic positions. I have no crystal ball from which to predict the future. But I do have access to the lessons of the past and of the present that may enable me to discuss my hopes and some possible trends for the future. Even in the best of times, predictions about the future seem hazardous, but this writing seems particularly difficult now. Certainly these are not the best of times for public school teachers. Nonetheless, we should think about the past, the present, and the future so that we may avoid a disinterested attitude. Whether the reader accepts or rejects that which is forwarded is perhaps of less importance than providing an opportunity for others to debate the advantages and disadvantages of certain propositions. It is my hope that from such debate, alternatives for the future may be addressed, goals determined, and changes for the betterment of teaching brought about.

Also, I agree with Postman (1983) who states, "I believe only that the future will be a consequence of what we do now as a response to our understanding of the problems we face." He suggests, "the future of the future is the present" (p. 311). We must examine the present carefully, glance back in the past as if peering into the rear-view mirror of a car, and then move forward into the future with the hope that the route we take will, in fact, improve public schools, teachers, and the students they serve.

Demography: Its Significance

J. Myron Atkin (1981) stated, "the health of the schools, particularly, public schools, depends on the condition of the nation" (p. 95). This thesis would seem to apply everywhere, but it seems particularly applicable to the United States, whose demographics may foretell the future conditions and effectiveness of our public school system and its teaching force. Haberman (1984) also suggests the importance of demographics:

> What we learn from demography is that America is in a continuous process of becoming a more diverse, shifting, fractionated culture. It is possible to put a positive light on this diversity as leading to options, new development, and ethnic richness; others view the same trends and see an unstable, segmented society at war with itself. (pp. 499-500)

In essence, although demography is ever-changing, it may forecast destiny, and Americans of today, in ways both obvious and subtle, are inventing the America of tomorrow. Consider some demographics from the last few years and the present associated with (a) American society and education[1] and (b) physical education and physical educators.[2]

The U.S. Population and the Family

- In 1983 the median age of the population reached 30.9 years, the oldest ever, and is expected to exceed 36 years by the year 2000.
- In well over half of American families, both parents are working.
- The number of children living with one parent grew by 69% since

---

[1]These demographics originate from: Boyer (1983), Gallup (1985), Gerdau (1984), Goodlad (1983b), Grant and Snyder (1983), Howey (1983), "Learning to read" (1985), National Commission on Excellence in Education (1983), Rosenholtz and Smylie (1984), "School Test: "Mine passes, yours fails" (1985), "Teachers need more respect, pollster says" (1985), and Yeakey and Johnston (1985).

[2]These demographics originate from: Dodds and Locke (1984), Gallup (1985), Garcia (1985), Goodlad (1983b), Graham (1982), Grant and Snyder (1983), Johnson (1985), Locke, Griffin, and Templin (1986), Kollen (1983), National Education Association (1982), Ross and Gilbert (1985), Ross, Dotson, Gilbert, and Katz (1985), Sage (1980), Taylor (1986), and Templin (1983).

1970. One out of every five children and more than half of all black children live in a one-parent household.

- The traditional nuclear family now accounts for only 11% of all households.
- One quarter of the children under 6 are living below the poverty line. In 1982 almost one of every six students enrolled in the public schools was from a poor family and almost one of every 10 was handicapped. One of every four was a member of a minority group.
- More than half of all serious crimes in the U.S. are now committed by youths 10 to 17 years of age.
- One quarter of our elementary school population are latchkey children.
- In 1983, only 28% of our families had children in public school; by the year 2000 there will be fewer such families.

Students

- Only 72% of students today graduate from high school, 85% white and 75% black students.
- Of our 25 largest school systems, 23 have predominantly minority students and are grossly underfunded.
- Students spend 5,000 more hours watching television than being in school in a 12-year school career.
- 67% of high school students are employed.
- 50% of high school students cut classes.
- The number of people ages 16 through 21 who read even part of a book during a year has dropped to 63%—a drop of 12% since 1978.
- Students of all races, age groups, and regions are reading better than was demonstrated on the National Assessment of Education's first two tests in 1971 and 1975. Yet, 55% of white high school students, 80% of the Hispanics, and 84% of the blacks have difficulty reading standard high school texts. Reading levels of 9-year-olds and 13-year-olds have remained almost constant since 1980.
- In a study of achievement in math and science, American 12-year-olds received the lowest average scores in math among children from eight countries.
- Children who come from homes of incomes below $5,000 tested at half the level of children who come from homes of incomes above $21,000. What's worse, they are expected to fall further behind as they go through high school.
- Functional illiteracy among minority youth may run as high as 40%.
- Between 1963 and 1980, verbal and math scores on the Scholastic Aptitude Test declined 50 and 40 points, respectively. These scores have now leveled off and are on the rise again (see point 8 under teachers and teaching).

Teachers and Teaching

- Although 72% of teachers graded their performance as A or B in a 1985 Gallup poll, and 50% of the public assigned these grades, 71% of senior high teachers indicted that public attitudes had a negative effect on their job satisfaction.
- In a 1985 Gallup poll, teachers rated themselves highest among 12 professions in terms of their contribution to society, but rated themselves as lowest in status. The public also rated teaching as the lowest status occupation.
- The median salary for an experienced teacher in 1982 was $17,000, half that for an experienced professional in private industry, and that gap widens as a teacher stays in the profession. In most cases it takes a teacher a full career to double his or her salary.
- Over the last decade, teachers have suffered a real loss in income of 13.7% while personal income went up more than 17% nationwide. It is estimated that 11% of teachers moonlight.
- More than half of our teachers say they would never choose teaching again—five times the percentage of 20 years ago.
- One half of those who enter teaching leave after 7 years, two thirds to three fourths of them within the first 3 years of teaching. These are usually the most able teachers. Money is cited as a contributing factor for teacher attrition, but low salary is subordinate to other factors related to work conditions that make a difference in student learning, factors such as lack of administrative and parental support and interest, and lack of student interest.
- The number of college students who would choose teaching is less than at any time in the last 30 years. Less than 10% of teacher education applicants are rejected.
- The 1984-85 average SAT verbal and math scores of college-bound high school seniors who planned to major in education were 441 and 446, respectively. The verbal average was 10 points above the average for all college-bound seniors, and 14 points below the average math score. These scores represent an increase of 50 points and 41 points (math) from 1979 figures.
- One million new public school teachers will be hired by 1990. At the same time, the supply of new teacher graduates is projected to decline by almost 20%. A recent Harris poll forecast a shortage of one million teachers by 1990.
- Less than 100 tenured teachers have been fired for incompetent teaching in the last 43 years in the U.S.
- Of the public school teachers polled in a Harris survey, 70% reported a desire to spend less time on administrative tasks and "inane rules and requirements that are imposed on teachers."

- Future teachers have been characterized as follows: (a) they tend to come from a smaller city, town, or rural area, (b) are monolingual, (c) are likely to have attended a college or university relatively near to home, (d) prefer not to teach a multi-ethnic student population, (e) and tend to be conservative, high in concreteness of beliefs, high in absolutism toward rules and roles, and high in the need to control others.
- The typical pattern in the classroom is that the teacher is the dominant figure in determining the activities and tone of a class, and is virtually autonomous with respect to classroom decisions. Teacher domination is obvious in the conduct of instruction; teachers tend not to respond in overly positive or negative ways to the work students do. The variety of teaching techniques is greatest in the lower elementary grades and least in secondary schools.

Physical Education and Physical Educators

The demographics cited above seem to signal warning shots for the future, but what indices may signal possible future directions in physical education and public school physical educators? Again, consider the following:

- Over a 20-year period, the percentage of secondary health and physical education teachers combined within the total teaching force has dropped from 8.2% to 6.5%. Furthermore, supply and demand estimates show no increased demand for physical education teachers through the mid-1990s. Shortages of less than .8% are reported for elementary and secondary teachers.
- Some 41% of health and physical education teachers report that they would not become teachers if they could start their college preparation again, and 18% reported that their chances of choosing a teaching career are about 50-50.
- One of every six American children is so unfit that he or she is classified as physically underdeveloped.
- One half of the children in grades 5 through 12 are involved in activity that would meet the minimum requirement for efficient functioning of the cardiovascular system.
- American young people have become fatter since the 1960s. Some 13 to 20% of American children between the ages of 6 and 11 are overweight, and as many as 24% have high serum cholesterol levels.
- Students like physical education but rank it low in importance and difficulty.
- One third of the schools in the U.S. have good physical education programs, although some people claim this figure is too generous.

- Although 80% of students in grades 5 through 12 are enrolled in physical education classes, only 36.3% take physical education daily.
- The physical education of elementary students reflects short weekly activity, inadequate time and facilities, and a heavy reliance on relays and informal games.
- The physical education of junior and senior high students reflects a heavy emphasis on group sports/competitive games and other activities that they are not likely to continue throughout adulthood.
- A 1985 Gallup poll revealed that 75% of public school teachers felt that physical education should be a required subject for 2.6 years. Of the public polled, 45% reported that P.E. should be a required subject.
- Physical education teacher/coaches are characterized as higher in prejudicial, absolutist, and authoritarian attitudes in comparison to secondary school teachers from other academic areas; aspiring physical educator/coaches have been found to be more dogmatic and rigid than other college students; physical educators tend to be conservative and mirror those traits and social backgrounds of teachers described earlier (Sage, 1980).
- A recent California study (Garcia, 1985) suggested that the morale of physical education teachers is low, due to budget cuts, reduced graduation requirements for physical education, absence of physical education from reform legislation, few opportunities for staff development, and student disinterest.
- A recent review of literature of "in house" criticism and evaluations from outsiders who peek into gyms suggests that physical education in our schools represents (a) an outmoded umbrella program with no real focus; (b) supervised recreation, glorified recess; (c) a criminal waste of time; (d) the primary reason for one's avoidance of exercise in adulthood; (e) a boring experience; (f) an irrelevant learning setting, where there are no teacher or curriculum effects; (g) a setting where custodial, inequitable teacher behavior is normative; (h) a setting in which embarrassment, humiliation, anger, discomfort, noninvolvement, apathy, rebellion, compliance, and irrelevant activity appear to be the norm; (i) a setting that reflects teacher struggle—one in which teacher isolation is high; (j) a setting where accountability for teaching and learning is minimal, if not nonexistent.
- The above information greatly outweighs the information on excellence in teaching physical education. Recent profiles of elementary and secondary teachers across the country reveal how various factors enhance public school physical education: learning progressions that integrate instructional concepts, incentive programs, student record-keeping, class management, the integration of physical education with other subjects, computer-assisted instruction, personal commitment and responsibility, positive role modeling, and high expectations.

Summary

Certainly these figures speak to our changing, postindustrial society. Although some of the news is good, the data are indicative of a society that seems to have placed education as its lowest priority even though one of every four citizens in the U.S. is directly involved in the educational process (Grant & Snyder, 1983). The data show that many students must cope with the disintegration of the family, many young children live in poverty or in the lonely world of latchkey children, or are raised by surrogates, and adolescents have a pop culture full of diversions that move them away from educational priorities. Small wonder that schools are more troubled and the practice of teaching has become more complex than ever.

Furthermore, these demographics speak of the present condition of teaching—low pay, isolated and burdensome work conditions, and disinterested students who are more tuned in to videos, television, records, and magazines than to education. The demographics also speak of a work force whose competence is being questioned. And they speak of colleges of education that are in danger of becoming academic wastelands because they have such open admissions policies.[3]

Finally, the demographics reflect a country that has been, as Borchert (cited in Haberman, 1984) states, "a controlled system in the technical sense, but (one which) to some extent . . . has been a relatively, uncontrolled social experiment" (p. 509).

While there are some encouraging data about excellence in public school physical education (Graham, 1982; Templin, 1983), again the demography appears to suggest that physical education and its practitioners have some major problems. Too many of our teacher training entrants are marginal academically. The teaching supply outnumbers the demand, and the benefits of physical education programs are being questioned and in fact seem to be negligible (Taylor, 1986). Furthermore, parents and students alike (and perhaps school administrators and educational leaders) see physical education as moderately important at best in comparison to other subjects. Physical education seems indeed to be a "subjecta non grata" (Dodds & Locke, 1984, p. 77) in education, and physical educators appear to be "persona non grata."

---

[3]A discussion of teacher education is not addressed here. However, one must acknowledge that the future of teaching physical education *could* depend on the degree to which preservice and inservice teacher education reform movements socialize teachers and affect the conditions of the workplace. The reader is referred to various references that have implications for the future of teaching in physical education (Clark, 1984; Howey & Gardner, 1983; Lanier & Little, 1985; Lawson, 1986; Locke & Dodds, 1984; Locke, Mand, & Siedentop, 1981; Tabachnick & Zeichner, 1984; Templin, 1985).

A New Scenario for Teachers

More Innovation?

One has to wonder whether the reform movement in education will promote the change necessary to remedy the problems cited above. Certainly most review/reform commissions have neglected physical education, and one can interpret this as a tacit message that either all is well within our ranks or all is not worthy of examination and/or reform (i.e., we're too far gone). I would prefer that the former be the reason for such neglect, yet am hard-pressed to support this line of reasoning. The scenario persists: Physical education appears peripheral to the aims of education, regardless of the rhetoric that may suggest otherwise.

Yet, would further reform and/or innovation assure a brighter future in education, particularly in physical education? Would physical education become more central? Perhaps, but probably not. Reform movements and innovations have yet to, and probably will not, change the face of most classrooms or gymnasia. Ravitch (1983) demonstrates that educational forecasts and innovations from the writing of Dewey's (1915) *Schools of Tomorrow*, through the predictions of the 1944 Educational Policy Commission, to the educational reform movement of the 1960s and the reforms of the "third wave" have failed as revolutions. Ravitch suggests,

> schools of the year 2000 will bear the same relationship to the schools of 20 years ago. If we consider how little schools have changed since 1966, then it seems utopian to predict that all schools might in the foreseeable future, be as good as the very best schools of today. (1983, p. 320)

Unfortunately, this seems no less true for programs of physical education and the teaching linked to our school programs. Our reforms and innovations have come and gone and more will arrive. Yet, as suggested before, most programs will remain similar to those of the past and epitomize the traditional physical education culture described by Hoffman (1971). I suspect only a few of our teachers are using or will use instructional innovations. Beyond legislative reforms mandating change, most physical educators will remain untouched, and even in the case of mandated reforms, adherence may be questionable.

Why? Even though an understanding of the culture of the school is said to be prerequisite to school reform, our understanding of the culture of physical education settings hasn't led to widespread reform within our schools. Over the last decade we have had access to various documents (Anderson & Barrett, 1978; Goodlad, 1983b; Graham, 1982; Hoffman, 1971; Kollen, 1983; Locke, 1974; Locke, Griffin, & Templin, 1986; Templin, 1983) describing the way of life or the behavioral and programmatic regularities within our gymnasia, yet a culture of mostly negative images persists. The demographics cited earlier seem to define the traditional and primarily custodial culture of physical education which appears to be reinforced by successive generations of physical educators.

Why is reform so difficult to bring about? Reformers of the past have been, and I suspect those of the future will be, individuals who have unrealistic expectations for and approaches to change. Reformers expect that students will be interested in their reforms and eager to learn. They expect that teachers will be competent and dedicated to reforms that are rarely teacher initiated. They propose reforms that are said to be "teacher proof," yet at times a subtle contempt for and patronizing of the teachers who must implement change assures the failure of such reforms. Reformers fail to consider that teachers perceive problems differently and that teachers and school organizations tend to continue established practices. It's interesting how some of us in teacher education may question or denounce various pedagogical practices in our schools, yet they persist, not only in our schools but in teacher educators' classrooms as well.

If reforms and innovations are to succeed at all, teachers must be made part of the initial reform or innovation movement. "Failure to involve teachers in all phases of new curriculum (and instructional processes) tend to inhibit—even destroy the effectiveness of innovation" (Ornstein, 1981, p. 49). Hence, the future of educational reform and teaching practice doesn't lie in the hands of scholars alone, or merely in the concepts of reform or innovation. It lies in scholars, teachers, school administrators, students, and parents trying to understand the school culture and joining together in all phases of curriculum and instructional planning, implementation, and evaluation within our classrooms and gymnasia (Bentzen, 1974; Berman & McLaughlin, 1975; Goodlad, 1983b; Sarason, 1982). Everyone must share in the responsibility of setting the proper conditions under which schools and teachers can function effectively.

Conditions of the Workplace

In all probability, the future of teaching in physical education does not lie in increased educational innovation. Certainly future technological developments will complement instruction, yet our real future rests in taking what is and developing it to its highest potential. Practice must begin to match rhetoric. As Ravitch (1983) states, "this challenge may be more radical than the call for an entirely new institution to replace schools" (p. 320). How do we realize this potential? As most of the literature on education suggests, we must improve the conditions under which teachers toil. I choose to address some of these conditions within a contingency, an "if . . . then" context. It is a short wish list for the future of teaching physical education related to recruitment, rewards, communication, instructional leadership, community involvement, student interest, teacher/coach conflict. In part, it represents a redefinition of our culture.

Teacher Recruitment

Weaver (1979) suggests that as the market demand for new graduates in a given field diminishes, the quality of the pool of applicants entering the field will also decrease. Furthermore, it is assumed that the institution of higher education adapts to a decline in market demand by selecting the best from a shrinking pool of talent. However, although the market demand has declined in physical education and will not improve for some time, we continue to admit most students under weak admission standards. We seem to do just the opposite of what Weaver proposes. If physical education is to improve the quality of its teaching entrants, then we must (a) reduce the number of professional preparation programs and (b) increase the admission and retention standards of those programs in existence. We will also have to consider the utility of a predicted future trend whereby liberal arts graduates will be able to obtain certification after completing inservice internship.

Finally, with changing occupational opportunities for women, we will need to find ways of attracting the best women into physical education. Even with these changes, we must recognize that the best students will most likely continue to seek other fields of study unless other conditions of teaching change as well.

Salaries and Rewards

If we are to attract above-average students, then the future must guarantee higher salaries for teachers. If state legislators wish to effect improvements in education[4] and the quality of teaching entrants, they must continue to pass legislation that increases the salaries of beginning teachers. "Many would enter teaching if the possibilities of and requirements for ultimately earning a decent living were clear" (Goodlad, 1983b, p. 314). Further, state legislators and especially local school systems will have to assure that teachers beyond their first year are rewarded equitably; that is, as they gain experience they will be paid equal to peers of similar experience and enough to offset inflation. Boyer (1983) suggests that average salaries for teachers be increased by at least 25% beyond the rate of inflation through 1987. Such increases would seem to decrease the teachers' need to moonlight in various jobs (or coach just to earn extra money).

This of course raises the issue of merit pay. Although I fully support increased salaries for teachers, merit pay may be justifiable only if clear

---

[4]There is considerable evidence across all 50 states that state legislatures have effected legislation in the areas of teacher salaries, teacher certification and professional preparation, performance-based payments, master teachers, teacher shortages, and the professional development of teachers (National Commission on Excellence in Education, 1983).

criteria can be developed and equitably applied in assessing meritorious teaching. When considering merit pay in the future, one must understand that there may be problems associated with such rewards. For example, Rosenholtz and Smylie (1984) found that not only does merit pay create measurement problems, but it also inhibits communication among those who work together, promotes intolerance of others, reduces encouragement of others, diminishes group problem-solving, and increases isolation among teachers. If merit pay is to be used in the future, then the problems cited must be resolved as we reward our best teachers. A reward system makes sense, but only if it doesn't create further problems for our teachers.

What about the reward of tenure? I believe that tenure also serves as a disincentive for many teachers. Hiding behind the security of lifelong employment (less than 100 teachers have been fired over the past 43 years for incompetence within the U.S.), the ineffectiveness of tenured faculty rarely becomes the target of negative sanctions. It has always seemed incredible to me that poor teachers are allowed to continue teaching. Tenure and a system that does not demand accountability seems to ensure this. By the same token, it seems incredible that good teachers rarely receive appropriate rewards (i.e., teacher merit and awards, positive feedback from administrators, colleagues, and students, peer mentoring positions with release time and increased salary). If teacher accountability and effectiveness is to be assured in the future, then good teaching must be recognized and rewarded while inferior teaching is resolved or terminated.

Recognition of teacher efforts and effectiveness must play a major role, but increased salaries alone are unlikely to retain our best teachers. Rather, it will be professional or symbolic rewards that will increase the likelihood of keeping our best teachers. If we are to retain the best teachers in the future, then their success with students, approval of administrators, colleagues, students, and parents, and assignment to paid advisory roles in recognition of competence are the keys (Boyer, 1983; Rosenholtz & Smylie, 1984). However important money is in the selection of other occupations, it has never been, and probably never will be, the primary criterion for one's attraction to teaching or the retaining of quality teachers.

Communication

Technology. Although most educational innovations or reform movements seem to leave teachers unaffected, today's high technology may have the greatest likelihood of affecting the physical educator of the future. As Goodlad (1983b) states, although "schools compared with other institutions, have responded very little to this technological revolution . . . . it is difficult to believe that schools can have a future apart from technology" (p. 322).

High technology has forced a communications explosion in our information society, which means teachers will have access to educational resources far beyond that available in the past. Computers, video recorders, and other forms of audiovisual technology have already had an impact on our profession (Sinclair, 1983; Tymeson & Hastad, 1985) and will probably continue to do so for those who avail themselves of such technology. Certainly if physical education teachers do not consider and provide technological aids for students' learning, they may be depriving those students of learning technologies that could give them an educational advantage. As Boyer (1983) states,

> The challenge is not to view technology as the enemy . . . . Rather the challenge is to build a partnership between traditional and nontraditional education, letting each do what they can do best. The potential of technology is to free teachers from the rigidity of the syllabus and tap the imaginations of both teacher and student . . . . In the long run, electronic teachers may provide exchanges of information, ideas, and experiences more effectively than the traditional classroom or the teacher. (pp. 200-201)

Furthermore, the technological movement may expand the role of the teacher to beyond the school whereby interactive technology will enable teachers to physically educate people both young and old in various settings (schools, homes, offices, factories) at varying times. With an expanded role, the physical educator of the future could be a very busy person.

Although physical education personnel will assume primary responsibility for directing and implementing this technology, one thing we must guard against is the deskilling of our teaching force (Apple, 1983). If teaching physical education only translates into one's operating a VCR so that Jane Fonda can lead a physical education class, or for students to press a computer key to direct their movement experiences, teachers will be deskilled. To do little more than execute someone else's conceptions is hardly the creative challenge of our future in teaching. Teaching physical education will still need to be a "high touch" enterprise in the future. As Naisbitt (1982) points out, "Whenever new technology is introduced to society, there must be a counterbalancing human response— that is, high touch—or the technology is rejected" (p. 35). People need people, and in our gymnasia, teachers and students will need to perpetuate interpersonal connections. In fact, I suggest that positive interpersonal relations will be more important than ever as more technology is introduced within our schools.

Collegial Relationships. Another important aspect of the future beyond the technology of communications concerns the professional relationships that exist among teachers. Although this may seem less true for physical education staffs at the secondary level, I am in total agreement with those who believe that teachers are isolated in their work (Feiman-Nemser & Floden, 1985; Goodlad, 1983b; Knoblock & Goldstein, 1971; Lortie, 1975). Although some may define teacher isolation as teacher autonomy, this autonomy seems to be, as Goodlad states,

> exercised in a context more of isolation than of rich professional dialogue about a plethora of challenging educational alternatives. The classroom cell in which teachers spend much of their time appear to me to be symbolic and predictive of their relative isolation from one another and from sources of ideas beyond their own background of experience. . . . There is little to suggest active, ongoing exchanges of ideas and practice across schools, between groups of teachers, or between individuals even in the same schools. . . . There are no infrastructures designed to encourage or support either communication among teachers in improving teaching or collaboration in attacking schoolwide problems. Teachers carry on side by side in separate activity. (1983b, p. 186)

Perhaps one of the greatest impediments to the future of the public school teacher is professional isolation. Lortie (1975) reported that 45% of elementary and secondary teachers have no contact with other teachers. Again, while I suspect that secondary school physical educators have more contact with each other, I also suspect their contact rarely involves work-related issues (Bishop, 1977; Little, 1982). It is well documented that isolation is a problem confronting elementary physical educators (Locke, 1974; Locke et al., 1986; Sanborn, 1985; Templin, 1986). For example, isolation of the physical educator is characterized by infrequent contact with colleagues, and the peer interaction that does occur is usually brief, social in nature, and rarely centered on curricular or instructional concerns. Equally important, the school itself does not facilitate collegiality by providing time for formal interaction on a regular basis. Physical educators for the most part must be self-reliant. Hence, day-to-day experience or trial and error learning becomes a means to professional development rather than pedagogical exchange or peer evaluations of colleagues. Finally, isolation will continue to be a problem in the future if we fail to recognize that the autonomy granted physical educators really reflects institutional neglect (Bain, cited in Lawson, 1986) or physical education's peripheral status in the school.

If professional isolation is to be reduced in the future, teachers will have to be given structured opportunities for staff development within the working day. If teaching physical education is to become a collective enterprise that favors the exchange of ideas versus "experience swapping" and sympathy between teachers, then our effectiveness will have to match that of teachers working in collegial environs (Little, 1982; Metz,

1983). Such a condition also points to the future of teacher selection and training whereby their "predispositions for working with others as well as (developing) the skills to do this may be important considerations" (Howey, 1983, p. 33).

Instructional Leadership

The effectiveness of the public school physical educator in the future will in many ways depend on instructional leaders who will also be responsible for establishing more fruitful collegial relationships with teachers (Graham, Faucette, & Ratliffe, 1985). Of course, this will require individuals who have the skills to evaluate teachers, who do in fact visit classrooms, who are not buried in "administrivia," who aren't bureaucratic functionaries, who have power and authority to develop competent staffs, who provide for staff development and promote collegial relations among teachers and administrators, and who truly support physical education and physical educators. These individuals must not be indifferent toward teachers or the process of teaching. The future of teaching in physical education lies partly in the hands of those leaders who are able to promote these characteristics that have been linked to leader, school, and teacher effectiveness (Bossert, Dwyer, Rowan, & Lee, 1982).

Community Involvement

The rising level of education has created a citizenry quite capable of collaborating with schools. As a consequence of the trend toward decentralization, this citizenry has and will become more assertive in demanding the right to effective education as well as their right to become more directly involved in the school. Hence, if physical education is to maintain its place in the future within the school curriculum, administrators and teachers will need to take the concept of collegiality one step further. We will need to discuss with parents, community groups, and business and industry the significance of school physical education, uniting as a body politic both locally and on a state level to secure our future. The constituency for whom public school physical education teachers work will be increasingly important, and if we are to improve the status of the teaching ranks with this constituency, we will need increased interaction, mutual respect, and increased coordination of goals and design of physical education. Partnerships must be formed.[5]

---

[5]The reader is referred to Goodlad's (1983b) discussion of "The Partnership," which has as one of its goals the development of "an understanding of education as a community wide rather than only a school based activity" (p. 355).

Student Interest

The teacher of the future will be responsible for maintaining students' liking for physical education, as documented by Goodlad (1983b). The teacher will also have to change students' perceptions that physical education is low in importance. An increased emphasis on quality and less emphasis on custodial programs that continue to be geared toward skill, fitness, and cognitive and interpersonal development is a beginning, but programs must stress affective development as well. Physical education students may continue to like our programs, but without a concomitant development of values that explicitly communicate the import of one's lifelong involvement in physical education/activity, our goals will remain unreached and the demographics of unfit children will persist. Physical educators must make the "why" connections between teacher demands and student activity.

Tomorrow's students (and some of today's) will demand to know why they are told to do something, and tomorrow's teachers will need to know the full reason. Physical educators must avoid knowledge obsolescence and move to a level whereby students see value connections that endure throughout life. They must teach values as an integral component of the physical education programs of the future.

Teacher/Coach Role Conflict

Within the last few years a great deal of attention has been given to the role conflict or strain that results from trying to fill the roles of teacher and coach simultaneously (Bain, 1983; Locke & Massengale, 1978; Massengale, 1977; Templin, 1981). We have documentation that varying types of conflict (i.e., value, status, self/other, load, teacher/coach) are perceived and actually experienced by teacher/coaches and such conflicts may be deleterious to either role. For example, load conflict defined by Locke and Massengale (1978, p. 164) as the "incompatible expectations deriving from the combined work loads of teaching and coaching" has been found to be perceived and experienced to a high degree by both male and female teacher/coaches on a variety of teacher/coaching levels. In essence, the duration and intensity of the combined roles weigh quite heavily on most teacher/coaches.

Furthermore, conflict due to the differences in the role skills and attitudinal disposition required in teaching versus those required in coaching appears to be a problem. Such conflict is linked to differences in clientele, rewards, and role requirements for both teaching and coaching, and this presents problems for the teacher/coach. Combined with conflicts related to value differences between teacher/coaches and their clients, the low status of teacher/coaches, and their blocked career aspirations, the consequences of role conflict can be quite damaging to the individual.

Maladaptive reactions such as lack of job satisfaction or motivation, poor job performance, stress and anxiety, withdrawal and apathy, alienation, absenteeism, and burnout are some of the severe consequences linked to role conflict and strain (Massengale, 1977; Newman & Beehr, 1979; Templin, 1984).

My opinion is that such conflicts are more deleterious to one's teaching role and will continue to be so for two reasons. First there is evidence to suggest that aspiring physical educators enter our field with a primary orientation toward coaching (Templin, Woodford, & Mulling, 1982). Hence, teaching physical education becomes a career contingency; that is, if one aspires to coach in a public school, one usually pursues certification as a teacher. Given such an orientation, one's interest in being an exemplary teacher is secondary. In essence, teaching in itself may be a conflict for many teacher/coaches, and I suggest that within our present organizational structure it will continue to be so.

Second, retreating by withdrawing to the coaching role will be reinforced by our society's emphasis on sport and the athletic syndrome present in most schools. The physical education teacher/coach's orientation toward coaching will likely be reinforced by those who see physical education as subordinate to interscholastic athletics. Again, physical education will be perceived as subjecta non grata.

What is the resolution to such a problem? Although a variety of options exist for the future (Templin, Cervak, & Marrs, 1982), consider a couple of strategies: If teacher/coach conflict is detrimental to one's teaching role, future employment staff scheduling practices must be developed that make it virtually impossible to occupy the roles simultaneously. Teacher/coaches could be hired separately (the college/university model), or practice schedules could be structured so that one would not teach while coaching; part-time activity experts with physical education training could be hired, or curriculum offerings could be modified or reduced.

Another possibility would be a system whereby athletics is taken out of the school and transferred to club teams serving adolescents. Although this does not preclude the possibility of teachers seeking coaching positions within such a structure, taking sports out of the school may help teachers whose occupational livelihood within a school system depends on their success as a coach.

If the value of sport continues to outweigh the value of physical education within the school culture, the status of physical education and the esteem given to physical education teachers as bona fide faculty members will remain negligible. Furthermore, the physical education student will continue to perceive the benefits of physical education as minimal. Undoubtedly, instructional leaders will need to become sensitized to teacher/coach conflict and help resolve it.

Summary

John Goodlad (1983a) states,

> For all schools, the priority item always to be on the agenda is the quality of life in the workplace—its assessment and subsequent continuing improvement. Creating a satisfying place of work for the individuals who inhabit schools is good in its own right but it appears also to be necessary to maintaining a productive educational environment. (p. 59)

The future of teaching absolutely depends on improving the quality of life of the physical educator's workplace. In order to bring about more positive demographics than those cited in the beginning of this chapter, it is critical that the following factors combine to establish a new culture within schools and within physical education in particular: increased funding and professional rewards, improved communication through high tech and high touch, improved collegial relations, improved instructional leadership, increased community involvement, increased student interest, and the resolution of role conflict.

Equally, a redefinition of our culture is critical. Without such a commitment the prophecies of Ravitch (1983) will come true—The physical education of the future will look no different than the physical education of the past. The physical educator of the future must recognize that beyond a better quality of life through improved conditions, one must be committed to that which occurs between the teacher and physical education students as well. The revolution in physical education in the future must also take place in our gymnasia and on our playing fields. Again, while it is certainly true that improved resources and support are necessary, no one outside the gym can make the revolution happen. Nor can anyone outside the gym prevent the physical educator of the future from making physical education truly effective.

Would I teach again? Absolutely, because I believe that conditions will improve and commitment to our roles will grow. I believe a different culture within physical education is possible. The distance between where we are now and where we can be in the future is great, but it is not beyond our reach. Change will occur slowly, but as the Tao (cited in Ravitch, 1985) says, "A journey of a thousand miles must begin with a single step." We know which way to proceed, but our problem will continue to be, as it has always been, whether we have the support and commitment to take new steps. Such steps will not only serve the teacher of the future, but most important, they will guarantee a better experience for the generations of students who pass through our programs.

The Business of Physical Education

Michael J. Ellis
University of Oregon

We physical educators have traditionally fought shy of business interests in our activities. We have resented any interest by the world of commerce as if it was in some way impure. Our complaints have sometimes been shrill and replete with words like "quackery," "charlatanry" and "prostitution." These terms, though rarely used, stick out like the tips of verbal icebergs hiding an internal resentment for the changes that have been brought to physical education by the forces of the marketplace. The resentment ought to be replaced with wonderment that physical education has moved so rapidly beyond the quieter backwaters of our programs in schools and formal institutions.

The nervousness seems to be concentrated in the physical educators who were recruited for service in the teaching of physical education knowing that the rewards were slim but that there was security in the profession; after all, there were always going to be children needing our services. That conservatism, the trading off of potential wealth for security and the pervading ethos that teaching was a calling, socialized many of us, myself included, into believing that physical education and profit were in some way immiscible. We are finding that we were wrong.

Physical education via its many new manifestations is rapidly coming of age. Many new avenues for service have either appeared or been created. This has been in response to the drastic changes in the demography and expectations of the school systems that formerly sustained the vast majority of physical educators. More and more physical educators must now practice, not in the quieter backwaters of academe but in the mainstream, buffeted directly by the turbulence of the economy.

Those who like the good old days when physical education was essentially school physical education bemoan the lack of control we now have over the large forces at work in our society that now influence physical education. This chapter will explore the nature and origin of these forces and attempt some forecasts that, with luck, will hold up through the next decade or so.

Our Roots

The historians of sport and physical education push far back into antiquity to trace our roots, but that is not called for here. The changes we speak of have their roots in relatively recent developments that have come with maturation of our industrial society. The roots of the changes affecting us do not reach much further back than the Depression or perhaps the end of World War II.

World War II, its ending ushering in the Nuclear Age, established the economic and military supremacy of the United States. It presaged a short troubled period of recovery, and then a period of optimism, calm, and growth that set the scene for many of the patterns we have come to take for granted. The population was growing, money was available for education, and the opportunities in teaching were plentiful at all levels. The baby boom created a bulge of opportunity for physical educators, as the 1950s and 1960s focused the bulk of our attention on matters that clustered around teaching and teacher preparation.

Then the baby boom generation reached graduation age, the birthrate declined, and the nation was divided by Viet Nam. During the late 1970s and early 1980s the student population shrank, people lost confidence, and the economy ran out of steam. The impact on the teaching profession was profound as education came under attack. The call, "back to the basics," represented a questioning of the role of physical education and many other subjects. Education did not have the money it needed; worse, it did not have the same support it had enjoyed earlier. For a while the general reaction was to try harder to restore the old systems. Teachers unionized in an attempt to force the economy and to protect their numbers. The populace began to question how their tax money was being spent and insisted on changes that were usually resisted by the teaching profession, including physical education. The changes rendered the profession less attractive and less secure. As a result, new physical educators were dramatically less inclined to commit themselves to teaching. They forced a rethinking of the profession.

Despite this tale of woe, the absolute number of teaching jobs in primary and secondary schools has been increasing throughout the last 15 years. In the 1970s the total number of teaching positions increased to 2,439,000, up by 151,000 despite falling enrollment. This gain was due to a reduction in the teacher-pupil ratio at a rate that exceeded the drop in the teacher corps created by dropping enrollment. For example, the change due to the reduction in teacher-pupil ratio in public schools was +15.9% while the rate at which the number was being driven down by declining enrollment was −10.6%. For private schools the figures showed even more contrast: +22.8% to −4.3%, respectively (Frankel & Gerald, 1982, p. 72).

The problem for the profession was not that the teacher corps had failed to grow, but that the numbers of new teachers far exceeded the demand. Figure 1 displays this relationship very clearly. Although the demand for new teachers fell slowly, the numbers available exceeded demand by about 600,000. The number of new graduates fell precipitately during the next 5 years, yet the backlog of would-be teachers, returning teachers, and new teachers flooded the market. Those physical educators unable to enter the teaching profession had to find some other way to earn a living. In turn, the curricula that prepared new physical educators had to respond to the falling interest in teaching careers. These two closely related forces strengthened the pressure to create alternative avenues to service and resulted in a revolution as physical education went into business.

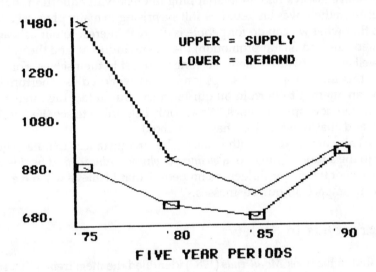

Figure 1 — Estimated demand for new additional teachers in elementary and secondary schools and estimated supply of new teacher graduates, 5-year totals (Frankel & Gerald, 1982, p. 71).

P.E. Goes Into Business

We now see a light at the end of the tunnel in education. There is a small upswing in the birthrate, the early recruits brought in by the baby boom are reaching the end of their careers and are beginning to retire in greater numbers, making room for physical educators once again. But it is too late. We have already sampled success in new fields, weathered some storms, and found that adults need and will pay for physical education services. The babies of the baby boom are once again a driving force. Now as young adults, they are altering our practice and our opportunities, this time via their purchasing power. Their interest in activity and leisure, together with their discretionary income, has created a new market outside the traditional schools and public sector recreation departments.

Physical educators, because of their knowledge about physical activity and its effects on people, have always stood at the confluence of four major streams in our society. How physical educators can benefit their clients is of concern to education, health care, the leisure industry, and the military. We have understood that in theory but have only recently understood that we had something valuable to contribute and would be welcomed if we did so.

Three of these classes of enterprise—health, leisure, and the military—have always had an overlapping interest with education, but our interest in them was limited. It is still surprising to many physical educators that what we can do for people is of great interest to our colleagues in medicine and health promotion, the leisure industry, and the military, as well as to individual clients seeking to invest in themselves. For some time this interest aroused suspicion. It was regarded as a perturbation or as an attempt to horn in on our territory. But in fact the interest has generated new opportunities. We are only beginning to see the possibilities, and that is what this chapter is about.

This chapter deals with some of the circumstances that have given rise to the sudden growth of a *business of physical education*. It begins with a survey of the major influences on people that I believe will have a significant impact on our businesses.

Macrotrends in Society

Naisbitt in his book *Megatrends* (1982) identified the megatrends that seem to be affecting our society. These trends can be boiled down into three macrotrends that will influence activity and the leisure industry: demystification, our changing market, and market segmentation. The megatrends are still worth the effort to understand, but for our future as a complex of businesses, some are more important than others. We will focus on these.

Demystification

Demystification of the esoterica of our profession will result from the intersection of two megatrends, the first stemming from the information revolution. Our collective capacity to assemble and distribute information in easily understood form throughout society will increase to levels we are just beginning to comprehend.

The information revolution is being created by three interlocked developments. First is the incredible reduction in the price of computers to the point that many people have access to them at work and/or at home. To this must be added the dramatic increase in the power of easy-to-understand software packages for managing information. Finally, we are poised on the threshold of a telecommunications revolution that will hook those computers and their software packages together interactively. The advances in fiber-optics, digital coding, and new processes that will be developed in the heat of the competition, thanks to a deregulated telecommunications industry, will speed up the information revolution. Information will be available as never before.

The second megatrend has been a consumer revolution. Consumers are not so willing to accept services offered them on face value. They question and seek second opinions. There is self-prescription, self-testing, and do-it-yourself. Their new self-confidence has resulted in changing attitudes to professionals, who formerly controlled a body of information and skills that were largely unavailable to lay people. To some extent the professionals hid that information to preserve the power it gave them. They created acarne procedures and jargon to preserve and mystify their professions. Now the consumers have access to much of the information and have recognized that professionals are, to a large extent, simply information retailers.

The result has been a trend toward demystification of the professions, and it will continue as more people gain confidence in themselves and access to the information formerly controlled by professionals. Demystification will occur even in fields that have regulations against practice by lay people.

Demystification will manifest itself in the spreading expectations that professionals will strive to satisfy, just like other service retailers. Increasingly, it will be considered acceptable for professional service retailers to compete with each other for clients. This has already begun to occur in the legal profession as lawyers compete, advertise, and reduce the price of their services. In the final analysis these trends will transfer some of the control of professional behavior to clients and the market forces they dictate.

Demystification will affect the activity and leisure industries. However, that will produce more change among physical educators than recreators. The latter, since the inception of their field, have had to practice in an arena where the client is in control. Recreation's very goals are to create situations in which the clients perceive their participation to be voluntary. Physical educators, for their part, have traditionally had captive clients. This captivity has been legislated in schools and other institutions, where attendance has been forced on the grounds of the higher benefit that will result. However, in so doing we have isolated ourselves and our practices from the pressures of client choice.

Physical educators have generated obligations to participate. The content of the field until now has largely been team sports and games. Loyalty to the team and the creation of a sense of belonging, while perfectly legitimate goals, have tended to guarantee attendance. Repeat business has also been enhanced by the structure of leagues and conferences that delay for as long as possible the ultimate resolution of the competition and the eventual dissolution of the team. A trend away from participation in team games and sports will accentuate those activities that are discretionary at each point of participation. Thus, physical educators will be continually reminded that each experience is the precursor to the next.

From now on we will be increasingly concerned with repeat business, though we will have less control over it. Creating a service in a setting that will encourage the client to return will be of paramount importance. Of course, the major aspect of this effort must be to track the clients' needs and wishes very accurately. We will use the marketing strategies established by the business sector to assess the wishes of potential clients, to locate those clients, and to monitor the effectiveness of our efforts to reach and serve them. Courses on marketing and monitoring will replace the classic tests and measurements courses. This new emphasis will focus on market development and program evaluation.

The current evaluation technology is built for physical assessment of groups of clients. In a sense, the outcome informs clients exactly how they are faring relative to a population. Since people like to perceive themselves as above average, they do not welcome any news to the contrary. A new assessment technology is needed that concentrates on demonstrating individual gains and losses without reference to a norm. The new emphasis would support an ongoing service relationship with a client who can at any moment decide the experience is not worth the effort or the fee and drop out immediately.

We have not fared very well when we have empowered the clients without changing our procedures and attitudes. Our field-wide concern with required and elective courses is a case in point. Traditionally, enrollment has dropped off when we permitted the choice. However, some time later as we learn to create attractive, client-oriented programs the enrollment returns. Another less pleasing example is the incredible dropout rate from youth sport programs and the virtual absence of adult organized and oriented club-sport systems outside of the universities. We have not yet learned to package sport programs to maintain the interest of clients beyond the early years.

The concept of fostering repeat business has raised the hackles of many physical educators for whom it connotes dependence or lack of individual initiative. However, repeat experience can have a positive side beyond the receipts that repeated attendance will bring. When the repeated exposure to physical education services brings with it learning, development, fitness, friendship, and a sense of belonging, then it is a positive process. As such it is a prized service offered for which the client is happy to pay for being well served. The darker side of this process occurs when a physical educator attaches negative consequences, threats to withhold friendship, status, advice, and/or access to development in order to foster dependence and fear. In the long run only the first kind of repeat business can be sustained, and we must teach ourselves how to generate it positively.

Why do we face these problems and have doubts about whether we will have clients? The answer is simple: Our field developed its methods, aspirations, systems, and recruits for situations in which the clients were captive. We never had to market and sell our professional services to clients with multiple choices, high standards, and ready access to our knowledge base. We now do. We are forced by changing circumstances to work in the mainstream.

Our Changing Market

Fortunately for us, just as the traditional fields of opportunity were closing down, new ones were opening up. The baby boom generation has grown up, joined the work force, and acquired a sense of self-worth. They learned from the turmoil of their youth and acquired knowledge and attitudes about the impact of their lifestyle decisions on their health and productivity. They are willing to invest some of their discretionary time and income to self-enhancing activities. To the extent these tendencies continue as the baby boom generation grows older, and to the extent that the ideas and attitudes spread to other cohorts, the opportunities for service will expand.

The windows of opportunity will naturally occur in the free market where potential clients spend their discretionary income. Of course, these same potential clients are also being bombarded with rival claims, and the competition for their dollars is and will be intense. It is appropriate here to consider the likely developments and size of the basic phenomena driving the market: discretionary time and discretionary income.

Discretionary Time. In the last 20 years the average work week in the United States has shrunk about 10%. In 1964 it was just under 39 hours. It had shrunk to about 34.5 hours per week by 1982. Since then it has edged up slightly to about 35.5 hours as we emerge from recession. There are three possible trends: a return to the 40-hour week, a return to the linear trend downward toward a shorter week that was interrupted by the recession, or some complex curve that results from something else.

The third choice will probably be the correct one. The amount of discretionary time will be created by the intersection of people's desire to work, changes in productivity, changing social consensus that there is not enough work and that it should be shared, and a willingness to accept marginal unemployment such as unpaid vacations, leaves of absence, official holidays, and early retirement.

The linear trend we can see in Figure 2 would, if other things are held constant, reduce the work week to 30 hours somewhere around the year 2004. However, it is becoming clear that people like working, and thus we probably will not move below a 32-hour work week in the next 20 years. We will see a greater variation in how the hours are worked: flex-time, 4-day work weeks, some work done at home, and so forth. This slight increase in and considerable redistribution of discretionary time has important implications to retailers whose markets are controlled by the availability of discretionary time.

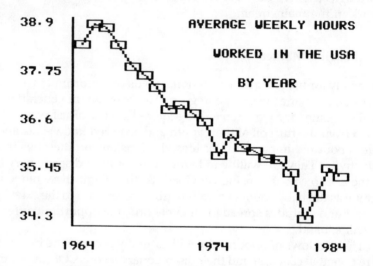

Figure 2 — Average weekly hours worked in the U.S. (Valentine, 1984, L13).

Although there will not be a dramatic reduction in the normal work week, other sources of discretionary time will expand. It is clear that people welcome extended periods of time to pursue some major life project. They want extended weekends and longer vacations, and if they cannot get them they are often willing to take them without pay. Stepping out of the work force voluntarily will become more common.[1] The

---

[1]Stepping out of the work force involuntarily via unemployment has also grown, and will probably remain large compared to conventional expectations of almost full employment. This will present problems in that these clients for our services have discretionary time but little if any discretionary income.

discretionary time this will create will also produce new opportunities for service. People will have time for supporting extended projects, travel, education, donating their service, social interaction, joint ventures and other such activities. To this source of discretionary time must be added retirement time. The number of retirees, their longevity, and the younger age at which people retire will dramatically increase this potential clientele.

Discretionary Income. Discretionary income when combined with discretionary time determines the absolute potential size of the market for activity and leisure services. During each year from 1974 to 1984, leisure spending in the U.S. has risen. It reached $191 billion in 1984, this growth representing a compounded growth rate of 11.9% over that decade (Valentine, 1984, L13). This growth in leisure spending mirrors the similar rise in real disposable personal income. By 1984 real disposable personal income rose to about $9,720 million, and approximately 2% of it was spent in the leisure market. We can expect leisure spending to continue following real disposable income in the future. As a quick rule of thumb we can project that the absolute size of the leisure market will be about 2% of real disposable income. (See Figures 3 and 4.)

The size of local markets can also be expected to follow real disposable personal income in those regions. The size of the U.S. market is of little consequence to an entrepreneur in the activity and leisure industry because he or she basically serves local clients face-to-face. Thus, opportunities lie with small business ventures seeking to create service

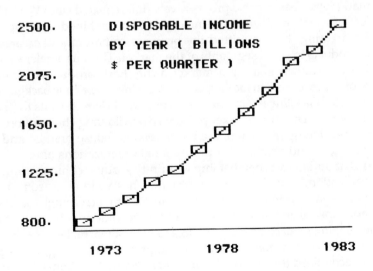

Figure 3 — **Real disposable personal income in billions of dollars—quarterly (Valentine, 1984).**

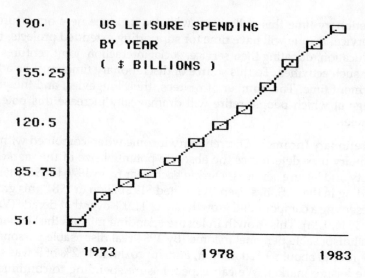

Figure 4 — U.S. leisure spending in billions of dollars (Valentine, 1984).

on a small scale in restricted locales. The secret will be to find small segments of the market and fill that need competitively, thus capturing some of the local leisure spending.

Market Segmentation

The marketplace has become progressively differentiated since World War II. More efficient production technology, when combined with sophisticated marketing, has permitted the business community to create and target products to small segments of the market. This has accelerated the number of products sharing a market niche. Each product is varied to satisfy preferences due to locality, social class, income, ethnic background, and so forth. Gasoline is "localized for you," and Detroit wants to "build a car for you." The supermarket presents a bewildering choice of breads, wines, and detergents. There are name brands, house brands, and the generic "no brand at all." Our professional organizations offer a smorgasbord of options for membership in affinity groups within the umbrella organization, and the magazine market has splintered from a few national magazines to myriads of titles targeted to increasingly narrower and more specialized markets. The choice is bewildering. In fact, people are developing retail counseling services to help others make wise choices.

The process seems to stem from improved marketing. Sales personnel recognized that although consumers wanted the benefits of mass production, they didn't want to lose their individual identity. Henry

Ford's early cars could be bought in any color—as long as it was black. But the need to express individuality asserted itself, and soon competition created choices. Carried forward into the present, one can now, for a price, order a car with so many options that it may well be unique.

Supporting the pressure from consumers to exercise options, the seeking of authenticity if you will, is the massive development of data handling systems. The amount of data required to support this level of consumer choice is enormous. Naturally the development of computers permitted the process to accelerate, but there were intermediate systems for remembering (e.g., addressographs) that started the process.

Associated with changes in production technology came changes in systems for developing markets via advertising and direct mail marketing campaigns. The development and sale of sophisticated directories of consumers, coded by demographic characteristics and preferences, bring us to the present with its large variety of relatively inexpensive systems for developing contacts with potential customers. The marketing is carefully targeted toward small segments of the overall market.

Segmentation Helps.   This segmentation of the marketplace has served both the consumer and the producer. The consumer gains real or apparent choice, and the producer is able to compete across a larger series of markets. It has also permitted smaller organizations to find small specialized niches and compete successfully. "Ma and pa" granola companies and yogurt producers were able to compete in segments of the market and survive and expand. There were more windows of opportunity, and the costs of meeting the specialized demand for a unique product or service in the local market segment was small.

This process has affected the activity and leisure industry similarly. In fact, it is substantially a retail distribution system. It delivers services in a face-to-face setting. There are few economies of scale, and thus small systems are at an advantage in designing products and services for tiny market segments. At the top of the scale are the tour wholesalers and cruise-line companies that must work hard to combat the impression that they cannot serve individuals exercising choices. In fact, these large leisure suppliers create matrices of options to maximize their chance of attracting clients. At the bottom of the scale are tiny organizations that serve just a few clients with highly specialized services: fishing guides and expedition leaders, coaches of small teams, golf pros, athletic trainers, and so forth.

Between these extremes most of the industry is organized into aggregates of a few to a few hundred professional employees. These organizations are about the same size as a small firm and have the same characteristics as they compete to develop their markets. These middle-sized organizations are the ones we are used to—school districts, recreation and park districts, universities, prison systems, health spas, nutrition and weight control services, health maintenance/promotion systems, youth clubs, and YMCAs.

Franchising. Franchising is a recently developed strategy for exploiting the opportunities created by market segmentation and bringing to small local businesses some of the economies of scale available to larger concerns. It is a centralized system for helping people start up and operate small businesses that serve a local need. Franchising supports a new business for a fee. It can purchase centrally on behalf of all franchisees, develop advertising and marketing strategies for local use, and provide managerial expertise and services. It uses local capital and the ownership usually is local, thus the motivation to succeed is high. The significant personal investment of the local franchisee ensures the attention to detail and organizational agility so necessary in the service retailing industries.

Jazzercise is one of the first, if not the first, activity franchising system. It offers franchisees a system to develop and market activity classes for a fee. It has spread nationwide with such success that it now has imitators. Franchising, as a method of creating opportunities for professionals to create their own businesses, increasingly will capture the markets formerly served by public sector organizations. The small private sector organizations, whether franchised or not, will generally be more aggressive and agile than the public sector agencies with which they will compete. As a result the consumer will be presented with more choice, and standards for the quality of the experience offered will rise.

Macrotrends Summarized

The three macrotrends of course will affect more than physical education and recreation. The changing nature of the professional relationship, its demystification, and the broadening of the clientele to include people of all ages will alter the kind of people we seek for the field. We will need people oriented to the enhancement of individuals throughout the lifespan, rather than people attracted by the glamor of elitism. The content of the field will be conditioned by the adult client. Team games and sports requiring neoadolescent vigor and foolhardiness will no longer be the staple fare of our field.

Segmentation of the market into very small niches will require the development of very different systems for identifying clienteles and maintaining them. A key feature of this change will be the recognition that participation by adults is discretionary and conditioned by their expectations for high quality service.

Public Versus Private Sector Competition

As a result of these macrotrends, the number of windows of opportunity for professionals in the activity and leisure industry have expanded and will expand further. New systems of franchising and marketing will result from the interaction of the new information technologies and the desire for people to receive services tailored to personal needs. As there are more ways to enter the business of physical education, we will see a startling rise in the number of paraprofessionals. The issue of para-professionalism is an important one but is not within the scope of this chapter. However, the forces of the marketplace will eventually drive out any para-professionals who fail to meet clients' rising expectations. The corollary is that professionals will also have to meet rising expectations if they are to survive.

The result of competition between the public and private sectors will be that the focus of the industry will shift away from the older agencies founded with public funds to meet the needs of the citizenry. As the private sector organizations increase in number and begin to compete with each other and the public sector agencies, pressure will develop to close the public agencies. The argument will be that the private sector organizations, driven by the need to be highly competitive, will be able to deliver their services at less cost.

As the private sector begins to displace the public sector, a new problem will surface. The public agencies were originally created to serve those who for various reasons were excluded from private sector services. The new emphasis on private sector provision will once again exclude the disadvantaged. In response to the groups of excluded citizens, new mechanisms will be developed whereby persons unable to purchase private sector services directly will be subsidized. Scholarships, "work for play," activity and leisure vouchers, and other imaginative schemes will emerge to enable broad involvement.

As a result of the shift away from public provision to private sector provision, the public agencies will need to find new rationales for their existence. They will have to find avenues to service that cannot be well met by the private sector. Since private sector organizations must realize a profit early or be forced out of business, the public sector agencies will have to concentrate on products and services that are not profitable, though desirable, or that require so much time to develop that small private sector organizations cannot raise the capital necessary to sustain them through to completion. These long-cycle, capital-intensive projects will provide the amenities and infrastructures upon which the private sector enterprises will be built. In fact, the public sector agencies should remove themselves from direct service and concentrate on creating the conditions for entrepreneurs (or intrapreneurs) to construct their products and offer their services.

An Example

Such a structure was experimented with at the University of Oregon and will be briefly described here as an example. The Department of Physical Education and Human Movement Studies was challenged during the recent budgetary crises to delete about 15% of its budget because the State of Oregon did not wish to fund service physical education. The service program was very large and important, and its loss would have challenged the continued existence of the department. So all possibilities for alternative funding were sought. One of the solutions described in Ellis and Ulrich (1983) was to use the infrastructure remaining in the budget, the faculty and the facilities, to support a system that would earn the portion of unfunded direct operating costs from potential clients who would pay for the services rendered.

The existing infrastructure was made available to any person who submitted an appropriate proposal to generate a program that could support itself from user fees. To gain approval to use the infrastructure, the proposal had to show that the program fitted comfortably within the educational mission of the university and that the budget for advertising, rental, proposer's salary, and so forth balanced the needs of clients with the needs to generate revenue. Approved programs were then advertised and operated. However, the proposer bore most of the risk that the program was not viable, since the salary portion was the last fraction of the budget to be earned from receipts. Thus, it was up to the operator to decide whether the program was profitable enough to run should enrollment not meet expectations. Programs that exceeded their budget enriched the operator with a significant fraction of the surplus.

In the language of business, the programs were joint ventures. The terms of an agreement were worked out beforehand in such a way that the department was bearing only the opportunity costs of its investment in administrative staff and facilities, but was not committing any direct funds because it did not have any. The majority of the risk and the potential reward was borne by the operator, who was rewarded for creating successful programs. The system was designed to unleash the imagination and effort of individuals who believed they had a service to offer. The nature of the program was to be tuned by market forces and was to provide physical education services that otherwise would not have been offered.

The University of Oregon program was the analog of the systems used by many businesses seeking to coordinate the activities of independent people or organizations to seek a profit. Real estate companies, medical practices, architectural groups, shopping centers, airports, and many other private sector organizations have developed such systems. A large system is organized to provide the infrastructure for many independent organizations to work in consort with each other to create and sell a service or product. The system works by harnessing the efforts of entrepreneurs who invest their talents and energies and are rewarded directly by the success of their efforts—the essence of the free enterprise system.

The program, given the acronym SHAPE (for Sport, Health and Physical Education), was allowed to compete with the SPE (short for Service Physical Education) program that continued to offer conventional term-long courses for credit, but also on a fee-supported basis. Both programs were tied directly to their capacity to create services/experiences that clients would pay for. Inadequate enrollment voided the contracts and of course resulted in the loss of potential earning by the program operators. The programs were set to compete with each other to ensure that both avenues to service, credit classes organized around the conventional three-times-a-week-for-a-term time schedule, and any other imaginative noncredit activity service were actively explored by all concerned.

Both SPE and SHAPE programs unleashed imaginative programs. However, the opportunity to earn credit for an experience, even though it took a longer time commitment on the part of clients, proved to be an overwhelming incentive, and the SHAPE program as originally conceived proved unable to compete. It was just more profitable to create and sell to the administration and the clients a credit class in SPE than a variety of smaller SHAPE experiences. It is still possible to use the mechanism to create unusual experiences, but after a year it was recognized that the SPE credit program had won the competition.

To save the advertising investment in the acronym SHAPE, the program was altered. It became the mechanism whereby people in the local communities could enter the existing credit classes by paying a fee. They did not have to be students and were not required to register with the university. They simply paid a fee and joined a class. They were not expected to do assignments, take exams, or meet attendance requirements. The clients had simply bought places in the classes and were responsible for their own level of involvement. However, since they could enroll in another class the following term, they were potential repeat customers. Thus there was strong pressure to create a climate of support for learning that was rewarding to each community client.

The effect on the budget was significant. The overhead remained constant, yet empty places in classes were filled with paying customers. Clients formerly excluded were now welcome. Classes were more heterogeneous and were more like the real world. More physical educators earned a living, because classes that may have been cancelled were now maintained. It was an all-win situation that arose by applying to our retail service physical education program some simple procedures that would have been used in the private sector of the economy.

Prognoses

The changes that have been identified will have very substantial effects on physical education, the main effect being to drive physical education's focus from the public to the private sector. This will come from the changes in lifestyle and an aging population. As such, the content of physical education will no longer center almost exclusively upon youth-oriented competitive sports. The core will become less demanding. Non zero-sum activities that sustain adult social interaction while contributing to their health and the quality of their lives will move to center stage.

Physical education will be reconceptualized as a retail service. It will have to follow the dictates of the market and will have to identify potential clients and turn them into regular customers. The curriculum will have to change to accommodate the new content and the new clientele. It will have to communicate the new managerial skills needed to survive in a postindustrial service economy.

The current divisions in content and skill fostered by the splintering of health education, physical education, and recreation will come to be seen as major impediments. Clients will not splinter their needs conveniently along disciplinary lines. They will want "one stop shopping" and we will have to learn to accommodate them by integrating our services for the convenience of a bewildering variety of clients.

The field of physical education, whether integrated with health education or not, will come under attack from the health care industry. The health care industry is being pressured to contain costs, in spite of its need to maintain profits. To accomplish this it is beginning to vertically integrate the industry and to seek new markets. One major market of course is the health enhancement industry formerly left to us. The competition will be intense, and one response from physical education will be to seek control of access to some part of the health and fitness market by accreditation and certification.

Despite competitive pressures, we will be competing from a strong position. For decades we have been building strategies and techniques for dealing with small groups as leaders. Outside business organizations will find it difficult to industrialize physical education. Physical educators have a relatively low cost professional preparation and have relatively low wage/salary expectations. These facts, together with the fact there are very limited opportunities to create economies of scale, dictate that physical educators will be able to compete successfully with physical therapists, nurses, and physicians for their clients.

In a nutshell, although there will still be many teachers of physical education in schools, that is not where the action will be during the next two decades. By then much of physical education will have gone into business.

Wellness Programs and Their Influence on Professional Preparation

Alexander W. McNeill
Montana State University

The term *wellness* is relatively new, but the concept was eloquently described by Ulrich (1976) as a "macrocosmic concept of fitness, . . . [fitting you] to live most so that you can serve best." In that presentation Ulrich acknowledged there was no easy formula to produce this macrocosmic fitness, but that we had the science of human movement as a potent force with which to effect total fitness. Unfortunately, the spirit of that message went largely unheard and physical educators still teach skills with the hope that all the other concomitants espoused by Williams in the 1930s (modality, process, and outcomes) will indeed take place.

The rapid growth of workplace wellness programs might well be interpreted as resulting from a failure of the health and physical education programs delivered in the public schools and universities over the last three or four decades. Why else would such programs be necessary, unless there was a lack of carry-over from the schools? We must take a critical look not just at what we are doing under the guise of health and physical education, but also how we are doing it. We have argued that physical education and health education should be retained in public schools because these programs contribute to the physical, mental, emotional, nutritional, and psychological well-being of participants.

Economic Influence

Although it would be appealing to think that the growth and development of the wellness movement in the United States stemmed from a sense of moral responsibility toward society, and that programs for health promotion were based upon principles of utilitarianism (i.e., the right to promote the general good), such a position would be naive. Undoubtedly there are individuals who pursue and develop such programs with a utilitarian ethic. However, the primary motive for the emergence of the wellness movement in our society is economic. But acknowledging this fact in no way diminishes the benefits derived by our society as a whole as the wellness/health promotion movement gathers momentum.

The physical fitness movement that began in the 1960s provided the impetus for the wellness/health promotion movement of the 1980s. However, the scope of wellness programs has transcended the general fitness goals of strength, flexibility, and endurance. The wellness programs of the 1980s include other physical components such as nutrition and body concept/body image, as well as psychological dimensions such as emotional well-being, stress management, and self-concept, and a metaphysical or spiritual dimension. The general tone of the wellness movement is that of an holistic approach to well-being, a true integration of body, mind, and spirit. The major purpose of wellness/health promotion programs is to shift the responsibility for wellness back to the person seeking to be well.

The physical fitness movement had its origin, as we might expect, in physical education. The wellness/health promotion movement encompasses physical goals, but the leadership for this movement has been provided by industry. The industrial and corporate fitness models have been the basis from which more generalized health promotion programs have developed in other organizations such as hospitals, clinics, agencies of state governments, and public schools. We might have expected colleges and departments of physical education, health and recreation to be in the vanguard of the wellness movement. Instead, they are better characterized as being in the caboose. While there are undoubtedly exceptions to this generalization, academic departments of health and physical education are still largely uninvolved in the wellness movement beyond their traditional roles, for example physical fitness and exercise as a means to weight control.

By examining the industrial model for wellness programs, it becomes clear that a primary motive for the development of health promotion programs is economic. Cost containment in medical care is a driving force that is consistently identified in conjunction with health promotion programs. Implementation of such programs provides additional benefits such as decreased absenteeism, improved morale, a better sense of community, and a feeling that the management cares about its personnel. But it is increased medical costs and the subsequent increase in health insurance premiums that forces companies to investigate cost-saving alternatives. Health insurance benefits are generally supplied by the employer, and the cost of providing this benefit has increased dramatically in the last 15 years and is predicted to double again before 1990.

In the United States, the term *health care* is commonly used to describe medical practices, but in fact medical practice was, and largely still is, centered around the treatment of disease. Thus when we read about increases in health care costs, we are really reading about the cost of treating disease. Very little money is dedicated to preventive medicine. This is hardly surprising, since the medical community has our tacit approval concerning the manner in which they control the medical care system. It is only natural that more money is spent on disease treatment than on disease prevention.

Because of this concern for the treatment of disease, the U.S. has the most advanced medical technology in the world. Our medical schools train practitioners to work with these technologies and treat disease. But little emphasis is placed upon disease prevention except in a few schools that train family practitioners. The average physician is unaccustomed to working with a healthy body and generally does not see a patient until a disease has produced observable symptoms. Technology and molecular engineering have provided means to eradicate many diseases that were rampant in the early 1900s. But we now have the chronic diseases that result from inactivity, malnutrition, and stress. Physicians rarely see patients during the years these chronic diseases are developing. Since there are no outward symptoms, the diseases develop undetected.

The availability of new technologies and the cost of developing them has had a direct impact on the cost of medical care. Medical costs are predicted to double again by the year 1990, a factor that will no doubt further raise public consciousness to the importance of health as the private and public sectors do all within their power to make their employees aware of mounting medical costs. Free or low-cost health insurance has been a traditional benefit provided by major corporations or state and local government. Adaptations of space age technology and medicine, genetic engineering and the controlled production of drugs and hormones only available 10 years ago as synthetic analogues, improvements in organ transplant techniques coupled with the advances in anaesthetic procedures revolutionized by semiconductor technology—these have all contributed to the miracle of modern medicine. Such advanced medical practices are available to more and more patients, but the cost of making them available is breaking the back of the traditional health care benefits package that is built around medical and surgical benefits. Thus, the growth of interest in wellness/health promotion appears to have an economic base, not a utilitarian ethic.

It is difficult to argue with the concept of health promotion programs. However, the move to wellness/health promotion programs is causing some concern in organized labor because many union leaders are afraid that health promotion programs will be substituted for health care benefits, or will take the focus away from health risks that predominate in some working environments. Wyatt Company of New York surveyed 1,115 organizations from a representative cross-section of American businesses and found that 52% of the employers provided free coverage under medical plans in 1980, whereas only 39% offered similar coverage in 1984. These results would seem to support the labor leaders' fears when considered in light of the increase in workplace wellness programs. However, there is not enough data to support true medical care cost reductions in businesses where wellness/health promotion programs have been implemented (Cox, Shepard, & Corey, 1981; Shepard, 1984; Wilbur, 1982).

Perhaps the greatest area for research in all of wellness is that of systematic evaluation of the reduction in medical care cost that is associated with participation in wellness/health promotion programs. A variety of positive outcomes are associated with the institutionalization of workplace wellness programs (O'Donnell, 1984; Wilbur, 1982): better job satisfaction, a general feeling of well-being, reduced absenteeism, and increased productivity. Thus, although the motive for instituting wellness/health promotion programs is economic, the outcome may well resemble a utilitarian ethic whereby society benefits. In the last analysis, however, little appears to have been done to reduce medical care costs.

We should question this lack of reduction in medical care costs. Undoubtedly it results from many factors. It is true that we have no control over the cost of medical care provided by hospitals and physicians. In fact, more sophisticated technologies are being incorporated into medical practice every day. Recent studies of organizations that have implemented wellness/health promotion programs indicate that the number of hospital and doctor visits are reduced for the employees who participate in the program—but the cost of providing the coverage for these fewer visits increases rather than decreases!

These increases can be explained in three ways: (a) Some cost increases reflect inflation. (b) Hospitals have relatively fixed costs in terms of physical plant and operation, and if they are to remain solvent they must transfer these costs to fewer patients. (c) Medicare and Medicaid pay only a fraction of the cost of hospitalization. With the federal government paying a smaller portion of these costs, more costs are then transferred to patients covered by private insurers. Medical care costs are more likely to be influenced by factors beyond the control of the individual than by the number of hospital or doctor visits.

Medical Influences

Despite my belief that the wellness movement stems from economic rather than profound ethical concerns, I have to acknowlege medicine's contribution to the growth of wellness/health promotion programs. The contribution is real, although somewhat oblique. Disease in our culture has changed over the years. Infectious diseases were the bane of the medical profession 40 years ago, but today many of them have been virtually eradicated. Now we have chronic diseases such as cancer, obesity, and heart disease and stroke; we know that many of these diseases are linked to life style (lack of exercise, smoking, alcohol abuse, drug abuse). The

Centers for Disease Control in Atlanta have suggested that roughly 50% of all deaths result from diseases that are associated with life style. Logically, if we can influence life style we should be able to influence these disease states. Most wellness/health promotion programs are built around this premise and seek to influence behavior and life style. But the traditional medical model attempts no intervention until a disease state is manifested.

This dependency on symptomatology for the identification of a diseased state cannot work for chronic diseases. By their very nature, chronic diseases are states that develop over a long period of time and persist, usually to become increasingly debilitating. Chronic disease states that are associated with the workplace have been developing over a considerable period of time, and dealing with them in the workplace may be like closing the barn door after the horse has bolted. Thus, a major opportunity for health and physical education is to establish healthy life styles in the formative years.

Wellness programs are built upon the premise that an individual should assume responsibility for his or her health and change life-style factors that contribute to chronic disease or other health risks. Wellness programs deal with physical, nutritional, psychological, intellectual, and metaphysical components of living. They involve a true integration of all components that constitute self.

Exercise is a key ingredient in any wellness program. As a single element it can contribute more than any other. However, physical fitness should not be confused with exercise, nor should physical fitness activities be considered the *only* activities suitable for a wellness program. Physical fitness results from participation in exercise and is usually measured in terms of aerobic capacity, and to some degree strength and flexibility. For some individuals, diet and inability to cope with stress combine to produce more deadly effects than lack of exercise. This statement is not meant to diminish the importance of sustained rhythmic activity that elevates the heart rate. Rather, it is intended to highlight other issues, such as stress and nutrition, which can have enormous influence on our health and well-being.

The need to cope, indeed to learn how, is expressed delightfully by Robert Elliott, a Nebraska cardiologist. Elliott has two rules when he discusses coping with his patients:

1. Don't sweat the small stuff.
2. It's all small stuff; if you can't fight and you can't flee, flow.

Coping skills may be as important to the student in school as to the worker in the workplace. We could equate truancy from school with absenteeism in the workplace, for both often reflect stress-related symptoms. Thus we can establish another link between problems in the workplace and problems in the public schools. Stress is known to be a major contributor to coronary artery disease, cancer, lung disease, accidental injury, cirrhosis of the liver, and suicide—six of the leading causes of death in the U.S. for all ages. Suppression of the immune system (decrease in the number of T-lymphocytes and macrophages) by chronic stress is, without question, linked to some of these diseases. Although we might argue that accidents and suicide are discrete events, they generally reflect a long-term erosion of either the ability to concentrate or the ability to see a sense of purpose in life.

The effects of stress are insidious. Slowly but inexorably they erode physical and mental well-being. Exercise certainly appears to alleviate some symptoms of stress, but so do other activities such as transcendental meditation, fishing, or collecting wildflowers. Exercise is not a panacea for the ills of modern life, but it is a powerful tool in our toolbox. Yet, we must not ignore the potential contribution of other activities in dealing with stress.

Stress management should be included in any health promotion program, and a variety of techniques should be explored so that individuals can adopt those best suited to them. We cannot avoid stress, but we can learn to channel our response to stress in a manner that minimizes its harmful effects. The earlier we learn these techniques, the less likely chronic disease becomes a necessary part of modern living. Children need to learn coping skills in their formative years.

Social Influences

When the President's Council on Physical Fitness was established in the 1960s, little did we know the extent to which diseases due to lack of exercise would affect the U.S. population. The major concern at that time was national defense: the launching of Sputnik by the Soviet Union on October 4, 1957, shocked the U.S. into an evaluation of its military capabilities, both in terms of technology and manpower. Films like ''The Flabby American'' emphasized the plight of the military. New recruits were found to be weaker, fatter, and less fit than those of previous generations. The push for fitness began. Unfortunately, it began too late for a whole generation of Americans who were beyond the draft age and who had established life styles with rich foods and little exercise during the relatively comfortable 1950s when good jobs were plentiful and inflation was minimal. This shift to a life style of plenty is understandable, for these were the children raised during the years of World War II. The tragedy is that these children were fed diets rich in animal fats and proteins, and labor-saving devices were replacing what little physical work was left in the home or in the workplace. The stage was set for chronic disease. Families share a common life style, which then becomes a source of learning for children; they in turn often pattern their own lives the same way. Exposure to high fat diets, cigarette smoking, and sedentary living habits in childhood may have a greater influence on coronary artery disease than genetic factors (Kirby, 1980). The real impact of these life styles is only now becoming apparent.

Despite a 22% decrease in death from coronary artery disease in the period from 1968 to 1977, 38% of all deaths for all ages in the U.S. in 1975 were a result of heart disease (DHEW, 1979). The dramatic reduction in deaths from heart disease is not just a reflection of the effects of jogging and exercise programs. It also reflects the changes in our society during the 1960s, when young people rejected such practices as smoking cigarettes and eating copious amounts of red meat or foods that were not organically grown. This decade also saw the beginning of the running movement in the U.S., and there is no denying the importance of aerobic activities in combatting heart disease.

We know that aerobic activity has a positive effect on the cardio-respiratory system and the muscular system (Booth, 1985; Clausen, 1977; Rowell, 1974; Scheuer & Tipton, 1977). We also know that exercise requires an increased metabolic rate, and increased metabolism requires more energy, and that elevated metabolism continues for some time after the exercise has ceased. Hence, exercise can help control weight. Aerobic exercise is also accompanied by changes in the lipid profile of the blood (Lehtonen & Viikari, 1978; Squires et al., 1979). People who exercise have lower levels of cholesterol and triglycerides and higher levels of high density lipoprotein (a substance that appears to protect against the buildup of atherosclerotic plaque), changes which help guard against coronary artery disease.

Measures of the advancement of our society include *perceived* better nutrition and an ever increasing number of labor-saving devices at home and at work. Both work to the detriment of our bodies. The perception that we practice good nutrition is erroneous. We are dominated by marketing and advertising; we are gullible travelers in a world of Lilliputian nutrition and Brobdingnagian burgers. We have come to equate good nutrition with more protein, especially protein from red meat. We consume fewer tuberous vegetables and legumes, fewer whole grains, and more refined sugar and alcohol. We are pawns in the hands of industry where corporate profits dictate corporate practices, where utilitarianism appears to be, essentially, extinct and the phoenix of corporate existentialism has arisen from its ashes.

We live on diets that have 30% more fat than our grandparents consumed only 50 years ago (Brewster & Jacobsen, 1978). Our palates have been cultivated to prefer a high fat diet to one low in fat. We know that saturated fats are undesirable, so we have substituted margarines and vegetable oils for butter and lard, yet our overall fat intake has increased.

We have come to believe that a 16 oz. steak and a salad is more nutritious than a baked potato, whole grain bread, a green vegetable, and a 4 oz. serving of meat. Athletic trainers of the 1960s and 1970s reinforced this perception; large portions of meat and eggs were routine for athletes in training.

Even nutritious foods can be overconsumed. Milk is an important source of minerals and vitamins. Whole milk also contains significant quantities of animal fats; yet milk is a nutritious part of any diet. It has been argued that it takes about 10 pounds of milk to make one pound of cheese, therefore cheese has 10 times as much nutrition as milk. It is difficult to argue with the logic. However, cheese is no longer used in the same manner it was originally. Cheeses were developed as a means to preserve milk before refrigeration or the manipulation of fertility cycles in cows so that we could have milk throughout the year. Cheeses were used in place of other animal protein and formed the main part of the meal. Today cheese has become an appetizer. It is consumed in copious amounts *before* a meal, compounding the fat and nutritional problems. Animal protein contains cholesterol, a substance noticeably absent in vegetable protein sources.

High levels of serum cholesterol are associated with heart disease and stroke. It remains yet to be demonstrated that high serum cholesterol levels are associated with high cholesterol intake (Flynn, Nolph, & Flynn, 1979; Simmons, Gibson, & Painoc, 1978). But there is evidence of a synergistic effect when high cholesterol intake is combined with high saturated fat intake, producing high serum cholesterol levels (Erschow, Nicilosi, & Hayes, 1981). Since cholesterol is present in the lean portion of animal protein, and animal fat is often associated with this protein, it is clear that eating large quantities of protein from animal sources could increase serum cholesterol levels.

Endurance exercise has a positive effect on the levels of cholesterol in the blood. In 1970 the term *aerobics* was virtually limited to describing a series of exercises designed to improve cardiovascular endurance. These activities received popular attention through Kenneth Cooper at his Aerobics Center in Dallas. Indeed, if there is a single figure who has had the greatest influence on the growth of the wellness phenomenon, it would almost certainly have to be Cooper. His medical credentials and commitment to healthful living, together with the extensive data and norms he has developed at the Aerobics Institute, have all served to further the cause of wellness.

Today, however, there is a proliferation of "health" spas and clinics where "aerobics" are taught. These aerobics bear little resemblance to the activities in early editions of Cooper's publications. They are a series of musical calisthenics taught by instructors whose only training was a course from someone else with similar credentials. Many of these instructors are not trained in the principles of conditioning. The activities themselves do contribute to cardiorespiratory fitness, there is no question of that. It is the level of instruction used to provide these activities that is being questioned.

Quackery abounds in the wellness marketplace, from the media hype concerning sauna belts and sauna suits to vitamins and protein supplements. Exercise is big business. Again, profit is dictating practice. The public needs to be educated concerning what is being delivered at the health spa and its contribution to healthful living. Many health spas are an extension of the same process that resulted in our adverse life-style changes. Few contribute to anything other than the cosmetic appearance of being well; they simply pamper us in a luxurious surrounding.

Professional Implications

This chapter is not meant to be a treatise on exercise or life style, but rather to serve as a brief outline of a problem that could significantly affect health and physical education and the manner in which we train professionals for the future. An evaluation of wellness programs reveals that they are as varied as the backgrounds of the individuals who manage them. Here is an opportunity for the fields of health and physical education; we can prepare professionals trained to implement health promotion programs.

The common elements in the opportunity are not health and physical education. They are the concepts of wellness that transcend the traditional boundaries of either health or physical education. We may argue long over which discipline should prepare professionals capable of delivering holistic wellness programs. But the point is, neither the health educator nor the physical educator, as traditionally prepared, is equipped to undertake the responsibility for developing healthy life styles, either in the formative years or in the workplace, although together they have more to contribute than any other two disciplines.

As physical educators we espouse the concept of total self and speak eloquently against the separation of mind and body, but we only teach to body. We still operate in the 1980s with the same philosophy articulated by Williams, that the other concomitant benefits of physical activity will occur. We do this implicitly in the way we prepare our educators to teach skills (McNeill, 1982). Surely we can do better. We can address the skills *and* the other dimensions we feel are important enough to justify physical education in public school curricula.

The wellness model is in the workplace, or least in some workplaces, but the educational process concerning health and well-being must begin with the public schools. Presently, physical education teaches skills. The philosophical basis upon which physical education programs are developed utilizes the principles of wellness and emphasizes the benefits that accrue from exercise. But wellness principles go beyond fitness. Somewhere between belief and practice we have lost a critical element. We have lost sight of the educational purpose; we have assumed the typical educational position of transferring knowledges and developing skills, but pay little attention to the true education of the child. We need to develop programs that nurture the decision-making process, programs that attend to the importance of self, not in a selfish way, but instead by responsibly assuming control of life-style factors that affect health.

Health education teaches many concepts of wellness. Certainly it espouses self-actualization, social actualization, and androgeny. However, health education is viewed by many physical educators and school boards as a bastard child of physical education, whose rights to practice are limited, if not outright denied.

The wellness movement is derived in part from a belief that medical care costs can be contained by individuals assuming responsibility for their life style. I believe the present arrangement with the medical model "health" care makes it unlikely that wellness/health programs will reduce medical care costs. However, health promotion programs can help reduce the prevalence of chronic diseases that plague us today. Redesigning school health and physical education programs to encompass wellness principles and teaching children how to make life-style choices that will enhance their health is an essential step for a better society.

The concept is deceptively simple. But professional differentiation may prevent our succeeding. More effort is going into defining new subdisciplines in health and physical education than is being expended to integrate the knowledges that these subdisciplines produce. The existential phoenix is alive and well in our profession as well as in the corporate marketplace. The need for professional identity will most likely destroy attempts at integration. At one level the bastard child seeks its own autonomy; within health and physical education, factionalism at all levels spreads like a cancer. To a degree, I believe that our professions have lost sight of their common purpose as helping professions.

No other curricular areas in our public schools and universities have the ability to influence the future of our society as profoundly as ours. Our uniqueness is that we work with people, not technology or machines. Our responsibility is to build a better society.

Sport Management: Its Potential and Some Developmental Concerns

Betty van der Smissen
Bowling Green State University

Sport Management has existed as an activity from at least the time of the ancient Greeks, reflecting the importance of sport in the lives of men. Sport management in modern times, however, has not developed professionally as rapidly as management in other industries, perhaps reflecting a continuing association in the public mind of sport with play and management with work. (Lewis & Appenzeller, 1985, p. iii)

To be true, this statement needs to have a phrase inserted: has not developed professionally *within physical education*. Sport has always been "managed," but not by physical education professionals. Persons directing physical education curricula have been content over the past 50 years to focus on traditional learning and programs in the schools, especially with the boom of education in the 1970s. They could not be bothered with sport outside the schools. Historically, sport (athletics), intramurals, and physical education instruction *in the schools* were conducted by physical educators. However, in the last 10 years athletics in colleges has moved away from physical education departments, there have been increasingly fewer joint coach/instructor appointments (except in smaller colleges), many women physical educators have failed to embrace women's varsity athletics fully, and fewer and fewer varsity athletes have majored in physical education. In a good number of institutions, intramurals and club sports have been realigned under student affairs/activities, often not directed by a physical educator. And in the elementary and secondary schools, physical educators are not wanting to coach, forcing states to authorize nonteacher certified persons for coaching positions and to utilize nonphysical education teachers. And in the private sector, one finds few physical educators in pro or amateur sport positions, in sales of products, in hospitality enterprises, or in health spas. Traditionally, physical educators have been employed in YMCA and

YWCA physical activity programs, and some corporate fitness programs also seek out physical education (graduate level) exercise physiology specialists.

Thus, it seems a paradox that physical education now wants to make sport management an alternative career for physical education majors. It has only been since the decline of enrollments in physical education in colleges and universities that physical educators have begun to look with envious eye at sport as an arena for jobs. These physical educators are saying to non physical educators in sport positions, "Hey, we're the sport experts—get off our 'turf'!" Whose turf? Occupancy is 90% of the claim to turf—one cannot claim turf merely by acclaiming ownership— particularly when one has denied interest previously. There must be performance; physical educators must exhibit ability to "manage" better than others who do not have a physical education background.

The subsequent discussion of sport management focuses upon (a) the development of sport management as an outgrowth of society, (b) a definition of what sport management is from various perspectives, (c) sport management as a career, (d) the curriculum components for preparing individuals for a career in sport management, (e) professional organizations and journals related to sport management, and (f) the future of sport management.

Sport Management—An Outgrowth of Society

Whether or not physical education as a profession can qualify for management of sport, sport managers are and will remain in demand, for sport management is not isolated from society but is an outgrowth of it. Sport in society is not thought of as physical education.

> Sport is a mind-set that involves leisure and recreation. It is part of the culture and is engrained in Western civilization. It represents a cross section of society and brings together all subcultures. . . . There has been little change in quality and a much greater change in quantity [in sports in the past 10 years]. New sports, as a result of technology, are in the process of being developed at an ever-increasing rate. . . . [While] discretionary income that is available to the family expenditure on professional sports has increased and the number of individuals has increased proportionately. . . . the main impact has been upon the interest in greater diversity of sport while still maintaining a high interest level in the traditional sports. (Byers, 1983, p. 32)
>
> *Sport does pervade life* as a vehicle in participation as a spectator and as a player toward the pursuit of happiness. . . . Participatory and spectator sports have a pervasive influence on the lives of a vast

majority of Americans, affecting the quality of marital relations, patterns of child rearing and the reading and television watching habits of millions. Seventy-four percent of the population watches sports on television at least once a week, and almost 70 percent say they engage in sport or physical education at least once a week. In terms of numbers, swimming is the most popular participatory sport in America, with 33 percent of the population swimming at least once a week. . . . Couples with similar levels of sports interests appear to be more satisfied with their marriages, and 75 percent of American parents encourage their children to participate in sports. Eighty-five percent watch their children compete and cheer them on. . . . One out of every four Americans surveyed said participating in or watching sports events brought the family closer together. In terms of leisure activity, the survey found that 50 percent of those families who share a high interest in sports express a high degree of satisfaction with their overall leisure time, compared with 32 percent of those who share a low interest in sports. (van der Smissen, 1984, p. 9)

The horizons of amateur sport continue to be expanded. "America's strength has always been found in its diversity, and that's as true of amateur sport as it is of any other segment of society. Nowhere else in the world do athletics proliferate under as many disparate banners, ranging from youth recreation programs to Olympic-class training centers ("Grass-Roots," 1985, p. 10). Grass-roots participation is essential to developing elite athletes.

Sport is a major factor in the economy of the nation and of many states. For example, according to its Division of Tourism, the Missouri economy in 1985 enjoyed a $140 million boost because of the state's 13 postseason baseball games in the major league playoffs and World Series (*Sports Industry News*, 1985). Clothing, equipment, food service, and so forth related to sport also account for many dollars in the economy not only of a state but also of cities and communities. The National Sporting Goods Association (NSGA) estimates that sales in 1984 for sporting goods and recreational transport (e.g., bicycles, snowmobiles) totaled $23.4 billion; a 7% increase was anticipated for 1985 (*Leisure Industry Digest*, 1985, July 30).

Economies for corporations give impetus to fitness programs in the corporate setting. These economies are both in health care cost containment and in absenteeism reduction and productivity. While health promotion has a number of elements, certainly one of the most vital is that of physical activity. Some corporations have incentive plans for employees that include aerobic workouts and other physical fitness activity. A fitness program also may affect workers' compensation/insurance rates ("Big Business," 1985). And of course, all are familiar with the increased interest in health and fitness by individuals. The exercise equipment market exceeded $1 billion in 1984, for the first time in NSGA's 10 years of surveys (*Leisure Industry Digest*, 1985, July 30).

This interest in sport and fitness has given rise to the entrepreneurial inclination of many persons. The report of *Recreation, Sports, & Leisure's* 1984 survey of managed recreation states,

> it seems that the business of managed recreation today is characterized by a number of paradoxes. For one thing, while many have told us that it's easier than ever to make money providing fitness and leisure services to Americans, it's also easier than ever to fail. And, while the public pursues new fitness and recreation activities with an avidity that continues to astonish observers, they have become downright business-like about it—demanding speed, convenience, and cost-concessions from operators.
>
> Add to this mixture a public appetite that can be as fickle as it is voracious, and you have an industry that is experiencing constant change. While many indicators lead us to believe that managed recreation is maturing as an industry, we're also impressed by its increasing competitiveness. Single-purpose facilities are rapidly becoming obsolete, as more and more operators attempt to provide a total range of services to consumers.
>
> As a result, we see private facilities (that pay taxes) competing with nonprofit, tax-exempt facilities; hotel/resorts offering fitness packages that compete with multi-purpose clubs; multi-purpose clubs with food and beverage operations that compete with stand-alone restaurants. Because the public appetite seems limitless, everybody appears to want as much of it as possible . . . not only to increase profit margins, but also to provide some insulation from ever-changing shifts in public tastes. (1985, p. 13)

Sport Management—What Is It?

Sport management is the direction given to the setting structure in which physical activity is offered to the clientele. One might distinguish conduct of the physical activity and management of the setting in which that conduct takes place.

There is no simplistic definition of sport management. Most commonly it is used in the physical education context as the use of physical activity for any of a large variety of roles when not a part of the school instructional program, that is, when not encompassed by traditional physical education. Some would distinguish physical activity when used in a formal, organized format as *sport*, and when not constrained by organizational structure, as *exercise*. However, sport should not be considered synonymous with formal competition with others, for there are many sports in which one engages for enhancement of skill, the psychological/intellectual challenges, or the exhilaration of peak performance, or simply the freedom of movement. Physical fitness, on the other hand, is a condition of a person derived from engagement in physical activity, whether of the sport or exercise type. Because the use of physical activity as exercise is often used to enhance physical fitness, some would prefer the term *sport and fitness management*. It would not seem appropriate to say "sport and exercise," since sport also is exercise. Certainly there are many managed settings for fitness enhancement and a considerable number of these are in multiservice facilities, which include sports. Use of both terms, sport and fitness management, would convey management of both formal competitive and informal sport, as well as other forms of exercise.

In order to better understand sport management, one must look at it from various perspectives. It is acknowledged that the descriptions may be simplistic and not discrete categories; however, the following perspectives are presented as discussion stimuli to provide a more analytical approach to sport management and thus gain greater insights.

The Perspective of Various Fields

The Leisure Industry.   Sport management is one aspect of managed recreation, of leisure industry management. It focuses upon recreational sports, both informal organized competition and individual leisure activities. The leisure industry provides opportunities for sport experiences, whether in (a) public recreation-sponsored leagues and tournaments or in public areas and facilities, (b) as an offering at resorts and private clubs, through commercial sport enterprises (particularly pro sports), or under the organizational aegis of amateur sport organizations and voluntary associations. The largest basketball league in the world is said to be under the direction of the Mormon Church. The leisure industry encompasses intramurals and club sports in schools, as well as nonschool sport activities that are less known (e.g., karate), are water-related (e.g., marinas, water skiing, white-water rafting, sailing, fishing), take place at the raceways (e.g., auto, harness racing), or that are snow-related (e.g., the ski resorts).

Paradoxically, the recreation major programs associated with HPER claim commercial leisure management in their domain, yet deny association with physical education, the "experts" of physical activity and sport. This denial is in spite of the fact that sport has been an integral part of organized public recreation since the beginning of public recreation systems in municipalities. Only now with the rise of sport management has recreation begun to look at sport as part of leisure industry management.

Perhaps a more underlying reason for organized recreation not having been involved more with commercial sport management has been the close, often singular association of professional recreators ("NRPA types") with public (e.g., city, county, state, federal) recreation and its underlying philosophy of "recreation for all" and at a nominal cost to the participant. Further, some have the philosophy that individuals should have a totally free choice of activities without any marketing of one or more activities to influence the individual's choice. The ethics of marketing public services, suggesting that it denies the essence of public recreation and the right to define one's own leisure style, has been discussed by Godbey (1984), a recreation educator. Recreation major programs also often have embraced the term "leisure" in their title, yet failed to expand their curricula to encompass the leisure industry. Some recreation researchers have preferred to ignore the whole leisure industry for the academic study of leisure. When recreation curricula have added commercial recreation as a track or option, most frequently they have not embodied sport management as a primary aspect of it.

Physical Education.   From the perspective of physical education, sport management has not really been management. It has tended to be sport education wherein the thrust/concern has been for motor development through sport activity, the learning of a skill in the development of motor control for younger children, whereas older youth might be directed more toward performance of a sport skill and strategy knowledge of the sport to enhance their lifetime sport capability. However, the extension of this into involvement of physical educators in youth sports in the community settings seems minimal. Intramurals has served as a laboratory for sport performance and gaining an understanding of sport organization. This philosophic concept of the function of intramurals at the college level seems to have waned about 1980. Also, participation by physical education majors in varsity sports to enhance their skill and understanding of strategies appears to have decreased substantially. Physical education seems to be in a quandry, uncertain as to just what role sport should play in its school program and what role physical educators should have in sport in nonschool settings, yet all the while the increase in sport participation spirals upward. The question appears to be, can or should physical education extend itself into sport management, or is sport management really a separate programmatic area?

Whereas sport seems to have declined within the field of physical education, physical fitness seems to have gained a role. Physical educators in the last two decades have latched on to the AAHPERD and President's Fitness Council fitness tests; however, some feel that to focus on the scores of tests has reduced the effectiveness of physical education and its contribution to human development. Such tests should be only one motivational tool utilized and not the curriculum. In the 1980s more attention is being given to motor fitness and health-related physical fitness for youth (Pate, 1983). Notwithstanding this concern for youth fitness and the national criticism regarding the fitness of our nation's children and the "failure" of physical education in the schools, the fitness specialist does not seem to have found a place in the school system, nor has total fitness taken a primary place among the objectives of physical education in the schools.

Fitness is different at the young adult and adult levels. At the graduate level of education especially, not the teacher educators but the exercise physiologists have found many career opportunities. The approach to fitness has been rather narrow, however.

> During the aerobics boom of the 1970s it wasn't considered difficult to select an exercise mode. But the most popular ones—running, cycling, swimming, and walking—were those that concentrated on improving cardiovascular function, and little emphasis was placed on improving the other components of fitness and health. Today aerobic training is just part of a fitness framework that includes proper diet and weight control, stress management, and reduction of smoking, alcohol, and drug use, as well as the four fitness components (cardiovascular endurance, strength, flexibility, and body composition). . . . An exercise program should improve all four physiological components of fitness . . . and take into account mode, duration, intensity, and frequency of exercise . . . must also determine why . . . wants to exercise and . . . personality characteristics that may affect motivation, compliance, and the perceived benefits of exercise. (Hage, 1983, p. 123)

Along with fitness, the term *sports medicine* has become popular, although, unfortunately, it often is used to enhance by terminology the athletic training program or is limited essentially to exercise physiology rather than the more complete scope of elements of sport medicine. Sport medicine embraces psychologists, dentists, physicians, optometrists, athletic trainers, physical therapists, orthotists, podiatrists, nutritionists, exercise physiologists, kinesiologists, and others (Lombardo, 1985). Nevertheless, the ACSM's certification program focuses primarily upon exercise physiology. Although physical education does provide the foundation of the sport sciences for the exercise physiologist, the applied exercise physiologist has affiliated more with various fitness organizations (business, industry, voluntary organizations, private) and the research-rehabilitation (including athlete injury rehabilitation) exercise physiologist with the American College of Sports Medicine rather than the American Alliance for Health, Physical Education, Recreation and Dance (AAHPERD), the primary physical education professional organization.

Athletics. From the perspective of athletics, sport management is the organization of formal competitive team and individual sports for the elite child athlete, high school and college varsity performers, amateur adult athletes (e.g., Olympic sports and governing associations of specific sports), and professional athletes. The focus is upon the structural setting in which sport takes place and the management of sport, including promoting it, employing coaches and support personnel, and controlling spectators. However, when associated with physical education, athletics has been approached primarily from the coaching aspect, except for interscholastic athletics whereby the athletic director is frequently a physical educator in the school system. Athletics has not traditionally been a college major curriculum, though normally there is a course in the administration of interscholastic athletics. Sport management recognizes the viability of the curricular program for athletic management/administration.

The Perspective of the Roles of Sport

Sport is an Activity. In the schools, in public recreation, in the YWCA and YMCAs, in the military, in amateur sports, in retirement villages and senior centers, in resorts and hotels, in employee recreation in business and industry, sports are just one of the varied leisure activities, characterized by the focus being on the conduct of the activity by the leadership. The leadership may provide services in the way of instruction, organization of the activity to get those interested in participating together, general supervision in individual participation on facilities provided, and so forth. It is essentially a people-to-people relationship, the joy of working with people in activity, of seeing them grow and develop and enjoying themselves. Individuals participate for the "good in" sport, exhilaration of peak performance, the "feeling good" (Harris, 1983). Leaders are concerned with budget primarily as adequacy of equipment, areas, and facilities, not a balancing of income and expenditures or profit; frequently income is derived from taxes or contributions, fees, and membership dues. Prerequisite abilities of the leadership are not management skills so much as activity leadership skills.

Sport is a Modality. Sport is a modality to achieve certain objectives. One might ask, "What is sport good *for*?" Some of the prime uses of sport are for stress reduction, cardiac rehabilitation, physical rehabilitation from injuries, general increase of fitness, control of obesity, and mitigating of certain diseases. However, normally it is not sport per se but the exercise that is prescribed. But, to get this exercise through sport participation usually is more pleasurable. Sport also may be used as a modality in dealing with behavioral and emotional problems. Research and empirical evidence support the effectiveness of sport as a modality, depending upon the individual's circumstances. As with sport as an activity, the focus is upon activity leadership skills rather than management of a setting or structure. The leader is often part of a professional team.

Sport is the Service.   Sport is a business enterprise—racquet clubs, golf country clubs, marinas, aquatic complexes, fitness centers, private membership clubs, and so forth. The person in charge manages the facility and hires others to conduct the activities, unless it is a small operation in which the manager also may conduct some of the sport activities. The essence of management is to service the clientele and turn a profit. Income and expenditures, and catering to the clientele's desires become critical elements in the operation. Although one has to provide sport the activity, the focus of sport as a service is upon the selling of sport services in the particular setting.

> The promotion of service represents a new dimension in marketing to many recreational sports managers. . . . The emphasis of marketing in the past has been the promotion of goods, not the promotion of services. . . . the difference between marketing goods and services. Goods have physical substance; they are tangible and can be seen, bought, used, stored, and used again. Services, on the other hand, are intangible to the customer and are usually produced and utilized simultaneously. A service can most accurately be described as: any task or work performed for another and the provision of any facility, commodity or activity for another's use and not ownership. It is, therefore, intangible and incapable of being stored or recalled for further use without enacting an additional transaction. (Marciani, 1985, p. 30)

In order to know clientele needs for services, which is essential to having a successful business, one must keep abreast of changing society. McCarthy (1985), executive director of International Racquet Sports Association, has stated,

> In order to identify the opportunities for continued growth in the investor-owned club industry, it is necessary to note three changes that the industry has undergone in the last five years: the movement from a single-purpose racquet club to a multi-purpose athletic/fitness/social club; the movement from indoor-only to four-season indoor/outdoor clubs; and the movement from an annual dues plus pay-as-you-go-play pricing system, to an initiation fee plus monthly dues system. . . . Future success lies principally in attracting three distinct markets: (the de-conditioned, the family, the corporate America—the country's business and professional work force). (p. 38)

Sport is a Tenant.   Sport is a tenant in a larger enterprise, such as a stadium, arena, or sport complex. In this role, sport is just one of the varied events. In reference to arenas, specifically the Tacoma Dome, the Dome's manager stated,

> making a profit—and it's doing so by taking a strong special events approach rather than relying heavily on sports programming. . . . Our driving concept is that everything in the building, whether it's an athletic event, a concert, an exhibit show, a truck and tractor pull or a rodeo, is in fact a special event. . . . Out of our total available usage, we are looking to do 25 percent in athletics. ("Sporting Palace," 1985, p. 36)

Sport is a Sales Product.   Sport is a sales product sold to persons engaging in sport to enhance their participation, whether actual or perceived. Markets are created by making individuals believe they need some sport product for performance or social reasons. It was reported that the National Sporting Goods Association trade show had about 45,000 dealers/retailers (*Leisure Industry Digest*, 1985, September 16). The sales representative can be a most important element in business success, particularly with high technology playing an increasingly more extensive role.

> As advanced technology makes its way into the sports arena, more sophisticated exercise equipment is appearing in fitness centers. Corporate fitness facilities across the country now boast computerized exercise machines, pulse monitoring devices, and hydraulic and air-pressurized weight resistance machines, all of which provide many, sometimes unexpected, benefits.
>
> Above all, the new equipment promotes employee participation and health, if for no other reason than that it acts as a lure to bring new participants into the programs. In addition, in most cases it provides more immediate, convenient and accurate feedback than does conventional exercise equipment. (Jameson, 1985, p. 37)

But sales in sport is not just equipment and wearing apparel; there also are opportunities relating to information of many types.

> Imagine the variety of educational programs that could be offered to employees: classes . . . lectures . . . instruction . . . self-improvement . . . Companies that already house libraries of audio-visual materials for job-related technical training can easily set up audio or video presentations on health and wellness to supplement their corporate fitness programs. . . . A successful audiovisual program can mean employee satisfaction both on and off the job. (Zauzmer, 1985, p. 30)

So, in addition to sales persons, there is a wide career field for technical writers and instructional media experts. Closely related is the advertising field with its generous use of sport as an advertising medium. One only has to see or hear television, magazine, or newspaper ads to realize how extensively sport is used in advertising.

There are other typologies of organization that might be used to discuss the scope and nature of sport management. Snyder (1986), a sport sociologist, has discussed structure of sport management using Blau and Scott's (1962) organization classifications based upon the primary beneficiary of (a) mutual-benefit associations—the rank and file members benefit; (b) business concerns—owners and managers benefit; (c) service organizations—clients or outsiders are the beneficiaries; and (d) commonweal organizations—the public-at-large benefits. He also applied Etzioni's (1961) twofold classification typology. The first dimension related three ways that organizations may induce members to participate: coercive (use of force), remunerative (use of monetary or other extrinsic rewards), and normative (moral and educational development of the participants). The second dimension is based upon three types of involvement by the members: negative (participants are negative to the organization), extrinsic/social (participation is based on extrinsic or social rewards), and intrinsic/social (participation is based on intrinsic and social pleasures).

Sport Management—A Career

Sport management must be perceived as a career in itself. It must *not* be considered as alternate employment for a teacher-educated person who cannot find a teaching position; to be successful in sport management, one should be educated *for* sport management. According to Clayton and Clayton (1984), there are some unique differences and some key similarities between sport management and teaching physical education. (See Table 1.)

> The term emerging careers, often heard in professional meetings is really a misnomer. The majority of the careers are not new; rather, they have been filled by other than the traditionally-trained HPERD professional. . . . Careers in HPERD can be placed into six broad categories: (1) education, (2) fitness, medical, specialities, rehabilitation and therapy, (3) sales, (4) management, (5) performance, and (6) communication. (pp. 44-45)

Melnick (1980) listed six professional opportunities that sociologists of sport should consider, and there are similar opportunities for physical educators: (a) recreational sport facilities development, (b) consultant services to community sport organizations, (c) policy formulation and im-

Table 1

Specific Job Titles and Typical Places of Employment

Education

1. Teacher or Leader
   • Health: grades 7-12; colleges; private¹ clinics
   • Physical education: grades K-6; 7-12; colleges, private sport clubs
   • Recreation: city recreation departments; agencies
   • Dance: colleges; private studios
2. Scholar/Researcher in health, physical education, recreation, dance: college
3. Coach: grades 7-12; colleges; age-group teams in swimming, gymnastics, etc.; pro teams; private sport clubs
4. Teacher of the handicapped: grades K-6; 7-12; colleges; agencies

Fitness, Medical Specialties, Rehabilitation, and Therapy

5. Fitness leader: colleges; private sport clubs, recreation departments, dance studios, spas, business and industry
6. Exercise testing technician: colleges, private clubs, clinics, hospitals, business and industry
7. Exercise physiologist: colleges, private clubs, private clinics, hospitals, business and industry
8. Medical specialties (wellness, sports medicine, fitness, orthopedic surgery): private practice, colleges
9. Cardiac rehabilitation specialist: colleges, clinics, hospitals
10. Athletic trainer: colleges, clinics, pro teams
11. Therapist
    • corrective: hospitals, agencies
    • physical: hospitals, private practice, agencies, clinics
    • recreation: institutions, hospitals
    • dance: institutions, hospitals

Sales

12. Owner/manager: manufacturers, wholesalers, retail stores
13. Salesperson; manufacturers, wholesalers, retail stores, pharmaceutical companies

Management

14. Owner: athletic clubs, sport schools, dance studios, health-related clinics, camps, spas
15. Chief administrator
    • health: clinics, agencies
    • physical education: college athletic or HPERD departments, private clubs, pro teams, sport groups, professional groups
    • recreation: camps, city recreation departments
16. Business manager
    • health: clinics, private sport clubs
    • physical education: athletic clubs, spas, college athletic dept.
    • recreation: agencies
17. Sport facility director
    • physical education: arenas/stadia, private sport clubs, colleges
    • recreation: camps, arenas, playfields

(cont.)

Table 1 (cont.)

Specific Job Titles and Typical Places of Employment

Performance

18. Performer: touring professional (ice shows, pro teams, bowlers, etc.)
19. Official: professional leagues

Communication

20. Journalist: newspapers/magazines, college sports information director, freelance writer
21. Broadcaster: TV/radio

---

¹*Private* refers to profit-making groups, *agencies* refers to nonprofit groups
Note: This table is reprinted with permission from the *Journal of Physical Education, Recreation & Dance*, 1984, Volume 55(5), pp. 44-45. The *Journal* is a publication of the American Alliance for Health, Physical Education, Recreation and Dance, 1900 Association Drive, Reston, VA 22091.

plementation for sport commissions and agencies at all levels from local to international, (d) retirement community recreation sports programs planning and development, (e) adviser to governmental agencies on policy-related sport issues, and (f) consultants to amateur and professional sport groups and organizations.

Much has been written in newspapers and periodicals regarding careers related to fitness, especially corporate fitness programs. Some would question that fitness should be included under the umbrella of sport management, preferring to label the area sport and fitness management. There is little question that many management-oriented positions relate to fitness, in addition to the fitness program leadership-type positions.

> Keeping executives in tip-top shape is a new career for many experts . . . . Choosing to work in a new and developing profession can have tremendous advantages. In addition to growth potential and career flexibility, . . . are currently in high demand. . . . The availability of jobs in the field of corporate fitness can range from directors and program managers of large in-house fitness facilities, to part-time exercise test operators who monitor cardiac and stress responses while participants run on a treadmill or peddle an exercycle. Exercise physiologists are by far the most employable professionals in this rapidly expanding industry. . . . Personality is one element that can make or break a career in corporate fitness. ("Health & Medicine," 1985)

In addition to directors and program managers of corporate fitness, fitness consultants also have excellent career possibilities. According to Udeleff, "Finding the right [fitness] facility consultant can be as important as buying the right equipment or gaining employee support. Consultants can offer specialized help for specific problems, or take over the planning for an entire facility or program, based on the needs of the company" (1985, p. 35).

Two surveys give some insight into career potentials for nonfitness areas. Quain and Parks (1986) surveyed six career areas: physical fitness, sport promotion, sport marketing, sport administration and management, sport directing, and aquatics. Questionnaires were mailed to 200 active practitioners in each area, with an overall response rate of 31%. From their data, Quain and Parks concluded that the sport and fitness industries appear to be flourishing; some 365 practitioners reported 128 vacancies for a 1-year span. They indicated that vacancy rates in fitness, marketing, and management were "extremely high."

The second survey by *Recreation, Sports & Leisure* ("Managed Recreation," 1985) focused on various aspects of personnel such as characteristics of the professional, salaries, job satisfaction, and education and professional membership. This survey, done in 1985, included both private and public settings and had 2,211 respondents. The responses indicated that professionalism is becoming a critical factor in distinguishing the winners from the losers in today's managed recreation industry. In the private sector, mean salaries ranged from a low of $22,468 in retirement/life care centers to $41,451 in resort hotels/motels. The more common mean salaries, however, ranged in the $20,000s; private golf courses $22,544, multipurpose athletic clubs $24,914, YMCA/YWCAs $26,036, and tennis/racquetball clubs $28,832. However, there is considerable variation in salaries geographically, size of operation, nature of the responsibility, and experience. Generally, women have not reached parity with men, and in management positions the ratio of men to women is 3 to 1. Salaries often are considerably higher for men as well. In another survey done the next year by *Recreation, Sports & Leisure* ("Salaries in the Industry" 1986), generalizing from the data, it was indicated that there were no great increases in salary during the year and that age, experience, and gender still were important factors. The mean salary for women averages about 70% that of men for the same type of position.

Executive directors of several national organizations were asked about the future directions of the "managed recreation" industry ("State of the Industry," 1985, p. 85). J. McCarthy of the International Racquet Sports Association stated the suburban clubs are being developed as multipurpose, multiservice, indoor/outdoor facilities focusing upon social needs, fitness needs, and athletic needs. However, he indicated there is still growth, particularly in urban markets, for the modest sized fitness center. Professionalization of personnel is primarily in the fitness aspect of the industry, with the definition of fitness being expanded to a comprehensive wellness program including stress reduction, diet management, smoking cessation, and so forth. But according to McCarthy (1985, p. 38), "There are also tremendous opportunities opening up for training and educating middle managers in the industry. Look at a typical club. It's got a general manager, a fitness director, a facilities manager, a food and beverage director, a marketing director, a program director."

The executive director of the Golf Course Superintendents Association of America also indicated considerable anticipated growth in golf course construction, but noted that the golf clubs are going to have to be run like a business. The job opportunities extend beyond golf: "More and more, private developers are including golf courses—along with tennis courts, handball courts and so on—in residential developments. The recreation sites help sell the surrounding homes and time-sharing condominiums." The spa and pool industry also is experiencing considerable growth, according to the executive director of the National Spa and Pool Institute, who says, "It's become critical for any first-class hotel or health club to have a swimming pool. . . . should also mention the aquadynamics craze sweeping the country. With swimming you get the opportunity to really enjoy an exercise program that doesn't pound and beat and subject your body to a lot of stress, with the same muscle-toning and cardio-vascular benefit you get from other forms of exercise."

The executive director of Club Managers Association of America, an organization for private country, yacht, and town clubs, indicated that country clubs have had to diversify. Whereas a club previously might have offered only golf, clubs now are adding swimming, tennis, saunas, exercise rooms, and fitness facilities. Increased services means increased job opportunities. These are membership clubs and thus are not operated for profit; however, the business management aspect has become quite important both to meet competition and to keep from raising prices to what a member might consider excessive.

A 1984 survey by Sawyer (1985) assessed corporate fitness program director position and career paths. It was found that the directors usually had long tenure with the same firm and had little geographical mobility, and that nearly two thirds who obtained jobs through application-selection processes were promoted from within the firm. This stability of personnel also was found by the 1985 *Recreation, Sports & Leisure* survey previously described.

With changing lifestyles and the role of recreation on college campuses, there appears to be more career opportunities with college student recreation. The following addresses college recreation programs:

> the growth of open recreation programs means the role of recreation administrators is changing as well. They really have to be a lot more creative in their programming. . . . the role of recreation professionals becomes one of education and direction. . . . Student

recreation centers seem more and more to be patterned after the private health clubs and YMCAs. . . . in the role they play as social centers. On campus, that role can be very important in creating the total environment for quality education. . . . We are looking at the expectations of students . . . in self-development. Students today are looking for outlets to socialize and develop lifestyles. For many students, the recreation facility is becoming the center of their social life. . . . I think it's gone far beyond the concept of fitness, although that's still a major part of it. . . . play and having fun . . . to meet each other in a different setting. ("Recreation," 1985, pp. 10, 12, 14, 16)

While the leadership in youth sports has been longstanding volunteers, there appears to be increasing opportunities for careers with youth sports through associations for various amateur sports and organizations that sponsor youth sports. The concern is for organizational structure, including the promotion of sport and operational rules and regulations, and for training (e.g., clinics, workshops, literature, audiovisual materials) volunteer coaches for injury management and enhancing the physical development and skill competence of participants. There is increasing concern that youth sports does not have the proper perspective of sport for youth in today's society. This concern has been expressed by a number of people. A Minnesota director of a school district's community services and recreation states, "too much competitiveness; play should be an end in itself . . . play for the fun of it" (Korfhage, 1985, p. 32). And a person who spent 10 years with the P.A.L. program in New York expressed it this way:

The age bracket I wish to emphasize are the 5 to 12 years old. It is my personal belief that at this point in time they are not 'professional or college scholarship materials,' to me they are still babies and should be afforded appropriate attention from adult coaches. Bearing that in mind, I do not believe the game of baseball or any other sport for this age level should be termed a sport, but the playing of a game. I think if we keep in mind the age element we are dealing with and look upon baseball as a game for kids, we might be more sensible and realistic in our approach towards rules and adult participation. (Krupsky, 1985, p. 16)

Pat McInally (1985), a pro football player giving much time to youth sports, expressed his concern:

I really didn't need any surrogate father, which is the way a lot of coaches like to be looked at. . . . The second problem was that I really played sports for fun and the thing I always ran into was,

"You could do better if you were more serious." Like, when I kicked a 49-yard field goal my junior year in high school, if I hadn't been out there laughing and having a good time, I would have kicked a 60-yarder, which is not true, of course. . . . The coaching profession has come a long way. . . . What I'd like to see more of . . . is coaches explaining to the kids *why* they take laps and *why* they stretch, rather than just making them do it. (p. 10)

While the volunteer coaches do play a very important role in the value of youth sports to the participants, they do need certain training regarding those "whys" of conditioning and skill development and injury management.

> most youth sports programs share one major weakness. While most collegiate and many high school sports programs recognize the need for injury prevention and management programs, community youth sports programs tend to overlook this need. Because they are volunteers, coaches generally have had little or no first-aid training, and do not have a degree in a health-care field. . . . Injuries should be a major area of concern, . . . League officers often believe volunteer coaches are difficult to recruit. If coaches were required to have additional training, some officers feel it would be even more difficult to recruit the required number of coaches. However, league officers seem unaware that injuries received during the early years can continue to plague an athlete through adulthood if not handled correctly. (Hackworth, Jacobs, & O'Neill, 1983, p. 59)

Another developing career area is that of sport for the disabled, not the temporarily disabled but the permanently disabled or, as some would say, "the differently abled." This career area is not limited to adapted physical education in the schools, but rather is servicing the disabled in the nonschool setting. One can talk about accessibility of facilities and integrating the disabled into activities for the able-bodied, but to really provide for the *needs* of the disabled requires leadership and organization/management of the setting. Opportunities are found both in an integrated setting where the able-bodied and disabled work and play side by side ("Sport Haven," 1985), and in specialized settings for only the disabled. There also are career opportunities, as well as extensive volunteer opportunities, in organizations focusing upon specific disabilities. Considerably more attention is now being given to the elite athlete who happens to be disabled in some way. These athletes have need for the same type of support services (e.g., coaching, athletic training/conditioning) as able-bodied athletes. The field of aquatics for the disabled, both as a sport and for fitness, has seen expansion and emphasis in recent years, a direction which appears to be continuing into the latter 1980s.

Sport Management—The Curriculum

As part of the physical education curriculum, sport management can bring new enthusiasm and perspective to physical education. Embracing sport management will enrich physical education by helping it to gain insights as to its own role in schools and society; it will make physical education more knowledgeable and understanding about what one is educating "for"—for a lifestyle throughout life.

It is logical for physical education to foster sport management, for it already has certain basic foundation courses; however, this is not to say that new aspects cannot be added to the curriculum. "The expanding field of sport management has created its own job market, demanding entirely new skills and preparation" (Parkhouse, 1984, p. 12). Well, the skills are not entirely new skills, rather some new skills with the old (van der Smissen, 1984). Sport management is not a subdiscipline of physical education, the teacher education curriculum, but of physical education the discipline.

To institute sport management does not mean the teacher education curriculum must be changed. However, the teacher preparation physical educators, who presently control the curriculum, must open their minds to the wider field of physical education potential. Rather than be defensive about what physical education has been and is, physical educators need to go on the offense, if they wish to stake any claim whatsoever in the field of sport management, and for that matter, also in the wider field of wellness. Already, in some institutions physical education has or is losing out to health education in the field of fitness and wellness only because it has not moved ahead. The base of fitness is physical health, and should be in physical education with cooperative efforts with health education, not vice-versa.

One must not look upon teacher preparation and sport management as in competition with each other, but rather as two opportunities. It has been shown in undergraduate programs that initially some physical education (teacher preparation) majors transfer to the new sport management program because they really did not want to teach but had no alternative as a major curriculum; but those students who are committed to teaching do not change. On the other hand, sport management can draw many students who have long been interested in sport but had no curriculum. In other words, sport management fills a real need for students seeking nonteaching sport careers. Sport management is an exciting area to be in at this time in our nation's history, the potential of which is restricted only by the limits of our creativity and our willingness to seek out the opportunities. The challenge is in being a leader, of giving direction to a movement and not in followership. Yes, this is a new ball game for many physical educators, but one providing stimulation and renewed vigor.

Programs

Do not get hung up on the title of your curriculum. There are many different labels, which vary by institution and thrust. A 1985 study found these titles: sport(s) management, sport(s) administration, health promotion/wellness/fitness management, commercial/corporate recreation, sport(s) management/athletic administration, sport(s) administration and facility management, sport and recreation administration and facility management, and athletic administration (Milewski & Bryant, 1984). Also, opinions differ about whether it should be sport or sports management.

Should the program be at the undergraduate or graduate level or both? Graduate programs have been around, although in limited number, for nearly 20 years! It is surprising that the push for more programs did not "catch fire" until now. Ohio University was the first in 1966 and has maintained a very strong graduate program, highly selective and highly successful in placement of graduates. The University of Massachusetts also has had a very successful graduate program of long-standing.

There is a role for curricula at both levels, undergraduate and graduate; however, the integrity of each must be maintained. Certainly the graduate program must not merely be a survey for the physical education (teacher-prepared) undergraduate major, or for persons interested in sport from other majors. The courses must indeed be of graduate level and must build upon a proper undergraduate foundation. There must be prerequisites to provide the base upon which a graduate specialization can be built, for a graduate program is only 1 year in length and thus cannot both provide the base and the specialization.

Because the present impetus in physical education programming sport management is at the undergraduate level, the remainder of this section is directed toward undergraduate programs. For description of graduate programs, see Mullins (1984), and for further discussion and description of undergraduate programs, see Zanger and Parks (1984).

Undergraduate Tracks

The National Association for Sport and Physical Education (NASPE) of the AAHPERD in 1985 endeavored to establish guidelines and standards for undergraduate physical education students preparing for careers in business and industry. The guidelines and standards have many excellent elements that should be considered in developing curricula. However, as one reviews the roles of sport and the career potentials, one realizes that a singular program cannot provide the necessary background; there must be tracks. Suggested are three tracks that cluster several emphases. The tracks are not mutually exclusive.

Track I. Fitness/Sport Medicine/Wellness. *Physical fitness* includes exercise physiology predominantly, but with work in all four components of fitness. *Sport medicine* includes injury management and optimal conditioning for amateur, school, and pro sports. One usually specializes and needs graduate work in areas such as strength, exercise physiology, sport psychology, and athletic training. *Wellness* is broader than physical fitness but includes physical fitness as well as work with health educators in health promotion and areas such as alcohol, drugs, and tobacco.

Track II. Sport as Activity and Modality.   The emphasis is upon skills/strategies of sport and human development in a variety of settings and different clientele, such as (a) youth sports, intramurals, student recreation, Y's, private clubs, (b) special populations as a modality for the disabled, and (c) aquatics.

Track III. Management/Administration of the Setting.   This includes two distinct emphases: *management* of a facility/area of the activities, and *marketing* and *promotion*.

Program of Studies

In addition to general education courses it is recommended that there be three groupings of courses: core of courses for all sport management majors regardless of track, a grouping of courses or core for each of the three tracks, and then a series of required/suggested electives in accord with specific career emphasis within the track. If one studies the three tracks, one will note there are fundamental foundations essential for each, such as Track I, the human life sciences, Track II, human development and performance, and Track III, management skills. The three tracks and career emphases within each will not be detailed here (see Parks & Quain, 1986; Zanger & Parks, 1984). (See Table 2.)

Following is more detail regarding the six recommended areas for the core background of sport management majors, regardless of track. The manner of providing the background may vary from use of general education courses, specially designed survey courses, or focused courses.

1. The scientific bases of fitness, conditioning, and wellness: There should be an understanding of human physiology, anatomy, and kinesiology. This might be provided through general education courses, a first-level exercise physiology course, or a specially designed "scientific foundations of sport" course. In addition, there should be a personal health course, which would include substance abuse and wellness, and some background in nutrition. Those students electing Track I would of course go into considerably more depth in these various scientific aspects.

2. Management: This core area should include an overview of the field of management, including marketing and promotion. The book, *Successful Sport Management* (Lewis & Appenzeller, 1985), gives such an

Table 2

Curriculum Content Outline

A. General education courses
    (approx. 1/2 of the credit hours, as required in your institution)

B. Core courses for all sport management majors

    (these courses do not all have to be specially designed courses taught by HPER,
    but may be drawn from general education and courses in other units of the college
    or university; content detailed in subsequent paragraphs)

    1. Scientific bases of fitness, conditioning, and wellness
        scientific foundations of sport (exercise physiology, anatomy, kines.) personal
        health, including substance abuse, wellness, nutrition
    2. Management
        overview of field of management, including marketing and promotion
        computer applications
        legal aspects
        injury management
    3. Human behavior/dynamics
        sport psychology
        interpersonal communications
    4. Sport and economics
        economics
        fiscal accountability, including budgeting, management of financial resources
    5. Societal aspects
        sport sociology, including ethics, political aspects of sport
    6. Practical experiences
        practicums (short-term throughout academic career)
        internship

C. Specialization tracks

    (student declares one; institution may choose not to offer all three, but perhaps only
    one or two; further description in preceding section)

    1. Fitness/sport medicine/wellness
    2. Sport as activity and modality
    3. Management/administration of the setting

D. Electives

    (in accord with specific career emphasis within track, or to enhance and enrich
    generally one's educational experiences)

---

overview. This course should not be confused with an introduction or
orientation to sport management, a course that surveys the career field
of sport management. It is suggested that such content not be in a course
but be covered through career counseling, student professional club meetings, attendance at professional meetings, and reading of professional
literature. Those persons going into Track III would have a series of
courses on specific aspects of management. Those in Tracks I and II might

take some additional work, depending on their career emphases. It must be remembered, however, that one is *not* providing a major in management or business administration. The courses should be selected well to complement the sport-focused courses. It is useful to have some senior seminars that integrate management principles and sport.

In addition to the overview of sport management, there are several areas of management/administration that all majors in sport management should have: computer applications, legal aspects, and injury management.

Concerning computer applications, there is so much software available to enhance both management/administration and evaluative assessment (particularly in the fitness and wellness area) that the new major coming out of college cannot afford to be ignorant of the potential of computers.

Legal aspects, the second area, acknowledges that this is a legalistic society. While it is good to have some business law, particularly for Track III, this course is not focused on business law but upon two other aspects: management of facilities and personnel in sport enterprises and amelioration of situations that give rise to lawsuits based on negligence. Wolf put it rather bluntly: "Many facilities are little more than lawsuits waiting to happen. . . . Most fitness facility enterpreneurs are waiting for their first lawsuit before they wise up" (Wolf, 1985, p. 26). Further, it is the individual who is conducting the activity (sport or exercise) who is the front line of defense against lawsuits.

The third area, injury management, addresses one of the greatest needs of sport programs: youth sports injury prevention and management (Hackworth, Jacobs, & O'Neill, 1983). Every facility manager and activity leader must have the competence to render injury assistance appropriate to the activity and client whether this is the most basic of first-aid or cardiac arrest. The importance of conditioning for fitness/exercise programs or youth sport participation must be understood.

As a point of interest, Keidel's book *Game Plans, Sports Strategies for Business* (1985) states on the jacket, "Everyone knows that when you join a business organization you become part of a team—[this book] shows how valuable the specific lessons from sports for business can be. . . . by showing how every corporation is organized like a baseball, football, or basketball team—or a combination of these sports—depending on the pattern of teamwork it displays. . . . explores the strengths and weaknesses of each team model."

3. Human behavior/dynamics: Understanding the dynamics of human behavior is essential to all persons regardless of track—from the motivation and adherence of those who exercise to the management of crowds; as Anderson states, "The element of human intervention will always be necessary in crowd management" (1985, p. 28). The role of

sport psychology is well known and was highlighted in the 1984 Olympics, but sport psychology is just as important to the local sport enthusiast. Another part of human dynamics is that of interpersonal communications, one of the top-rated competencies that practitioners indicated was needed, according to Parks and Quain (1986).

4. Sport and economics: Sport is a powerful influence upon the economy of the nation, and vice versa, the state of the economy determines to a large extent the participation of people in sport. Further, one must understand the difference between public and private goods and what this means as a manager of a sport service. In addition to the economics basic to financial enterprise, one must have a competency in fiscal accountability, including budgeting and management of financial resources.

5. Societal aspects: As indicated in the first part of this article, sport plays a vital role in society; thus it is essential that those involved in sport management have some understanding of the sociology of sport and the ethics practiced by various segments of society as related to sport. No small part of the involvement of sport in society is political. An understanding of how sport is used in world politics, as well as the politics of sport management in the local and state setting, is essential.

6. Practical experiences: Higher education has frequently been assailed for its so-called ivory tower and theoretical approaches to the real world. Direct experience for students is critical throughout their 4 years of college, first to give greater insight into the various career potentials of sport management and what competencies are required, and later to engage in the realities of day-to-day operations and performance. (For further discussion, see Zanger & Parks, 1984.)

Cautions

There also are some cautions for those who would have a sport management curriculum. First, sport management cannot and must not be everything in sport and physical activity that is not teacher education. Some aspects are more appropriately part of the leisure industry, often offered by recreation curricula. Second, in eagerness to manage settings, one must not mistake management of the setting for organization of the participant and activity; in other words, overorganization of the clientele will "kill" the participation. The focus must be on providing opportunities of many varieties for the clientele, both organized and unorganized, but at all times permitting the client/participant to make the choices. The third caution is that private enterprise long ago learned that the challenge of marketing is change and meeting the needs of the clientele. Curricula that do not keep abreast of the times will soon be obsolete and graduates will not have placement.

Fourth, sport management is a very popular major with students, and physical education faculty are instituting it in many colleges and universities. This can result in two undesirable situations: oversupply of graduates for the number of positions available, unless one is astute as to the needs of the field, and lack of quality control. Bigger is not necessarily better. Quality control of the curriculum and of the students being admitted and retained in the curriculum is essential. Fifth, while sport is engaged in extensively, it must be remembered that it is in competition with other leisure activities for the time of individuals. Sixth, the curriculum of sport management must be a demanding one and must have academic respectability or it will not be long a major program.

No illustrative curricula currently operational are set forth inasmuch as each institution has its own structure and course organization, but in constructing new or evaluating present curricula, one should assess them against the aspects described in this section. Further, curriculum is dynamic in relation to the profession and society and must be updated regularly.

Business–University Relationships

The relationship between business and higher education must extend beyond the practical experiences of internships and practicums. Vogt (1984), a former Dean of a college of business administration, in speaking to a sport management curriculum symposium, stated that three relatively new additions to the interface of business and higher education interface warrant special attention. These are (a) establishment of business–university joint venture enterprises to promote research in high technology and/or to further develop commercial potentials resulting from scientific breakthroughs; (b) creation of partnerships consisting of business–government–higher education that provide the organizational base to promote and support regional economic development; and (c) development of cooperative educational programming to support businesses' training function. Most colleges and universities do have professional advisory boards, particularly essential for sport management. Some institutions also utilize professionals in the field as adjunct faculty.

Sport Management— Sharing Through Organizations and Journals

The number of undergraduate programs in sport management is burgeoning and the graduate programs are being developed further in the mid-1980s. There are a number of periodicals and organizations, most focusing on a singular aspect of sport management, but none emanated from physical education. Recognizing this need for those who have been involved in physical education to share together, a number of educators from Canada and the United States initiated both an international organization, North American Society for Sport Management (NASSM), and a journal, *Journal of Sport Management*. The first annual conference was held at Kent State University in June 1986. The first Executive Council has been established with the following members: Bob Boucher (president), University of Windsor; Carl Schraibman (president-elect), Kent State University; Earle Zeigler (the "organizing" president), University of Western Ontario; Beverly Zanger (secretary), Bowling Green State University; Joy DeSensi (treasurer), University of Tennessee; Ted Coates, The Ohio State University; Terry Haggerty, University of Western Ontario; Janet Koontz, Rutgers University; and Rich Quain, Bowling Green State University. The semi-annual journal's first issue was published in January 1987 by Human Kinetics Publishers, for NASSM. Its co-editors are Gordon Olafson, University of Windsor, and Janet Parks, Bowling Green State University.

The Future of Sport Management

According to the U.S. Bureau of Labor Statistics ("Jobs," 1985), leisure and recreation services, of which sport management is a part, is one of the key industries in the next 10 years. The Bureau has estimated that leisure and recreation services will be up 27% by 1995 in number of job opportunities. Only computer electronics (35%), health care (29%), and high tech (28%) had a greater projected increase. Considering the many opportunities as set forth in the section on perspectives of sport management, its future as a career opportunity is indeed great. Thus, the potential for a curriculum in sport management also should be great *if* it is carefully planned and executed.

But the more important question, as posed in the opening paragraph, is whether sport management will prosper within physical education or HPERD. If the content of the three program tracks is taught well, then those graduating from such programs should be able to manage better. But, to establish physical education as a primary delivery system for sport management depends upon physical educators. Four attributes of leadership are required.

1. Insights and entrepreneur aggressiveness—There must be an excitement about pursuing sport management opportunities; physical educators must be analytical and reach out to all types of potential opportunities.
2. Commitment and dedication—Physical educators must be committed and dedicated to development of the physical being in all contexts, not just children in school settings. They also must recognize the con-

tribution of sport to the well-being of persons of whatever ability, age, or condition, as well as to the economy of the nation.

3. Comfortableness—There must be a comfortableness outside the school environs with other disciplines in health and well-being, and in the behavioral sciences of society, particularly in the business world.

4. Leadership—This involves giving time and energy to the movement, including preparation of persons who can teach at the university level, involvement in research related to sport management, and establishment of a professional organization and journal which becomes recognized as "the" sport management organization and journal in the field.

Dreaming the Impossible Dream:
The Decline and Fall of Physical Education

Shirl J. Hoffman
University of North Carolina at Greensboro

A.D. 2020 was the year the Board of Education in Murrysville, Florida, finally threw in the towel and abandoned the notion that physical education should be part of the local educational enterprise. Florida was the last state to require the subject anyway, and for the past 2 years Murrysville had been the state's lone holdout, maintaining professionally trained physical educators on its teaching force. Its passing earned a scant 2-inch announcement in the "Community News" column of the local paper and occurred without special notice save for one passionate letter to the editor from a resident who pleaded that the board reconsider. The few good points the fellow made were later blunted when it was learned his brother-in-law was one of the physical education teachers losing his job.

Physical education had been on the wane in Murrysville for well over a decade, and what remained in 2020 was only a tattered vestige of a once glossy and (some said, but never proved) effective program. So assured was its demise that before board members even voted on the matter, they had hired an architect to draft plans to convert the middle school gymnasium into a new science and information center. Nearly 15 years earlier, gymnasia in two Murrysville elementary schools had been remodeled to meet academic needs, one being converted into a botanical garden, the other into a library annex. The newest elementary school, built 7 years earlier, had no gymnasium. The board decided against converting the gym at Crestwood (the most affluent of the town's schools) into a cultural arts center, not to preserve physical education but to accommodate an educational innovation that originated near the turn of the century on the West Coast.

For more than 10 years, the Murrysville district had been among the thousands that had followed the lead of California schools by offering "Self-Directed Play" ("SDP," as educators called it), and the gymnasium, though not absolutely essential, proved convenient on rainy days. The concept of SDP was born out of union resistance to the practice of requiring elementary classroom teachers to supervise students during the two state-mandated recess periods each day. As so often happened, a vocational void (in this case the need for quasi-professionals to supervise the unstructured activities of schoolchildren) gave birth to a formal certification program, and before long, local community colleges were processing students through a course of study called "Self-Directed Play Management."

Although SDP managers lacked specialized training in pedagogy or in-depth training in the science of movement, they were for the most part enthusiastic, given to loud and expressive conversation, and competent in the fundamentals of large-group organization. Exit competency tests for SDPs required them to demonstrate successful management of three "trouble free" recess periods out of the five they were assigned. Trouble free was assumed to mean no injuries, no fights, no destruction of school property, and no sitting down; in the trainees' lexicon, these were known as "the big four." To many superintendents, SDP was not all that different from their recollections of physical education in the 1980s and 90s. In fact, during the meeting at which the board decided to adopt the SDP model, the 75-year-old superintendent of the Murrysville board recalled that as far back as 1984 the Massachusetts State Board of Education had counted recess (something very similar to SDP) toward the state requirement for physical education (Dodds & Locke, 1984).

Any reservations the board might have harbored about scrapping the elementary physical education program in favor of SDP vaporized when a consultant compellingly explained how much the fiscally wrenched community could save by hiring SDP managers instead of physical education teachers. The consultant had primed the board by dusting off a federally funded research study conducted in 1989 which showed that children placed under the largely passive care of teacher assistants learned fully as much as children taught by physical education teachers with doctorates. At least that's how it was interpreted by school administrators and summarized in USA Today. Those knowledgeable in statistics more accurately interpreted the study to have demonstrated that neither type of instruction produced significant gains in learning. Furthermore, those close to the scene were not surprised at the results, having known that many of the physical education doctorates used as subjects in the study were exercise science specialists who had never taught physical education. Some thought it sad that such gross misinterpretation of data was allowed to influence the board's decision, although an unidentified official claiming to be in the know said the study results really had made no difference. "Administrative decisions never are based on research data," she confided. "Why, we would have to modify our operations every year if we were to seriously consider what researchers tell us."

As it turned out, diehards, who had hoped the null results would spur the board to upgrade the quality of teaching in the schools, rather than eliminate it, only were set up for further disappointment. They might have had a chance had they possessed data on the effects of their programs over the past 10, 5, or even 2 years, but systematic measurement of achievement in physical education (physical fitness scores, now the responsibility of health educators, were an exception) had never been high on teachers' agendas. This, plus an inability to reach consensus over what or how they should teach, or how it should be measured, could not long evade the penetrating eyes of educational policy makers.

And so it was, that on the strength of spurious evidence gleaned from a study conducted in 1989—ironically, the 100th anniversary of the historic Boston Conference—the last surviving elementary physical education program was replaced by SDP. That it had lasted more than 15 years following the study's publication was truly remarkable in light of the swift surgery performed on most programs between 1990 and 1993.

Commercialization of Varsity Sports

It was a victory of small proportions for physical educators that the Murrysville board had decided not to follow through with plans to remodel the high school gym into a theater. This decision had nothing to do with the high school physical education program. It had survived elementary physical education only by a scant 5 years, something of a surprise to those who had predicted secondary programs would be the first to go (Dodds & Locke, 1984; Siedentop, 1981). Sentiment to preserve the high school gym arose initially from a small group of parents—"hopeless romantics" one board member had called them—who were interested in reviving the school-sponsored varsity athletics that had bitten the dust in the mid-1990s, a few years before funeral services had been held for elementary school physical education. Physical education purists, who had always viewed athletics with a certain contempt (some were reported even to have cheered when the varsity program was phased out) learned too late about the vital symbiosis that had sustained both programs for over half a century. It is a long story, but worth telling:

Interschool athletic programs had been victims of the economic "detrusion" of the mid-1990s. Republicans had gained control not only of the White House but also both houses of Congress in 1988, and had remained in power ever since. They refused to call the current economic condition by its proper name—a depression. As the economy went into a tailspin, Murrysville, like most communities, could only wince under the pain of an eroding tax base. The average age of taxpayers in the town had risen 5 years beyond the average age in 1980, and to make matters worse a cloud of suspicion hung over everything connected with the public schools. This was due in large part to a succession of education commissioners who were private school devotees, one of the dubious legacies of two-term president Pat Robertson. Under the circumstances, most of the citizenry of Murrysville had few dollars to contribute to school tax coffers and even less to frivolous athletic programs. Those who could afford to did so, but only after tightening the political screws on their school board representatives.

The decision to drop interschool sports was least popular with parents of athletes who had been counting on college athletic scholarships to defray what had become outrageous college tuition costs. They reacted by lobbying for a pay-for-play plan. "If the school can't pay for the program, we'll pay for it ourselves," the well-heeled father of the school's star wide-receiver told the board. This pay-for-play plan (soon known as P³) held intrinsic appeal for the board: it was very much in the spirit of the emerging trend toward increased parental involvement, but more important, it promised to get them off the hook on a delicate issue. Few would have imagined the doom this seemingly harmless innovation spelled for interschool sports, and even fewer would have guessed it would grease the slide for plummeting public support for physical education.

Problems exploded the first season P³ went into operation in Murrysville. Because school-age children from low-income, predominantly black families found it difficult to come up with the $1,000 required to purchase a spot on the football team, or the $800 for the girl's basketball team, the quality of performance declined noticeably. Just how drastically was evident the second year after the program began. In a throwback to the old Negro Baseball League, black athletes from Murrysville banded together to form an independent basketball team which, when allowed to compete against regional school-sponsored teams, slaughtered them rather unmercifully. For parents and school officials whose interpretations of "success" seldom reached beyond the season won-loss record, the "success" of the independents only served to magnify the colossal "failure" of P³. To worsen matters, players on the independent teams always seemed to have more fun than players on the school-sponsored teams, an observation noted by more than one envious Murrysville varsity athlete.

Before long parents seized total control of varsity programs, reasoning that if they were footing the bill they should have complete say in how the program would run. Thus, what had started as merely parental input by a parents' advisory committee soon became absolute domination by men and women who, despite their good intentions, were equipped neither educationally nor emotionally to perform the job. Parental control, as it turned out, was short-lived. From its inception, P³ had relied heavily on local businessmen to cover regular shortfalls in the operating budget, a product of poor management and gross neglect by parents who had become disillusioned with the enormous amount of time and effort required to coach and manage school athletic programs. Thus, in a short 2 years, parents relinquished control to a group of local business-men who were able to report a decent profit by the third year of opera-tion. In educational circles, "profit" and "success" had become synony-mous, given the bleak financial picture confronting educational institu-tions, and the owners of the Murrysville teams proudly displayed the teams' financial statements alongside their schedule of contests.

By 1993 in municipalities across the nation, businessmen were getting involved in school athletic programs. The enormous financial potential of youth sports was the subject of a feature article in the *Wall Street Journal*, and by 1998, Pedasport, Inc., a P³ nationally franchised, wholly owned subsidiary of Anheuser Busch, Inc., had signed its 1,000th contract with a school district. Pedasport, Inc., had begun in the mid-1980s as "Scat Fat," a fitness and exercise emporium that targeted its limited range of services to body-conscious yuppies. In 1990 it moved into the field of youth sports, and by 1995 had become the largest single deliverer of youth sport programs in the United States, far outstripping the declin-ing programs offered by the schools. Curiously, parents who in 1985 balked at spending tax dollars on school athletic programs willingly forked over huge sums to Pedasport, Inc. The dollar return somehow seemed to justify it, a perception no doubt shaped by nifty commercials wedged between nationally televised athletic contests.

Unfortunately, the business model expunged the few remaining drops of educational philosophy that flavored the rhetoric, if not always the conduct, of high school athletic coaches. By 1990 it had become a prac-tice of longstanding to hire coaches who lacked professional training in sport, exercise, or pedagogy. In retrospect, a pivotal case had occurred when Paul Blair, former New York Yankee All-Star and Golden Glove recipient, was denied the opportunity to coach the 1982 Port Chester, New York, high school varsity team because he was not a certified teacher. Blair's argument, published in *The New York Times* ("School coach," 1982), was persuasive: "Why should a guy who has been a major leaguer for 16 years be denied the right to coach, when a teacher who never played the game can coach?" That same year the New York Board of Regents passed a regulation permitting the hiring of uncertified varsity coaches when a certified teacher is unavailable for the job. This rent-a-coach poli-cy, only sporadically and half-heartedly denounced by professional physi-cal education associations, spread rapidly and, in the process, set the stage for the deprofessionalization of athletic coaching.

With the influx of coaches who lacked allegiance to the school board and who had little if any sympathy for the notion that sports should be opportunities for personal growth and learning, the split between sports and education was finalized. The enormity of the split was evident when, in 2010, Delbert Oberteuffer's prophetic utterance of 1963 was entered as an item in the 7th annual edition of *Oddities and Oddballs: Strange Views on Education*:

What we in physical education must come to understand is that no one, but no one, will take us seriously until we begin to take ourselves seriously and become truly intelligent about exploring the contribution which the world of sports, games and dance can have to the education of man. (Obertueffer, 1963, p. 28)

In retrospect, ethical compromise always had been part of the life and times of school coaches but it had been buffered by concerns for educational propriety. When these buffering effects disintegrated, it wasn't long before a scourge of sleazy practices that would have shocked the most hardened cynics of the 1980s spread through the ranks. The problem was compounded by a heightened interest in success and a dwindling concern for the methods used to attain it, a phenomenon some blamed on the decline and ultimate disappearance of liberal education in the universities. The urge to win, thought by social critics of the 1980s to have reached a zenith in their time, continued unabated well into the 21st century and showed little sign of changing its slope or acceleration. The Lombardian dictum that had guided coaches in the 60s and 70s, "Winning isn't everything, it's the only thing," gave way in 1996 to, "God, family, and winning, only not in that order," a saying popularized by the coach of the Las Vegas Roulettes, winners of Super Bowl XXX.

Gradually, differences between the goals for high school programs and those for the Roulettes diminished to hair-splitting philosophical distinctions. Coaches caved in to raw survival instincts. Soon high schools were struggling with the same problems that had plagued colleges and universities in the 80s. State investigators leveled an assortment of charges against Murrysville, although they were judged to be relatively mild. For example, it had been discovered that poorer athletes who couldn't afford the P^3 fee were illegally enticed with "scholarships" paid from a slush fund generated by siphoning off cafeteria milk money and library fines. The school principal claimed no knowledge of the incident, blaming it on some well-meaning alumni.

The advent of the voucher system in 1989 gave parents considerable choice concerning which schools their children would attend, and those whose progeny were gifted athletes often were influenced by deals sharpened under the table. In one of the more celebrated cases, the illiterate father of a standout halfback was given a position coaching holders for kickoffs even though everyone knew his services were required only on windy days. His wife was appointed to the lucrative post of "academic counselor to the cheerleaders," responsibilities for which were never quite clear either to the school board members, the cheerleaders, or as it turned out, the woman herself.

Under the circumstances, the idea of reviving the school athletic program, as one of the romantics given to flowery speech put it, "to rescue athletics from the vipers whose venom is obsession with winning," held little appeal for the Murrysville School Board. Members could well imagine the hours to be consumed in meetings resolving disputes and charges brought with increasing frequency by the recently commissioned National Association of Youth Sports, and they wanted no part of it. "Better to let Pedasport handle these problems," commented the board chairman, "than to waste our time dealing with them. They aren't *educational* problems, anyway."

Commercialization of Physical Education Programs

The commercialization of high school physical education followed naturally in the wake of commercialization of sport programs. Once it became obvious to independent contractors that they could deliver an effective, profitable, and competitive sport program, it was only a matter of time before they ventured into the sports instruction business. So it was, then, that in the fall of 2001 the Murrysville board signed a contract with Pedasport, Inc., to deliver a basic instruction program in sport and exercise to the local high school. The plan appeared to work well and save money at other school districts across the nation, inspiring the Pedasport public relations representatives to remind board members of their moral obligation to adopt the Pedasport plan.

By the mid-1990s, Pedasport executives realized that the market for high quality, basic instruction in sport and exercise promised an even larger return on the dollar than competitive youth sports programs. Management consultants, hired to scout the territory, had submitted a report that left executives licking their chops. The report's earliest pages pinpointed the crucial issues:

> Physical education professionals have been awash in a sea of confusion for years. No two of them can agree on what should be taught. What passes for physical education at any particular school is likely to depend on the whims of the teachers. Since its inception, the National Assessment of Educational Progress at Educational Testing Services has omitted physical education from its assessment program because there is no national consensus concerning curriculum content in the school program. We can only imagine what might happen were math, science, and English teachers to follow the same destructive course.

The report went on to underscore the lack of sequential curriculum structure, noting: "in our visits to schools we were struck by the similarity between high school classes and what we could remember of elementary classes; the same skills were taught, the same instructional strategies were employed, and the students appeared to be performing at about the same level."

The report documented a long history of dissatisfaction, noting that much of the criticism emanated from physical educators themselves. Among the citations was a 1986 article penned by a physical educator-turned National Institute of Education (NIE) official (Taylor, 1986). The article summarized prevailing views of educational researchers toward physical education: "it is glorified recess," "physical education teachers are highly paid, educated teacher aides," "the purpose of physical education is to help fill the school day and give students a breather." The reaction of one researcher provoked loud cheering around the Pedasport board table:

> Since people outside of physical education are attracting, motivating, and getting money for encouraging people to become more active physically, the school should contract out services to these people and businesses for students' education.

The report went on to note the results of a poll that probed public perception of the specialized knowledge and competencies of physical education teachers. This piece of data was viewed as critical by Pedasport executives who recognized the need to establish training programs for the teachers they would employ. To their surprise, the list of specialized skills and knowledge was conveniently short; a grasp of first-aid procedures was at the top of everyone's list, and an appreciation of legal implications of acts of negligence was second. Approximately half felt that teachers should master some basic skills in organizing large groups of people, and about 30% mentioned they should have a smattering of knowledge and performance capabilities in the wide range of skills they were expected to teach.

Results of the poll underscored a reality not fully appreciated by physical educators until too late. The mystery once surrounding their profession had been swept away with a flood of self-help books and video tapes on exercise, fitness, and sport instruction. "I had always thought that sports, exercise, and the like were really complicated," said one middle-age respondent. "Now that I've read about it I would feel comfortable teaching classes in sports that I know something about, like tennis, for example. After all, I was a two-time runner-up in my club's tournament and I've taught both of my daughters to play. Our high school teacher tells me she's never competed in a tournament in her life." The report went on to point out that it was not difficult to find laypersons whose knowledge and expertise on the activities in physical education ranged far beyond those of teachers themselves. If physical education teachers had any special talent at all, it seemed to be the ability to teach a broad range of skills at an introductory level in environments that promised little hope of success. They appeared to be "specialists in generalism," possessors of talents no longer in demand or even appreciated.

From a marketing perspective, the transition from varsity athletics to physical education was natural. Businessmen, lacking the benefits of a principles of physical education course, never drew fine distinctions between the two. They reasoned that both were aimed at improving performance competence and fitness, albeit for different populations of students. "Coaches," noted one of the R&D technicians, "simply try to do what physical education teachers try to do with a different class of athlete. We have proven that we can staff school athletic programs with coaches who can manage instruction at the highest levels; surely we can staff physical education programs with people who can teach at the introductory level."

Thus, by the turn of the century Pedasport had contracted with high schools across the country to offer instruction in sport and exercise. The Pedasport approach was not the feeble gesture offered by school districts in the 1980s to satisfy state requirements. Classes were small and students were taught in the same fertile pedagogical settings traditionally reserved for varsity athletics. After-school and weekend classes of sufficient length to ensure learning replaced the impoverished intermissions that had been crammed between academic classes under the old regime. Pedapedagogues (called P^2s) were serious about teaching. They had little choice. After all, teachers were paid on a commission basis and their reputations as teachers were the only magnets attracting students to their classes. Like tennis and golf professionals of an earlier era, P^2s' survival depended on their ability to meet the expectations of their clients. Students flocked to the good teachers while lazy, uninteresting, and incompetent teachers were quickly eliminated.

As a prospective employer of teachers, Pedasport was stridently "anti-credentialist." Executives saw little logic in the old system of correlating teaching success, increasingly referred to as "customer satisfaction," with state certification or years of college training. Pedasport executives had visited teacher education programs at three major universities and had come away wondering how anyone could expect graduates of such programs to be expert instructors in either sport skills or exercise. The programs were too theoretical, lacking a foundation in the content teachers were expected to teach. By applying modern management training techniques, well-honed in the financial districts, Pedasport found they could hire expert performers—with national and international competitive experience but who lacked pedagogical pedigrees—provide them with packaged training programs on the rudiments of skills teaching, first-aid, and legal liability, and guarantee improvements in performance. Furthermore, they could make a bundle.

In the end, the decision not to convert the Murrysville high school gymnasium into a school theater was, like most school board decisions of the 21st century, a practical rather than a philosophical consideration. The treasurer of the board, a diligent guardian of the bottom line, explained that Pedasport, Inc., would rent the gymnasium at a rate that would cover mortgage payments on a brand new facility which could be constructed to house a theater. In addition, Pedasport had recently expanded its services to provide comprehensive liability insurance for all teachers and coaches, legal representation for employees charged with negligence, a field and equipment repair and maintenance service, and locker room supervision complete with towel service. All of this, plus a "performance improvement or money back guarantee." It was, the board concluded, simply too fine a deal to turn down.

The demise of physical education in Murrysville was a sad story, and not just for the committed souls who had invested a lifetime teaching the subject. It had a most emphatic impact on those who had entered the profession in the 1990s who, with 20 years of experience, found themselves experts in a subject no longer in demand. Fortunately, the writing on the wall had loomed in large print for years, giving most teachers adequate time to prepare for alternative careers. By the time the ax fell in Murrysville, many had accumulated enough credits to become certified as math, science, or social studies teachers. Those who had been selling real estate on a part-time basis for years decided to go full-time, although if the truth were told many had been selling full-time for years.

Some displaced teachers sought employment with Pedasport, Inc., but most found themselves unqualified to deliver the particular services expected of Pedasport instructors. Parents who were forking over $300 per month for gymnastic, tennis, and swimming lessons had fairly high and specific expectations. Physical education teachers found themselves uncomfortable with what they considered unreasonable parental demands.

Some of the more perceptive teachers had enrolled in school administration courses long before physical education was phased out in their districts. So, by the late 1990s physical education teachers had moved into administrative posts at a rate John Conant would have believed impossible. One of the more ironic and unforgiveable features of this turn of events was that many of these same administrators, culled from the ranks of gym teachers, helped plot (and in some cases even celebrated) the elimination of physical education from the school curriculum. A few decent administrative appointments with sentimental ties to the profession were known to have complained privately, but none made a serious attempt to resist what had come to be regarded as an irreversible and logical trend.

Life and Times and Biokinetics at Old Comp U.

Hindsight is always 20/20, and in the year 2020 it was easy to trace the course of developments that resulted in the extinction of college departments of physical education. However, as developments were unfolding, their significance was not so apparent. True, some had fretted publicly about the future of the profession as early as 1979 (Bressan, 1979; Hoffman, 1985), but even they could not have foreseen what was coming. Events in the Department of Physical Education at Comprehensive University, the primary supplier of teachers for the Murrysville system, were fairly representative of developments at most colleges and universities across the land.

As early as 1980, teacher education faculty had detected a decided shift in student career selection away from the traditional interest in teaching, toward exercise science and life-style education. The national passion for health and fitness and the bleak economic considerations of pursuing a career in education were obvious causes. But other, less obvious, factors had contributed at least as much. For example, changes in state regulations provided career possibilities in coaching to students from a variety of disciplines. In the old days, those who aspired to coaching careers accounted for a large percentage of physical education majors. Under new regulations, students no longer felt obliged to pursue careers in physical education. Social studies or industrial arts were equally acceptable routes to a coaching career.

Teacher educators identified it as a recruiting problem and laid the blame at the feet of public school teachers. They enjoyed pointing out that physical education teachers of an earlier generation had been powerful role models, charismatic and enthusiastic proponents of sport and physical activity whose dynamic influence was a strong force for recruiting students into the profession. They were idealists who loved their work and were committed to the broad values of physical education. More than that, they believed they could be a force for good and that their subject matter could change the lives of students.

Teachers of the 80s seemed not only to doubt the value of sport as a life-changing experience, they doubted the power of their own influence on the young people they taught. Idealism had been supplanted by cynicism. The seeds planted during undergraduate years by agnostic professors had been watered after graduation by the ugly realities of the gymnasium. Now teachers seemed satisfied to get through the day without major incident, let alone burden themselves with lofty goals of shepherding bright and talented students into the physical education profession.

Public school teachers were willing to bear some, but not all, of the blame. From their perspective, teacher educators wouldn't know what to do with a good student were they to find one. Rather than teach trainees how to perform and analyze sport skills, teacher educators seemed fascinated with the art of communicating and organizing. Problem-solving, applying knowledge from exercise science, and keeping abreast of technical information contained in journals like *Golf Digest*, *Swimmer's World* or *Modern Gymnast* never was considered very important.

For years they and their research were irrelevant to everyone except their small group of colleagues who gathered annually to talk about research and deliver pep talks. Research studies rarely focused on important variables. As a measure of how pathetic things had become, the last issue of *Journal of Teaching in Physical Education* carried an article entitled, "RRS: Teacher Pick-Up of Physiological Urgencies." The investigator, following a well-defined trend charted by previous descriptive, "acromaniacal" studies, had developed a new observation system for detecting student "rest-room signalling." Fittingly, he divided his data into Categories I and II. The results were inconclusive.

By 1992 the ranks of teacher preparation programs were virtually depleted of academically talented students. Witnessing the steady erosion was unbearable for teacher educators, especially the veterans who could recall the glory days of the 1960s. At Comp U., a veteran professor of 30 years sought, and regrettably found, the coward's solution. Her body, found at the base of Alumni Tower, bore a terse note lamenting the awful trend: "Nothing is as it used to be. No one cares about teaching and everybody wants to be an exercise physiologist." At memorial services, the department chair, who never quite realized the psychological calamity of it all, made matters worse by characterizing the departed as "the last of a dying breed."

Like many department chairpersons of his era, Art Aerosus had risen through the ranks of exercise science to become a strong leader in the Comp U. department. He was a tough-minded, no-nonsense empiricist whose background included a BS in biology, MS in epidemiology, and PhD in cell physiology. During his first 5 years at Comp U., Aerosus had authored only 47 research articles and 2 books, a spotty record that barely earned him tenure under the strict criteria governing advancement at the university. However, his career had blossomed on the strength of research in insect physiology. His seminal paper on the topic, "Slow and Fast-Twitch Muscle Fibers in Trained and Untrained Young Grasshoppers," had been a hit at the annual meeting of SIPE (Society for Insect Physiology of Exercise), one of 300 subgroups of the American College of Sports Medicine. Though his research was far removed from the world of sport, movement, and human exercise (Aerosus himself acknowledged the lack of conceivable applications of his work, a confession that earned him points with the liberal arts faculty), the work promised to open up an entire new line of research for exercise physiologists, who by this time were starved for possible new topics.

The fact that Aerosus had no background in physical education was considered by the Comp U. faculty as not too unusual. Since the late 1970s, college departments had regularly admitted to their faculties scholars who lacked any training or understanding of physical education. At a Comp U. faculty meeting in 1989, someone jokingly observed that of the 12 faculty assembled, only 4 had any undergraduate training in physical education. Aerosus felt it important to respond by pointing out that infiltrating faculty ranks with outsiders had noticeably strengthened the department's position in the national rankings and in university politics. (Little did he realize that by 1995, responsibilities for teaching exercise science at Comp U. would be assigned to the Medical School. The department's political position wasn't as strong as Aerosus had imagined.) Keeping with Aerosus' philosophy, the faculty in 1990 voted to phase out the basic instruction program in sport and exercise and to change the department's name to fit more closely the revised departmental mission: "to study and teach the effects of training and bodily response to exercise." The new name, "Department of Biokinetics and Training Science," like the mission, failed to acknowledge the teacher education arm of the department. Teacher educators decided not to challenge the action, appreciative as they were of the exercise scientists' willingness to include them on the faculty.

That the fitness movement continued under a full head of steam through the first two decades of the 21st century was a surprise to those who in 1985 had judged it a fad. Sales of exercise clothes, health fitness magazines, and health club memberships climbed steadily every year. Around 2001 some social scientists and philosophers began worrying publicly about the spirit of self-absorption embodied in the movement, while others wondered whether it should be considered a movement at all especially in light of a recent survey revealing that the percentage of people engaging in high levels of regular physical activity actually had declined steadily since 1980. A curious development, embedded deep in the data, bode ill for exercise science faculty. Beginning in the early 1980s, exercise scientists began their own professional training programs, preparing "exercise leaders" and pointing them toward careers in health fitness centers. During this early period, managers of establishments like Easy-Time, one of the dozen or so health spas in Murrysville, had been trained by the Comp U. Department of Biokinetics and Training Science. A dual course of study in exercise science and management was good preparation for operators of facilities where exercise was the principal concern. But by the mid-1990s these establishments had expanded their range of services far beyond exercise. In fact, exercise was a relatively minor feature of the clubs' programs.

Customer interest shifted from exercise to meditation, yoga, and other Eastern modalities, and Easy-Time's owners responded by converting the club's racquetball courts to "silent gyms." (One of Aerosus' colleagues had published a research study purportedly showing increases both in max $\dot{V}O_2$ and strength as a result of meditation.) Swimming pools were retained but used mainly for "psychonautistics," a form of underwater psychotherapy. Some clubs retained their Nautilus rooms even though they were seldom used. Customers maintained that exercises were boring and pointless, so at Easy-Time the exercise machines were put in storage and the exercise room converted into a "J & T" (juice and tofu) lounge.

By the year 2001, exercise scientists no longer were in the business of preparing health club managers. Individuals trained as exercise leaders were ill-equipped to manage the broad range of consumer interests catered to by establishments such as Easy-Time. Instead, graduates of hotel, club, and restaurant management programs with expertise in food and beverage purchase, kitchen and dining room management, and delivery of luxury club services were considered more viable alternatives.

As a result of changing demands, Aerosus and his colleagues were forced to relinquish control of clinical exercise physiology to the Medical School and cardiac rehabilitation to the Department of Physical Therapy. Developments in the health club business had diminished the department's role in preparing exercise leaders and managers, and soon exercise scientists found themselves struggling for survival. A possible career window, pried open briefly in the late 1980s by exercise physiologists, had closed even more abruptly than it had opened. In the mid-1990s exercise physiologists began attacking elementary school physical education programs even though few of them had ever visited one. Wearing the white coats of science to enhance their legitimacy, they pronounced traditional programs that emphasized skill instruction to be a waste of time, even implying they were dangerous. One Big Ten exercise physiologist, who had been awarded a sizable grant to test an experimental fitness program in the schools, seized the occasion to drive home the following point:

> Too many physical education programs amount to little more than organized recess periods. They emphasize sport skills, like shooting baskets, when they could more productively be emphasizing lifestyle concepts. (University of Michigan, 1985)

Before they had time to circle their wagons, elementary school physical education teachers found themselves displaced by "life-style educators." New state regulations specified 3 hours weekly of life-style education in place of traditional physical education. Exercise scientists had assumed they would be the logical choice to prepare life-style educators. After all, they *had* been the principal lobbyists for the new regulations. However, by the time state officials had their say, exercise scientists were out in the cold, shivering with the elementary physical education teachers. The State Board of Education viewed training programs in exercise science as too specialized. Life-style was a broad concept (which seemed to grow broader each year) that included exercise as only one of a number of topics. It was decided that certified teachers would be drawn from schools of home economics, which, as it turned out, were teaching their own course in exercise science: "Exercise Physiology for Life-Style Education." It was a devastating blow to exercise science.

Some exercise scientists managed to land positions with other university units that already had absorbed various subfields of physical education. The best of the exercise physiologists, for example, were hired by medical schools. Some biomechanists with engineering degrees were admitted to the Comp U. engineering faculty—along with teaching assistants, they were assigned introductory courses. Motor learning and control faculty had effectively transferred into departments of psychology by 1995 and were not interested in developments in their old department.

As early as 1990, sport historians, sport sociologists, and sport psychologists began to feel uncomfortable with the heavy emphasis the department placed on health and fitness. As the number of students interested in studying sport as a phenomenon declined ("What kind of job is a sport historian qualified to do?" was the familiar query), these subfields were phased out. Aerosus had little appreciation of their value, and it had never been clear to university administrators how sport historians, sport sociologists, or sport psychologists differed from historians, sociologists, or psychologists who studied sport.

Looking back over the rise and fall of physical education in both public schools and colleges, one couldn't help but be struck by the welter of causes and interrelated effects. Bressan (1979) had predicted the eventual death of the profession, either at its own hands or at the hands of others. However, as things turned out, it was neither suicide nor murder that did the profession in, but death by natural causes. The profession contracted what can best be described as Organizational Alzheimer's, leaving it confused, disoriented, and unable to put together an effective strategy for accomplishing reasonable goals. Professionals consoled themselves with the notion that the profession had lived a long and fulfilling life but that professions, like people, do not live forever. It wasn't until 3 years after its passing that word finally reached the AAHPERD, who immediately assigned a committee to study the matter. . . .

At that moment, I was jolted upright as my feet slipped off the desk and hit the floor with a thud. What a relief to realize I had been asleep and dreaming. How reassuring to look out my office window and see physical education classes in full swing. I glanced at my watch and realized I'd better hurry. There was a meeting with the teacher education faculty within the hour, a luncheon appointment with our resident exercise physiologists, and a ton of mail to be opened and read—letters from colleagues as well as flyers and brochures from equipment companies and publishers. As I rose to leave, my eye caught one envelope among the litter—from an organization called "Pedasport, Inc." Obviously a piece of junk mail; I pitched it into the wastebasket and walked out the door.

Dreaming the Possible Dream:
The Rise and Triumph of Physical Education

Donald R. Hellison
Portland State University

Prologue

It seemed like a good idea at the time. Writing this chapter, that is. Editor John told me to pull out all the stops and describe a future characterized by "complete optimism, utopia at its best, enthusiasm uncontrolled," a future that will "enable the field of physical education to take its rightful place as a major contributor to the establishment of the 'best of all possible worlds'." What fun, I thought. Now it's done, and as I read it over I see oh so many problems and gaps.

I think the major difficulty I'm having is my own commitment to an experiment of one (Hellison, 1983). For the past 15 years or so I have conducted my own brand of offbeat research (some say pseudo-research, or worse), sort of a combination of case study and participant observation, in which I have always been quick to point out the idiosyncratic quality of my work and to offer it as an alternative, in the spirit of "only taking one case to prove a possibility" (Hellison, 1978, 1985, 1986). But here I am, staring at a manuscript that purports to represent everyone's best sense of the future; how contradictory!

Can I extricate myself from this dilemma, or do I call Editor John and tell him to forget it? Hmmm . . . Maybe I can get away with saying that this is one person's view, that it is punctuated with the biases of personal experience, and that I'm iconoclastic enough to be off in some other direction should this future become a reality by some unlikely turn of events. Better yet, I can say that the whole purpose of this exercise is to dissonate you, to create or stoke up a dialog that might help all of us think about the future of physical education and perhaps influence that future, rather than let it just evolve in its own way. Perhaps, even better yet, I should just share what I've written—since it is already done—and let you judge its merit as a future direction, as a dissonator, or as a fantasy story.

The Dream: An Overview

Here in a nutshell, basking in unbridled optimism, are the major future trends I see for physical education:

1. Physical education in higher education will return to an applied mission.
2. Physical educators in higher education will collaborate with teachers, coaches, and other practitioners at their worksites on an ongoing basis, gaining more of a whole-person perspective as they contend with real people and real problems.
3. Research in physical education will emphasize the transformation of research results into concepts and strategies useful to practitioners, will make more use of case studies and informal field studies, and will pay more attention to questions that practitioners are asking, especially in relation to on-the-job problem-solving.
4. The trend toward the separation of physical education from health education and recreation education will reverse direction, bolstered by a joint helping profession/whole-person perspective.
5. Public school physical education programs will be characterized by smaller classes and elimination of the teacher-coach role conflict, and physical education teachers will assume creative leadership for the development of their own curriculum and instruction models.
6. Physical education practitioners in all settings—schools, competitive sport programs, wellness programs, programs for special populations—will reach more people by employing clinical skills as well as didactic instruction, by paying more attention to client inner thoughts and feelings, by promoting the development of moral and humanitarian qualities in support of—and to offset the excesses of—self-development, and by encouraging clients to take responsibility for the program and their own lives.

That's about it. Without further apologies for what I've left out, the rest of this chapter will sketch out how these trends relate to each other and how they could become realities in our future. I will narrate my view of the future as an historian charged with chronicling and evaluating recent events.

Toward an Applied Mission in Physical Education in Higher Education

In my scenario for the future, the superspecialization trend that had spawned a number of subdisciplines with separate parent disciplines, languages, research questions and methods, preparatory coursework, and all the rest evolved without a great deal of interference—with apologies to McNeill (1982), Bressan (1982), Broekhoff (1982), Hoffman (1985), and others who tried to interfere—and proceeded to its logical conclusion. That is, the subdisciplines along with their journals and conventions were gradually subsumed by the parent disciplines. The only subdisciplinary scholars who stuck around were those who couldn't get an invitation to join another academic unit, and therefore were impotent forces in physical education's future, and those who really valued physical education and even liked its name!

The exodus of many scholars provided an opportunity for national organizations to take action. Both NAPEHE and AAHPERD decided, after years of skirting the issue, to deal with the question of mission. It was easier for NAPEHE; their organization was smaller and shrinking each year. They needed to do something, and small numbers allowed for quicker consensus. Of course, the breakdown of the subdisciplinary movement gave them courage. It was easier to argue for the return of physical education to an applied focus when those who were not interested in application were leaving the field in droves; in a sense, it became the only game in town. The study of sport or human movement or human performance, they argued, sounded academic enough but hadn't provided much of a central focus. Each subdiscipline had pretty much gone its own way. They were able to reach general agreement that, despite the variety of fancy names adopted by academic units across the country, physical education was fairly accurate: contributing to people's lives by educating them in and through the various forms of movement (e.g., sport, exercise, dance) was indeed the central focus of the field. Physical education was a helping profession, and the role of scholarship was to support this mission. Thus, exercise scientists, sport psychologists, and other subdisciplinary scholars who could make this commitment were embraced as part of the new family. Others were politely excluded.

It was a hard line, made easier by the recent departure of many subdisciplinary scholars. There were some lively debates that year, of course, as there would be in future years. A few held that this decision was a giant step backward to what one referred to as "the stone age of fizz ed" with its education of the physical versus through the physical debates, lectures to P.E. majors on how to pull out the bleachers, university physical education programs characterized by service rather than scholarship, and so on and so forth. One wag responded that it is high time the field recognized that its job is to sell Chevrolets, not Cadillacs! On a slightly more serious note, a bit of a debate broke out over the fine line that divides applied and "pure" research. A comment once made by Larry Locke (Siedentop, 1976) was invoked and seemed to satisfy most who were in attendance: The intention of the researcher should determine whether the inquiry is applied or not.

Although scholarship in university physical education must be pointed in the direction of the improvement of practice, such research need not be immediately useful. However, the vast wasteland lying between research and practice needed immediate attention so that research findings could be transformed, not just translated, into practice (Locke, 1969). Descriptive studies, for example, only describe the current state of affairs, not what kinds of changes to make nor how to make them. The absence of subdisciplinary scholars who were not interested in practical applications of their work greatly reduced the intensity and acrimony of these debates.

NAPEHE's decision was implemented immediately in a modified policy for *Quest* and in future formats for national meetings; and AAHPERD, after a bureaucratic struggle, followed suit with a more loosely worded applied mission statement, some internal reorganization (see below), and some changes in journal and convention policy. However, perhaps the most significant boost to implementation of the applied mission came from changes in university promotion, tenure, and merit pay guidelines.

Again, external forces played a part in greasing the skids for change; the publish or perish mentality that had spread to most universities by the 1970s was under increasingly heavy attack by students, taxpayers, alumni, and even commissions composed of university faculty and administrators. As a result, heads of academic affairs were open to revisions in promotion and tenure guidelines, and the adoption of an applied mission for physical education provided the basis for guideline changes in the field. Collaboration with practitioners and applied research were heavily weighted in the new guidelines, and this change by itself encouraged particularly young faculty to delve into the various work worlds of the practitioners. Other changes were also made in the promotion-tenure guidelines, most notably an individualized process so that faculty, in conference with administrators, could determine the weight of various activities in their evaluation.

Professor-Practitioner Collaboration

As these guidelines were put into place, in-service activities for practitioners who were coaching, teaching, and providing leadership for various sport, exercise, and movement programs both in and outside schools increased considerably. At first, university professors tended to hold show and tell workshops based on their research and the development of theoretical models, much as they had in the past. Although some of these activities gave practitioners new ideas and renewed energy, those who attended began to complain about the irrelevance of many of the ideas for their work world. Some dialogs ensued, especially among outspoken practitioners and professors who genuinely wanted to help even at the expense of having to change their ways. Such dialog was structured into a few workshops, and slowly, workshops began to take the practitioners' problems into account and even to develop around problems identified by practitioners.

Eventually this led to professors visiting the practitioners' workplaces, at first very tentatively from the sidelines but then, slowly, rolling up their sleeves and working alongside the practitioners. What began to happen was far different from the on-site data collection and student teaching/practicum supervision of earlier days. Professors had begun to actually experience the world of the practitioner, a world totally foreign to those who went straight from undergraduate studies into one specialization or another.

National organizations provided leadership for the field by clarifying and supporting a central mission that the evolution of the subdisciplinary movement had made possible, and changes in promotion and tenure guidelines encouraged physical education professors to put the mission into practice. However, what really altered the future of physical education was the new model of collaboration. The success of professor-practitioner teams—as judged by the participants themselves, by clients' and other publics' perceptions of the social significance of this work, and to a lesser extent by the data—encouraged other teams to form and work together. The departure of many subdisciplinary scholars set the stage, and national organizations and universities provided an important bridge to implementation. But the future was altered by those who did the work, who modeled the changes and reported their successes and failures. The changes that resulted were not mandated from above but modeled by those on the front line, providing powerful leadership for others who were to follow.

The Changing Face of Research

Professor-practitioner collaboration led to an increased awareness on the part of professors that their research wasn't being taken seriously by practitioners. First of all much of it had to be transformed, not just translated, to be useful. That meant filling in the gap between where the research ended and the practitioner's work world began. Practitioners needed specific concepts and strategies that they could try out and support to do so. Second, they were more persuaded by specific cases than by generalizations derived from data (Shulman, 1986). That meant conducting more "experiment of one" case studies (Hellison, 1983) and, in line with Cronbach's (1982) argument that the role of social research is to help with specific problems in specific contexts, illustrating the findings of more traditional research with specific cases. Third, professorial research often ignored the questions practitioners were asking. In particular, practitioners wanted to become better on-the-job problem solvers. They needed help in making sound professional judgments (Raywid, Tesconi, & Warren, 1984) and in becoming more competent at "reflection in action" (Sykes,

1983). The transformation of research and various case study approaches was increasingly aimed at helping practitioners in these areas.

Changes in the role and direction of research were facilitated by face-to-face interaction with clients in the practitioner's work world. Professors found it difficult to isolate their specialized interests while working with real people in real situations; too many other factors intruded. Whether they were little kids or retirees, whether an aerobics class or a basketball team, individuals responded not only with their bodies but with their thoughts, emotions, perceptions, and a host of other factors as well. Some needed social approval. Others needed body image or body boundary repairs. Still others were searching for personal meaning, for health enhancement, for a means of achievement, for stress reduction, for a drug abuse replacement. Some were in love with a particular physical activity. Others were anxious or afraid. Moreover, these problems presented themselves to practitioners in a never-ending series of idiosyncratic interactions with specific individuals in unique situations.

Practitioners needed the insight to deal with often-hidden needs and aspirations, a wide view of the potential roles of sport and exercise in people's lives, the skills to problem-solve "on their feet," and a deep abiding interest in and concern for their clients. Further, even if research could have an impact on these areas, practitioners needed a great deal of support and feedback to field-test new ideas in their settings; for most, reading a journal article or attending a workshop was not enough to bring about change. Professors gained more of a helping profession perspective and a better understanding of the whole person as the result of these observations; all this influenced their research, their collaboration efforts, and eventually their relationship with professors in other fields.

More traditional research concerning the influence of physical activity as an intervention medium (e.g., for heart health, depression, stress, body image, and a number of other psychological and physiological factors) was not scrapped during this period despite the emphasis on individuality and the idiosyncracies of physical education practice. However, research paradigms and procedures were loosened, and research generalizations were applied very cautiously. In particular, a physical eduation imagination (Mills, 1959) was nurtured, resulting in all sorts of field studies employing all sorts of research methods. Self-reports and other qualitative methods were treated every bit as valid as high-powered statistical manipulations, and in many cases they uncovered the variance in responses more effectively. Results were often reported as "Here's what happened in such-and-such a setting when we did such-and-such . . ." This paradigmatic looseness encouraged more practitioners, with or without professorial assistance, to replicate other studies, often with creative twists, and even to try new approaches. Meanwhile, professors not only collaborated with practitioners but brought their students along and, in so doing, combined research with service and teaching in one activity.

The consequence of these efforts was a significant increase in the use of physical activity as an intervention medium—in hospitals, psychiatric wards, diversion and detention facilities, homes for the elderly, preschool programs, and so on. Experimentation was in vogue and many were involved, sharing and celebrating the positive results of others similarly engaged.

Health and Leisure Education: Toward a New Focus

AAHPERD, with its 100+ substructures, up from 80+ in the mid-1980s, had no difficulty seeing the need for a central focus, and NAPEHE's decision encouraged the AAHPERD leadership to tackle the problem head on. Of course, action got bogged down in the various levels of bureaucracy and by the lobbying of various special interest groups. Some headway toward an applied focus was accomplished, however, resulting in a loosely worded mission statement and, more important, some consolidation of substructures into, or more accurately back to, health, physical education, and recreation. AAHPERD then began to push for these three fields to identify common values that would provide a sound basis for maintaining the Alliance. These gap-bridging sessions were marked by the usual turf battles, especially at the university level, but because university physical educators had already identified themselves as a helping profession with an applied mission, had become aware of the need for more of a whole-person perspective as a result of working with practitioners, and had begun to loosen their research paradigms and protocols, the stage was set for more collaboration with professionals from the other fields who were working toward these same goals. Some progress toward a health and leisure education helping profession alliance was achieved as communication continued, and lines between the three fields eventually began to blur.

Teaching Physical Education in Public Schools

For some time it had been widely recognized that physical education classes were too large (as were classes in other subjects) and that a fundamental teacher-coach role conflict existed. The collaboration of professors and teachers strengthened these arguments, and the media continued to pepper the public with messages regarding both the failure of schools to teach kids who needed help the most and the excesses of big-time athletics in public schools and universities. With the success of small alternative schools (Raywid, 1983), most of which served kids in trouble, middle-class parents began to complain that their kids ought to enjoy the benefits of these schools without first having to develop a record of misbehavior, low grades, and absenteeism. When middle-class parents spoke, administrators and school board members listened!

Experimental schools patterned after these alternative schools began to emerge and were immensely popular. The schools were small, none over 100 students, and class size was held to 15 or under with a few large lectures. Unlike large schools with bureaucracies and specialized roles, the few teachers in each school taught several subjects, counseled students, and carried out administrative duties. Both teachers and students felt a greater sense of belonging; if anyone was absent, everyone knew and wondered about it. After-school sports existed to the extent that students wanted a team and some faculty member was willing to sponsor or coach them. If the kids did want a team, they had to recruit some of the rest of the school to participate. With few to choose from, more were involved. There were no leagues. Phone calls were placed to other schools and to youth agencies: "Wanna play a basketball game Tuesday after school over here?" The many hats each teacher wore helped to keep after-school sports on an informal basis; they just didn't have the time to devote to organizing a big time program. If the kids wanted an athletic team, they had to do much of the organizing. The coach could lend whatever expertise he or she had in the activity itself.

Although not all school districts adopted the small school model, even on an experimental basis, most radically altered their interscholastic sports programs. For a variety of reasons, including cost, repeated criticism of big time athletic practices, publicizing of the teacher-coach role conflict, and the small school model, some school districts disbanded their interscholastic athletic programs, which were then taken over by various agencies in the community. Other schools began to hire full-time coaches and to reorganize morning and afternoon practice times in order to create full-time jobs (Kneer, 1985). Those teachers who preferred coaching could now elect to fill full-time coaching positions in schools or community agencies.

Curriculum Models

The reign of the traditional 3-week unit ended rather abruptly during this period. Even with small classes and the absence of coaching responsibilities, curriculum goals that aimed at student development were difficult to pursue when activities changed every few weeks. Students needed to be involved in the pursuit of curriculum goals over a longer period of time. That meant developing themes that ran throughout the year, once or twice a week or as part of every class period, as alternatives to the 3-week unit.

Capturing the mosaic of physical activity motives, meanings, and benefits in year-long themes proved to be an impossible task. The joy of movement was of paramount importance to some teachers, while others wanted to help students prove themselves in challenging situations. Physical activity could be used as an outlet or a place to "strut one's stuff."

Health could be enhanced, fair play taught, leisure skills acquired. However, if programs tried to do all of these things, surely little would be accomplished. Moreover, teachers held their own values and were informed by their own experiences; they preferred to teach certain activities for certain reasons and were less capable of fully supporting other activities and ideas. Little by little, teachers, often in collaboration with professors, were encouraged to adopt a major theme or goal for their program—for example fitness, sport skills, conceptual understanding, self-responsibility. Curriculum models developed at an earlier time (Jewett & Bain, 1985, pp. 41-89) served as a beginning point, but some teachers began to create their own models of major and minor themes and to articulate minor themes with teachers in their own or other schools. This approach, which became known as the 51% rule, allowed teachers to concentrate on their strengths and values (the 51%) while also teaching toward goals they felt obligated as physical educators to share with students (the other 49%). Students benefitted from increased teacher enthusiasm and from being involved in one theme intensely enough to experience improvement.

The subdisciplinary trend had split curriculum and instruction into two separate special interest groups who worked under largely different assumptions (Jewett & Bain, 1985, pp. 293-295). This division still existed to some extent, permitting some specialized research, but changes in mission, promotion, and tenure guidelines—and in particular professor-teacher and professor-professor collaboration—reduced the distinctions and greatly improved the link between curriculum models and instructional strategies. As a result, instructional specialists in collaboration with teachers worked to identify and try out teaching strategies that would support the 51% rule. Teaching strategies compatible with different curriculum models and with the development of year-long themes were field-tested and the results were shared at workshops and conventions and printed in journals.

During this period, the professionalism of the physical education teacher received quite a boost. "Teacher-proof" systems of instruction mandated or advocated from above (i.e., by school district administration or professors) were largely replaced by support for, and collaboration in, the development and implementation of curriculum and instruction models by preservice and inservice teachers individually or in small groups. With trends toward smaller classes and separation of the teacher and coach roles, teachers were less burdened and more interested in these kinds of activities.

Inclusion in Physical Education Classes

The problem of inclusion had always plagued physical education. Some kids moved better for a variety of reasons and, with the usual variance in self-perceptions, tended to develop more confidence in their bodies in response to positive reinforcement. As they grew older, the gap between the haves and have nots in competence, confidence, and persistence (Bressan & Weiss, 1982) widened, and sensitivity to peer approval heightened. While teachers were trying to teach their students to run and throw and play fair, students were learning their status as a physical education student and how their bodies measured up. A student-directed hidden curriculum was indeed alive and well (Dodds & Locke, 1984)! Teachers tended to reinforce the differential inclusion of their students by behaving positively toward skilled and fit students and paying less attention to those who were "busy, happy, and good" (Placek, 1983).

Teachers were impressed by visible signs of physical prowess and by compliance. What students were feeling and thinking was less visible and therefore more or less ignored. In addition, many teachers had strong sport backgrounds and valued competition, so they tended to judge students by comparing the performance of one student to another or to some standard. As members of the middle class for the most part, they were also influenced by the middle-class wellness movement that had not yet spent its force. As a result, the various competitive trappings of the wellness movement—standards for acceptable percent body fat, fun runs that ranked how participants performed by sex and age, double marathons and other iron-man contests—found their way in modified form into the many gyms.

Professors and practitioners who collaborated to analyze the inclusion problem saw the need for four changes in order to bring about greater inclusion. First, teachers needed to learn how to be clinicians: how to help individual students who were not progressing satisfactorily, how to diagnose and prescribe for specific problems. The trend toward smaller classes afforded more opportunities for tutorial work, but teachers needed clinical skills to tutor effectively. Didactic teaching skills and even individualized instructional techniques were insufficient to help students who were having difficulties (Adler, 1983).

Second, teachers needed to pay more attention to what was going on inside students' heads rather than what their "outside selves" were doing (Thomas, 1983, pp. 122-135). Each student's outside self consisted of a surfeit of statistical measurements including test scores, win-loss records, body fat percentages, and batting averages as well as answers to questions such as "Who do others think I am?" and "Who should I be?" This could be contrasted with their inside self, which was neither visible nor very quantifiable, for example the confrontation of personal motivations and fears, the struggle against external forces, self-evaluation by both internal and external standards and in relation to one's own history (deCharms, 1976), and questions such as "Who am I?" "Who can I be?" and "Who do I want to be?" (Hellison, 1978). The very visible self was merely the tip of the iceberg; the inside self, submerged under water, was the iceberg itself.

Third, teachers needed to promote a climate that recognized effort and social support as well as competitive achievement. Too often, effort was overlooked in favor of achievement and self-development was pursued at the expense of others in a win-loss environment. Emphasis on courage, persistence, self-control, sensitivity to others, and helping others was necessary to encourage the self-development of all students and to offset the exaggerated sense of self-concern that often results from focusing on self-development. These moral qualities (Loy, McPherson, & Kenyon, 1978) were an integral part of professional rhetoric, but since they were not measurable in the same sense as body fat or base hits, they tended to be ignored in practice.

Fourth, as earlier research had suggested (deCharms, 1976; Rutter, 1979; Strother, 1983), students needed to be given more responsibility for planning, implementing, and evaluating their physical education classes and their own sport-exercise programs. They needed to help decide what kind of an environment they wanted to work in, and they needed to take more responsibility for the direction of their lives. With responsibility would come a sense of ownership and therefore greater inclusion in the program.

These four changes received considerable attention in journals, at conventions, in workshops, and in collaborative field studies, resulting in preservice and inservice implementation of the following:

- Clinical skills to augment didactic instruction;
- Socratic instructional techniques (Adler, 1983) to help students reflect on peer and other external pressures and their own needs and values in physical education (with considerable assistance from health educators in the growing liaison between health education and physical education);
- Self-reflection strategies to help students focus on their inside selves (Hellison, 1985, pp. 22-23, 87-99);
- Strategies designed to help students become less critical of each other and more cooperative, supportive, and helpful (Hellison, 1985, pp. 33-49, 131-153);
- Self-responsibility strategies to help students strive toward personal goals despite the presence of external forces (Hellison, 1978; Hellison, 1985, pp. 69-129).
- Strategies designed to promote joint teacher-student ownership in planning, implementation, and evaluation of the program (Hellison, 1985, pp. 139-141, 155-159).

The 51% rule was modified considerably by these changes. Although teachers were reluctant to give up their newfound leadership in curriculum development, many began to see that teacher-oriented themes precluded the full inclusion of students and therefore were just a step in the progression toward student ownership of the program. Students could participate immediately in the development of minor themes (the other 49%) and give input into the development of the major curriculum theme. However, students also needed to learn to develop their own goals and programs. As time allowed and with the improvement of clinical skills, teachers began to do a better job of helping students to plan and implement their personal plans. Gradually, students had some influence not only in planning curriculum themes but in planning and implementing their own physical education programs as well.

Competitive Sport

The inclusion movement profoundly influenced competitive sport both in and outside the school. Recognition of each person's inside self led schools and community agencies to offer more options to correspond with individual differences in motive and meaning. "Blood 'n guts" competition was offered for those who wanted to train and play all-out and to be judged by their achievement individually and collectively. "Play fair-play hard" competition was offered for those who wanted to blend courage and persistence with cooperation and social support. This was a more process-oriented perspective, heavily influenced by the moral qualities of the inclusion movement. Fair play and effort were applauded in these games; winners were given no formal status nor were individual statistics kept. "Hit 'n giggle" competition was offered as a third option for those who did not want to try so hard, who wanted to play rather than work, who wanted to have fun. Score was kept loosely, but no league standings or statistics were recorded, and if players were of age, beer and wine drinking was permitted during the game, and some said even encouraged. Not surprisingly, some excellent play could be seen in these games along with the dregs of the motor skill world, but either way, play it was, not work. Pressure to perform was absent, because all who signed up understood and were committed to the same purpose: assume a reasonable effort by everyone (under the circumstances), support everyone, and stay loose! None of these three options was new; what was new was the freedom of choice and the extent to which all three options flourished.

Following the lead of the small schools, athletes assumed more responsibility for running many of the competitive sport teams and programs. This included determining the level of competitive intensity, putting together the schedule, making and modifying the rules, selecting a coach if they felt some expertise was needed, and handling various problems and disputes as they arose. In many blood 'n guts programs, various efforts to get a competitive edge—drugs, bending the rules—became the responsibility of the athletes.

In the new spirit of humanitarianism, some competitive sport teams devoted part of their schedule to performing for special populations in hospitals, homes for the elderly, inner city schools, and so forth. They also held fund-raisers for various humanitarian causes.

The end result of these changes was more variety in purpose at all levels, more emphasis on less measurable moral qualities, and more ownership by the players. As coach-practitioners assumed more of the leadership for these changes, they began to help athletes look at their own motives and meanings, become aware of the limitations of an outside self-perspective, and make better choices for themselves. These changes gradually found their way into youth sport as well; young children were reinforced for their efforts and for supporting others, and were able to play on teams that emphasized having fun if they so desired.

Wellness Programs

Many of these changes spilled over into wellness programs. Early critics of the wellness movement (Carlyon, 1984; McBride & Hellison, 1986; Minkler, 1983; Vertinsky, 1985) complained that disease prevention was only one aspect of wellness, that the wellness movement was aimed at the middle class, that wellness information was biased and not truly scientific, and that wellness tended to promote body narcissism, excessive guilt, arrogance, and extremism. These criticisms paved the way for the inclusion trend with its emphasis on individual attention, the inside self, and moral qualities.

Exercise, weight control, and nutrition advocacy were softened by a widespread plea for moderation and more attention to individual differences. Small group discussions were organized to deal with external pressures such as the promotion of thinness in advertising, the arrogance and elitism of achievement-oriented wellness participants ("You ran 3 miles? I ran 5"), and the guilt associated with such pressures. Wellness was redefined so that the needs of the inside self and the development of humanitarian concerns were not only included but ranked higher in importance than disease prevention. Dunk tanks (for hydrostatic weighing), leotards, and triathalons became options rather than obligations. Fun runs that were truly fun—shorn of splits, race results, and trophies—along with events in support of various humanitarian causes, became commonplace. In all, wellness began to be viewed more as a process involving people's struggle with purpose rather than a product to be achieved.

As practitioners received preservice and inservice training along these lines and collaborated with professors at their worksites, these changes were incorporated into more and more community programs.

Private health and athletic clubs saw the inclusion movement not only as the latest "in" thing but as an opportunity to appeal to more people. To succeed, they sent their practitioners to workshops and conventions, hired people with degrees in physical education, and requested the collaboration of professors.

Social Problems

Physical education did not come to be viewed as panacea for societal ills such as poverty, crime, terrorism, the threat of nuclear war, and all the rest. Physical education's efforts to ameliorate racism, sexism, handicappism, and ageism had been less than noble up to this time (Siedentop, 1980, p. 212); but many social problems such as the pervasive exclusion of the lower class in the mainstream of American society were at least partly structural in nature and as such were beyond the influence of physical education (Burnham, 1984; Eckstein, 1984). However, the missionary zeal and commitment to the outreach process that characterized this period were not dampened by physical education's past performance or the likelihood of success. In fact, more activities were conducted for the disfranchised than ever before. More professors went into the slums and hospitals and homes for special populations to conduct research that might help, to lend support to practitioners, and in some cases to start new programs. To whatever extent possible, the disfranchised were given responsibility for program development, were encouraged to reflect on and express their private thoughts and feelings, and were reinforced for their courage and persistence. Newly learned clinical skills helped physical educators to individualize and deal with special problems. Perhaps most important, these services were provided in a context that protected human rights and promoted concern for others.

In schools, the smallness trend also helped. Minorities, females, males—in short, everyone—were more difficult to stereotype in small schools and classes; familiarity bred better understanding rather than, as the old saying went, contempt. Sex roles were also affected. Moral qualities being integrated into physical education programs contained both hard (e.g., courage, persistence) and soft (e.g., sensitivity to others, helping others) qualities; both sexes were encouraged to develop a better balance of these hard and soft qualities. Moreover, personal needs that followed or crossed over traditional sex role guidelines were attended to by physical educators more thoroughly than in the past, due to the emphasis on the whole person and on the inside self. For example, progressions toward blood 'n guts competitive events and challenges were developed to meet the machismo needs of males and the achievement needs of females. Violence was neither encouraged nor discouraged; instead it was offered as a dance (Leonard, 1974) for those who wanted or needed it.

Epilogue: A Future Without Computers?

"Where's the high tech?" you ask. "High touch without high tech?" you object. What you have just read is a description of my dream for the future, not anyone else's. It is what I would like to see, not what current trends suggest. It is not very radical. Everything I have described is currently going on to some extent. In my view, we just need more of it. Most of all, I guess, we need to try harder to help. We are part of the social structure; we do have influence. What we do and value make a difference in people's lives. Perhaps the most we can offer is a tiny click of increased opportunity for emotional and social well-being, but with a more concerned effort the click could be louder. Perhaps much louder.

Epilogue: A Future Without Computers?

Three Dreams:
The Future of HPERD at the Cutting Edge

John J. Burt
University of Maryland

Liberation From Narrowness

My contention in this chapter is that we in health, physical education, recreation and dance—that centaur known as HPERD—desperately need to widen and scrub off the windows through which we view the world. My belief is that our vision is narrow and blurred, leaving us muddleheaded and exposed to the sharp edges of professional life. We have not yet been able to see far enough to clearly realize our place among the professions.

My thoughts on what to do about this problem are stimulated by an observation from Pablo Picasso:

> We all know that art is not truth. Art is a lie that makes us realize truth—at least, the truth that is given us to understand.

Perhaps a different approach, one not limited to truth, will serve to free our thinking from its present boundaries and help us to realize truth. Accordingly, the three pieces that make up this chapter are not truth; they are imaginative narrations—two dreams and a fictitious letter received in a dream—all intended to initiate discussions among those interested in evolving a perspective for the future of HPERD. For that reason the dream fragments are sometimes brief, and they may be somewhat dogmatic in tone. Each sets forth a "position" with relatively little explanation or defense. It is my hope that the dreams will provoke discussion that will counteract any dogmatism they may contain.

Dream One: The Subpoena

A town house in Maryland. The evening has been spent preparing a speech on the future, a speech to be given at a national conference of administrators of

HPERD programs. After long hours of struggle, I drift off to sleep—soon to dream. Soon to be assaulted by a nightmare that has reoccurred many times since that frightful night.

About 3 a.m. a subpoena arrives. It directs me to appear at once before the Academic Attorney General. Arriving at a monstrous complex of buildings, somewhere out in space, I am escorted to the Chief RAW Officer. My guide tells me to wait outside her door.

While waiting, I look up and discover what RAW stands for. My heart sinks. It stands for—Are you ready for this?—*Removal of Academic Waste*. Terrified, sweat pouring from my forehead, I enter her office. A fully-in-charge woman invites me to remain standing in front of her desk. It is clear that I am here to listen. She speaks.

"I am in charge of the removal of academic waste. You and your colleagues are administrators of academic areas marked for elimination. I mean for you to take this personally," she says, looking at me with obvious contempt. Then, hesitating for a moment, she goes on: "I guess you are no worse than the other mental pygmies who serve as chief executive officers of HPERD units. But since you will be meeting with them soon, we have selected you to take a message to the entire group. You are to see that they receive it at once! Is that clear?"

With repeated movements of my head, I indicate that I understand, saying to myself, "Who does she think she is?"

Astonished, I suddenly realize as she cuts into my thinking that she can read minds: "Let's get something straight: My powers are limitless. Unless you wish to be wasted, I mean right here and right now, then pay attention. And stand up straight."

There can be no doubt: I am overmatched. I stand up straight. She goes on, "Fifteen years from today, the Academic Attorney General will bring a class action suit against all colleges and divisions of HPERD. You will be charged with three counts of academic waste and recommended for elimination. Between now and then, you can either rethink what you are doing or come prepared to defend the fluff that you are now engaged in. But let me warn you: We have stood about all we can stand. And we will be pressing hard for your elimination."

Looking me straight in the eyes, she says quietly, "That is the message of which I spoke; take it to your group."

Again I make the mistake of thinking to myself. I am thinking, "There is no way that my colleagues are going to believe this dream. Furthermore, she hasn't told me what the three charges against us are." At this point she again breaks right into my thinking: "If for any reason the bimboes in your group question the validity of your message, we are prepared to work a little miracle. Here is what you do: Just write the names of any five colleges or divisions of HPERD on a plain sheet of paper. Then cross out the names with a red pencil. We will take care of the rest. These programs will be eliminated at once."

Taking a note pad from her desk, she writes with a black pen: *University of Washington.* Then she crosses it out, saying, "like this." I get the point.

In a different voice, she goes on: "Now to the three charges against you:

I. In violation of the *Code of Academic Usefulness,* colleges and divisions of HPERD have failed to see far enough to recognize the central issues of the time and to connect with these issues.

"In the full history of HPERD, we are hard pressed to find examples wherein you have been helpful, helpful in the solution of any significant human problems. As far as we can tell, you are useless! You haven't even been helpful in the solution of problems of intercollegiate sports. You are waste."

I try to think of a way to sidetrack her. But the message is clear: We have failed to connect with the central issues of our time. No chance to play with words here. No chance to ask, what is fitness? What is wellness? The charge is clear, too clear.

It is hard to explain how I feel each night when this part of the dream reoccurs. It's like when I go cycling each morning at 6 a.m. I have a 12-mile course with three big hills. When I get to the top of the first hill, there I am: out of breath, heart pounding, legs burning, relieved that it is over but already starting to worry about the next two hills. That's kind of the way it is in my dream each night, each night as I stand in front of her desk. My heart is pounding. I am glad it's over. But my mind is racing on to the next hill, to the next two charges.

One difference though. One big difference. As I stand there, the worst of all emotions descends upon me: SHAME. Shame because I realize that we are guilty. I look at the floor, hoping I will be able to make it up the next hill.

Then a pleasant thought. I remember that on my biking course the first hill is by far the toughest hill. Perhaps it will be like that here. But again reading my mind, she says: "It doesn't get any better" and goes on to the next charge:

II. In violation of the *Code of Academic Usefulness,* colleges and divisions of HPERD have become internally disjunctive, have lost all philosophical clarity, have compromised their birthright.

I don't fully understand. But reading my mind, she offers further explanation. "Let me make it simple enough for folks in HPERD to understand." With an expression of disgust she goes on: "Not only have you failed to recognize and connect with the central issues, but worse, in an ill-advised attempt to gain academic respectability you have subdivided HPERD into silly little walled-off compartments, like sport psychology, sport sociology, sport history, sport management, exercise physiology, motor learning, health psychology, health promotion, outdoor recreation, indoor recreation, upstairs recreation, downstairs recreation, modern dance, old dance, and who knows what else."

Shaking her finger at me, she says, "HPERD units are totally ineffective! In no case does the whole exceed the sum of those little compartments, those little pockets of waste."

Were we that bad? Were we nothing more than self-serving pockets of waste? I thought that was overkill. But this woman, she was too smart to be confronted with superficial arguments. She had given us 15 years to prepare a defense. Perhaps we should use the full time.

"I hope so" she said. "You need all the time you can get."

It is not easy being in the presence of someone who can read your mind. She went on to the third charge:

III. In violation of the *Code of Academic Usefulness*, colleges and divisions of HPERD—unlike the useful professional schools, unlike medicine and engineering and journalism and law—you have failed to concentrate your efforts and resources on the development of a high quality practitioner.

"One might have thought," she said, "that even mental pygmies like you in HPERD would have recognized the need for professionals who could apply the very best that your silly little compartments have to offer. But you showed little interest in application. You failed to realize that if we had only wanted research we would have gone to real psychology, to real sociology, to real physiology, to real history. What we wanted, what we fully expected from you was a high quality practitioner—one who could advise people of all ages on how to liberate themselves from the impediments and risk factors that might otherwise prevent them from being the best they could be. And a practitioner who could advise people on how to compensate for those impediments that are immutable. Instead, you have almost entirely perverted the task that you were given. Now those silly little compartments that have emerged have become ends in themselves, ends that look with disdain on powerless practitioners from whom they have embezzled vitality. Frauds! That's what you are. You have appropriated, fraudulently and for one's own selfish use, resources entrused to you to promote the common good.

"What's even worse" she says looking right through me, "is that not one of those silly compartments, not one of those embezzlers, has even made a significant discovery. Thousands of unrelated little studies signifying nothing. And not only has your research failed to address significant questions, but as far as we can see, you don't seem to be addressing any questions in a systematic and orderly way. HPERD is an academic wasteland!

"See you again in 15 years," she says as she abruptly walks out. Well, that's my nightmare. It leaves us with some serious questions:

- In the past, have we failed to recognize and to connect with the central issues of the time?
- What are the central issues in our immediate future?
- How can we connect with these issues?
- Are we internally disjunctive?
- Have we lost sight of a common purpose?
- Have we compromised our academic birthright?
- Have we created individual compartments that are now in danger of running away to become ends in themselves?
- Even worse, are these ends now embezzling the vitality of HPERD?

Dream Two: The Practitioner

Deeply troubled by the first nightmare, I spent many sleepless nights thinking about the need for a high quality practitioner in HPERD. I have the feeling that some of the subdivisions of HPERD have come a long way. I feel pride, for example, in the progress of exercise physiology and behavioral medicine. But that RAW officer was right: We simply were not preparing a high quality practitioner. We were more comparable to a medical school that prepared PhDs in anatomy or physiology or biochemistry or pathology but did not prepare practitioners of medicine. We prepared professionals in a variety of subspecialties—more people like ourselves—but what about the practitioner of wellness? However impressive our acquisition of knowledge, however proficient our graduates in research, if we were unable to marry theory and practice for the purpose of promoting wellness, we were in trouble. This because a profession is judged, inevitably, by its largest concern, and our largest concern seemed to be producing more people like ourselves. Could it be that the greatest threat to HPERD was our smallness of purpose? With these thoughts reverberating in my head, I have a second dream.

In this dream I am attending a convention. The year is not clear, but it is somewhere out in the future. Health, Physical Education, Recreation, and Dance are all grown up now. There has been another merger, a big one. AAHPERD has been joined by music and art and literature and drama and sculpture. In this second dream I am at a meeting of AAHPERDMALDS. Whatever we are, we are a large group. At first I have the feeling that I have passed to another life, to a place where God has collected all the low status professions. It's a kind of Academic Hall. Mother always said I might wind up in a bad place, but I never thought my profession, in toto, would also. But here we are!

Too late to worry. I just sit in my seat and wait for the first general session. A very tall man, the Chief Devil I assume, approaches the podium. His manner of smiling suggests that he knows something we don't. "You are a curious collection of people," he says, looking us over. "You are well-meaning, good-natured, inclined to be helpful, and somewhat motivated." Obviously he is building up to something. You don't get sent to hell for being well-meaning, for being good-natured.

"The trouble is," the tall devil continued, "you just haven't been very smart; you never understood what made people really tick; you understood your subject matter, of course, but not the persons to whom your facts and skills were addressed. That was your tragic flaw!"

I hung my head, knowing in my heart he was right. Very truthfully, we didn't understand what made people tick, and if that lack of understanding got a teacher sent to hell, we had no defense. I prepared for the worst.

But the speaker didn't seem the least vengeful. He went on, very relaxed: "I am here to tell you what you have failed to discover on your own; I am here to explain what makes people really tick; I am here to explain the *Law of Human Connectedness*. Once you understand this law, you will be able to help us with an important mission."

A law to explain human behavior—that made me very uncomfortable. I knew about laws in physics (things like special and general relativity), laws in chemistry, and even physiology. But my most respected philosophy teacher had convinced me that humans were agents with free will, agents whose behavior could never be described by laws. Was the devil a behaviorist? I could be in great trouble.

The know-it-all-devil went on, *"The Law of Human Connectedness* states: Given a full experience of any set of human options, a person will ultimately select the option most helpful in overcoming aloneness, the option most helpful in establishing connectedness. This because the feeling of connectedness is the highest of the affirmative emotions, an emotion so pleasurable that all others will be put aside in favor of it."

Now I thought I knew who this man really was! The talk about pleasure tipped me off. This was Mephistopheles; this was the same devil that appeared to Dr. Faust; this was the same Mephistopheles who offered Faust earthly pleasures in exchange for his soul. I could guess his mission! Mephistopheles would try to recruit those of us in AAHPERD-MALDS to work for him. Our mission would be to trade pleasures for souls. He thought we would be too dumb, too poorly read, to catch on. I would show him. I raised my hand and prepared to attack his silly law.

"Who says connectedness is the most affirmative emotion?" I addressed the devil as if he were a graduate student. "Where is your evidence?" "What about an alternative hypothesis, that creativity is the most affirmative emotion?" These questions, I supposed, would slow him down, at least until I could think of some more.

Mephistopheles, however, was not thrown off by my questions, or offended. Indeed, he appeared ready for them. "Creativity as an affirmative emotion does not even come close to connectedness," he said. "Michelangelo, the most creative mind yet—an acclaimed master of painting and sculpture and architecture and poetry—said at the peak of his popularity, 'It would have been better if I had been a matchmaker.' Michelangelo wanted to be connected to something useful! Unconnected creativity is nothing. Ask Vincent Van Gogh. More than anything else he too wanted to be useful."

Thus spoke the devil, and all could see that he was right. I had chosen a bad example. But that didn't prove that connectedness was the most affirmative emotion. What about love? I was about to ask when it hit me: Love was probably the highest form of connectedness.

Well what about sex? Mephistopheles had said that a person given full experience of any set of human options would always choose the one that afforded the greatest connectedness. Now that might be generally true; but sex, I thought, would be a special exception. As with Einstein's relativity, the general theory must presume the validity of the special case. I had him! I shot the question. "Does the *Law of Human Connectedness* hold if one of the options is sex?"

Mephistopheles, to my great surprise, seemed to welcome the question. "Consider," he said, "the following set of sex-related options: autoerotism, experience with a prostitute, casual sex, and sex with a person who is loved and respected. Now, all moral questions aside, which option would be more pleasurable? Which would produce the most affirmative emotion?"

The answer was obvious. I had asked this question of my own students at least a thousand times, and for even the most liberal, the answer was clear: "The stronger the connection to the other person the greater the pleasure. The weaker the connection, the less affirming the experience."

I was no match for Mephistopheles. I understood for the first time what Faust meant when he said,

I have, alas, studied philosophy,
Jurisprudence and medicine, too,
And, worst of all, theology
With keen endeavor, through and through—
And here I am, for all my lore,
The wretched fool I was before.

Knowledge was impotent if it couldn't get us to the affirmative emotions. No matter how much we studied and researched, we were still wretched fools if we didn't understand what made people tick, if we didn't understand human motivation. And we didn't. It was all so clear now, but apparently too late. I would keep quiet. No matter what his mission, Mephistopheles was smarter than I. Moreover, it was nice of him to explain where we went wrong. Why we had been sent here. There was pleasure in knowing, even at this late date.

Mephistopheles went on uninterrupted. "There are three types of connectedness:

Type I is connection to meaning and purpose;
Type II is psychobiological connection to other people;
Type III is connection to one's genetic and cultural past.

Mephistopheles made things so clear. He would have been a wonderful teacher. He really knew how to communicate. There was connectedness to purpose, connectedness to people, and connectedness to one's genetic and cultural background. And establishing these connections constituted the highest affirmative emotions. It was so simple. Why had we never discovered this?

Mephistopheles next gave some examples of people who had accomplished Type I connectedness: "Where are our examples of this type of connectedness? Let me give you three: Gandhi, King, and Carver. Gandhi was a person connected to purpose—so much so that he was willing to starve to death if necessary. He noted that life was made up of many journeys and that those who didn't keep their minds on the destination often got lost. Martin Luther King had a lively perception of Type I connectedness. No one has described it more clearly: 'If a man hasn't discovered something that he will die for, he isn't fit to live.'

"Now," Mephisto was very serious, "let me give you an example of how the *Law of Connectedness* influences human choice. The example comes from the life of Washington Carver. Starting as a slave, he worked his way through elementary school, high school, and college. All this under the most adverse conditions that you can imagine. Nonetheless, he finally arrived at the top, a college position, his own laboratory—an impossible dream come true. Then one day a call came from Booker T. Washington. The conversation went something like this:

— "Dr. Carver, I am starting a college in Alabama. I would like to have you head one of my departments."
— "I see," said Carver, "and what kind of department would it be?"
— "Well, to tell you the truth, it only exists on paper. You would be the department."
— "I see," said Carver, "and what kind of labs would I have?"
— "Well, to tell you the truth, you would have to build your own."
— "I see," said Carver again, "and just what did you expect me to do at this school with no department and no lab?" (Carver was a little leary.)

— "Well," said the man on the other end, "I would like to start a college for blacks, a place that could change their apprehensions about the future into anticipations."

"Of all the options," Mephisto was intense, "that a college professor might consider—tenure, lab space, salary, moving expenses, secretaries—these were all put aside. The moment Carver connected with the mission of Tuskegee, he said, 'I am on the way.' Not only did he go there to teach, but most of the time he gave his paycheck to a student in need.

"What you could never understand," Mephistopheles looked straight at his audience, "is what made a man like Carver tick. The *Law of Connectedness* explains this. Carver actually chose the most pleasurable option! Once you have fully experienced an option that gets you to connectedness, you want none other. Carver's life was not a sacrifice; it was a great pleasure. His epitaph is really a statement of Type I connectedness:

He could have added fortune to fame, but caring for neither, he found happiness and honor in being helpful to the world.

"Given a full experience of the kind of connection found by Gandhi and King and Carver, all people would move toward these options; but alas," Mephisto's expression was stern, "most have never had this opportunity. Most have been blocked by teachers."

I covered my face in shame, beginning to understand why I was in hell. Education did get in the way of connectedness. It occupied 12, 16, 20 years of life—and missed the point. Faust studied law and medicine and philosophy, but realized he was a wretched fool in spite of all his knowledge.

So were we! Funny, there was a certain perverse pleasure in realizing this, even if you had to come to hell to find out about it.

Mephisto went on to Type II connectedness: "Hans Selye, the Canadian biologist, once suggested that what's most important in life is the gratitude of others. People may say that they work for fortune or fame or science, but what they really seek is the gratitude of others, their love and respect. This is the essence of Type II connectedness. Whatever our talents—artistic, athletic, intellectual—they are all of little value unless they somehow connect us to others."

Mephisto was right. History was indeed a record of human attempts to overcome aloneness. That's why we worked and played and made love and war. It was really kind of simple. That's what we all wanted, a little respect. That's what AAHPERD had struggled for. And blacks and women and homosexuals. That's what everybody wanted: to be more than just an anatomical and physiological thing that existed for 72 years. We wanted to be connected! Mephisto was damn smart.

"Type III connectedness," he continued, "is connectedness to your prior programming. We are each programmed by our genes and by our values. We behave to reduce hunger and thirst because it is pleasurable to do so, because it is painful not to do so. We behave to achieve our values because it is pleasurable to do so, because it is painful not to do so. Our feelings are signals, reports of how well our behavior accords the way we have been programmed. We are free to write other programs, at least those related to our values, but once the program is in place, then it's a matter of behavior and feeling. Type III connectedness is a state of being in which we understand why our behavior produces certain kinds of feelings. In a popular sense, Type III connectedness means being in touch with the cause of your feelings.''

Mephisto was brilliant. I felt uneasy respecting the devil, but what the hell, he was plenty smart. I just had to be alert when it came to this mission he was recruiting for. It was one thing to admire his knowledge, another to join forces with the devil.

Just in time. Mephisto is getting to the mission.

''Now that you are acquainted with the LAW OF HUMAN CON-NECTEDNESS, let me explain the mission that I want to recruit you for. We are currently experiencing one of the most destructive diseases in the history of the world. Bubonic plague, cancer, heart disease—all these pale when compared to this modern malady. For the year 2000, the world has but one goal: Stop this disease.

''The problem to which I refer is a loss of will, a loss of will to continue striving for connectedness. When a person tries and tries to find meaning and fails, when a person tries and tries to connect with others but fails, when a person tries and tries to understand prior programming but fails, such a person often gives up—stops trying to connect, becomes a victim of what we now refer to as the *Corruption of Consciousness*, or CC for short. CC is the dreaded disease of which I spoke.

''In advanced CC, victims often attempt suicide, become alcoholics, turn to drugs, become depressed. In milder cases, Corruption of Consciousness victims exhibit little interest in fitness or health or medical compliance or social compliance or leisure or work or music or art or literature or drama or sculpture. CC victims do what they must to survive, and fill up the remaining hours with passive pleasures. The healthy will that once sought active connection is corrupted by this disease; it no longer seeks the affirmative, it seeks only to avoid pain; it would prefer not to feel at all. The CC victim does not anticipate the future—no, that is not exacting enough—the victim's anticipations are all changed to apprehensions.

''In a world in which 80% of the population now work for someone else, in a world in which morality has been reduced to law, in a world in which science and reductionism are king and queen, in this kind of world CC is pandemic and spreading wildly.

"Your mission, should you decide to accept, is to stop CC. Through sport and movement and drama and art and music and sculpture—through all the things you represent—we hope to stir up the emotions and return people to healthy consciousness, to a will that again seeks joy.

"It is our intention to establish a network of rehabilitation centers, centers designed to end the corruption-of-consciousness plague that is now sweeping the entire world. The purpose of these centers will be to acquaint people with an expanded set of options. Options, the full experience of which may return them to a healthy consciousness. Ultimately, we hope our centers will lead people to connectedness.

"I am currently searching for professionals to staff these centers. That's why I am here. Let me tell you about the kind of people I am looking for. I call them teaching artists, but don't let the title throw you. For purposes of this project, I define an artist as a person who walks for the emotions, a spokesperson who is able through the use of some medium to describe or symbolize a path to connectedness—a path to the highest of the affirmative emotions.

"Art, by this definition, takes many forms. For example, a healthy person is a limited edition of a human work of art, a work of art that portrays wellness. Health artists utilize the medium of health to sculptor themselves into works of art. Thus they create works that speak for their own emotions and for the emotions of those who have not yet reached health, which is to say, a well person serving as a work of art transmits the 'gestures of the spirit'—rather like a good painting. Moreover, this art, rather than hanging in a museum, actually walks among people. Likewise, movement and sport and dance are mediums through which artists may create—mediums through which paths to connectedness can be created. As you might guess, a major problem among those who suffer from CC is that they have no spokesperson for their emotions. That's where you come in. AAHPERDMALDS could walk as spokespeople for the emotions of millions.

"But I am looking for more than just practicing artists; I need teaching artists, people who in addition to working in some medium can also utilize the work of other artists to help people establish connectedness. I need people who can put movement and dance and sport and health and art to work. People who both practice and teach.

"I hope this won't offend you, but I have no interest in teachers who don't also practice their art. You don't have to be an acclaimed master, but you must struggle with some medium—struggle to give expression to human emotion. I can't use health educators unless they at least struggle to be healthy. I can't use physical educators unless they struggle to expression through movement. I can't use dance teachers unless they struggle to expression through dance.

"I simply cannot use a teacher who is not also an artist. Likewise,

I have no interest in artists who are not struggling to teach people how to use art to establish connectedness.

"I am sorry to be so blunt," Mephisto said, "but it has been our experience that a professional who is not a teaching artist often loses sight of what he or she is about. A few examples will illustrate. For a time, physical educators tried to help people discover the affirmative emotions through movement. Then, for some reason they got so preoccupied with the science of physical education—physiology of exercise, sports medicine, sport psychology, kinesiology, test and measurements—that they lost sight of the original goal. Health educators got so preoccupied with risk factors and disease and compliance and longevity that they literally lost sight of the meaning of health—of health as wellness. Rather, they saw health education as "the good care of cattle." Teachers of literature got so preoccupied with literary criticism, with motivations of writers, with the influence of culture on writers, with the comparison of writers, with development of a taxonomy of literature, that they forgot that literature could be a way to the affirmative emotions. Recreation became so preoccupied with recreational activities that it lost sight of the affirming aspects of recreation. Art that once attempted to express the temper of the times, that once spoke for the emotions, got separated from purpose. Now, for the most part, it is simply the excrement of the artist. It is difficult to find an artist who even wants to entertain the notion of walking as spokesperson for the emotions. Bernard Shaw said the dramatist had something more important to do than simply entertain, he had to interpret life. But try to find such a dramatist. There aren't many.

"So if you are interested in being a teaching artist, whatever your field, we can certainly use you. Finally, let me tell you what's in this mission for you. I am the Director of the Museum for Human Connectedness, and at the entrance to my museum is an inscription from Albert Einstein. It reads,

> Is there not a certain satisfaction in the fact that natural limits are set to the life of the individual so that at its conclusion it may appear as a work of art.

"Now I am offering you an opportunity to create with your life a work of art. I am offering you an opportunity to walk as spokespersons for the emotions of those whose emotions have no spokespersons, a chance to help others achieve connectedness. And I promise you this: You can experience no greater joy than that which comes from first being connected yourself and then helping others to get there. That's what's in it for you—the greatest joy a human can experience."

With these words the tall man faded from my dreams. I don't really know who he was, but it was clear in the end that he was no devil. Some kind of museum director, he said.

Well, that was my second dream. It leaves us with some serious questions:

- Should HPERD focus more attention on what makes people tick?
- Is wellness behavior as important as what we now study? More important?
- Will the central problems of the future evolve around a lack of skills and knowledges? Or will the larger problem be a corruption of consciousness? A loss of will to continue striving for wellness?
- Even today, is the problem a matter of knowing about risk factors and how to get to fitness? Or is the problem a matter of will? Perhaps a better reason for moving toward wellness? Perhaps a lack of experience with the affirmative emotions?
- Does HPERD have anything to offer in this battle against the corruption of consciousness? Should we take the lead in this fight?
- What about this notion of the teaching artist? This idea of trying to be a model spokesperson, not just a spokesperson? Does that have merit in today's world?
- Should the HPERD practitioner be a teaching artist?
- Will the future world have need of such a practitioner?
- Is this corruption of consciousness plague real? Is it all around us today? Or is it just a bad dream?

Dream Three: The Letter[1]

Life becomes more restless after the first two dreams. More and more my attention drifts away from the professional problems of HPERD. More and more I think about the problems of people in general—about what they are really up against, about our failure to address their concerns.

I read a line from Norman Cousins:

"The purpose of education is to create a higher sense of the possible than would occur to the undifferentiated intelligence."

That's what we need to do. Help people find a higher sense of the possible, a higher sense of the affirmative emotions. Feeling that I am finally starting to make progress, I fall into a restful sleep, only to dream again.

In this dream a man comes to my door to deliver a letter. Wait. It's not just a man. He has a thousand faces. He is everybody. As he leaves, I quickly tear open the letter:

---

[1]This letter first appeared as a portion of a chapter by John Burt in "Metahealth: A Challenge for the Future." *(Behavioral Health: A Handbook of Health Enhancement and Disease Prevention,* edited by J. Matarazzo, S. Weiss, A. Herd, N. Miller, & S. Weiss. New York: Wiley & Sons, 1984, pp. 1239-1245.)

"To Those Concerned With Health Enhancement and Disease Prevention:

"I am writing a single letter to all of you who are closely connected with my physical, mental, and spiritual health. Through this letter I hope to explain why I am, like millions of others in the world, so utterly desperate. You have advised me to put a curb on my pleasures, to resist the desire to engage in behaviors that will jeopardize my health and spiritual rightness. But I do not believe that you are fully aware of the implications of your well-intended advice. That is why I am writing to you. Let me begin by reminding you of a fact that you seem to have forgotten: I am not the maker of my own temperament, which unceasingly invites me to pleasure, an invitation that is more compelling in every sense than your invitation to longevity and spiritual enlightenment. For as long as anyone can remember, those of you in health enhancement and disease prevention have deflected and dispirited people through your teachings and promotion campaigns. I feel certain that this is not your intention; nonetheless, when you go down the list of pleasures known to or available to most people and one by one attach a risk to each and thereafter offer a strategy whereby behavior can be changed to avoid that risk, it is tantamount to saying that pleasure and health are necessarily at odds with each other. Thus, in attempting to promote health, you have simultaneously promoted an attitude—you must choose between health and pleasure—that thwarts the very health you seek to enhance. Intentionally or not, you have caused most of us to think that ill health and bad luck are punishments for pleasure-seeking, that it is only just that those who indulge the pleasures of eating should come to look funny (fat funny) and have their arteries clogged, that those who drink too much should be rendered impotent as a warning and develop cirrhosis of the liver if the practice continues, that those who smoke should develop emphysema and lung cancer, that those who have many sex partners should have herpes for life and syphilis and gonorrhea as short-term punishments, that those who eat sweets should have bad teeth, that those who gamble should end up broke, and that those who drive fast should have accidents.

"What I am trying to tell you is that the health problems of today's world do not result so much from an ignorance of risk factors or an ignorance of strategies to change behavior as from an ignorance of pleasure options that are not attended by a snag. In the battle for control of the human will—persuader vying against persuader—those of you in health enhancement and disease prevention have not been much of a factor. You have no sensitivity to the positive side of health: You don't understand the human will.

"To prevent your getting off on another wrong track, let me hasten to add that although my temperament unceasingly invites me to pleasure, this does not negate my free will. This point is worth emphasizing:

The invitation from my temperament is in every sense an invitation, nothing more. But I must tell you, with complete honesty, that as a free agent I am interested in pleasure. In truth, I weigh all my options to determine their pleasure content. You seem to have a bias against pleasure, but it is a bias that I do not share. At my very best, I am an intelligent consumer of pleasure options, and a major portion of my mental life is spent evaluating invitations to pleasure. Moreover, I somehow have the feeling that I am far more skillful at this matter than you give me credit for. Because you are preoccupied with promoting longevity and spiritual rightness, you have a tendency to judge my choices as stupid. They are not really; you would understand if you stood in my shoes. The trouble is that, being just a common person, my invitations to pleasure constitute only a short list, and due to your extensive research and teaching, nearly every pleasure on my list is now marked: "caution—this may be dangerous to health or spiritual rightness." What I desperately need is an invitation from someone who really understands health enhancement—an invitation to pleasure without a snag, without a caution sign. But it never comes. I have waited and waited—watching you destroy the few pleasures that I have discovered while remaining totally insensitive to my real problem. Don't you care? Can't you see that humanity places little value on longevity and spiritual rightness that is devoid of pleasure? What do you have against pleasure?

"I know that you are very busy discovering new risk factors, teaching about old ones, propounding new models of health behavior, and writing books about health enhancement, but would it be asking too much to request that the next time you shoot down one of my pleasure options you replace it with a new one—one without a snag? That is, unless it is true that health and spiritual rightness must forever be at odds with pleasure. In which case, I will just continue weighing pleasure options against longevity options, pleasure against spiritual rightness. Continue asking myself what, if not to enjoy pleasure, is health good for? And wondering—wondering if you are really trying to help me.

"Let me end my letter with this observation. The English humorist John Billings once suggested that no person who lived to break a hundred years was famous for anything except living to be a hundred. That is not entirely true, but it points to an important presupposition held by people like me: Health is something to be used for the accomplishment of goals, and pursuing self-selected goals represents one of the highest forms of pleasure-seeking. So you must understand that health is a means; the end is pleasure. And if pleasure and health conflict, so much the worse for health. I know that you don't see it that way, but most of us do."

Sincerely,
An Unhealthy Citizen

That's the third dream. It leaves us with some serious questions:

- Is it possible that gentle people like those of us in HPERD have with the best of intentions injured the interests of those we wanted to help? Could it be that we have deflected and dispirited people by our efforts to promote health?
- Have we inadvertently given people the impression that health and pleasure are incompatible?
- Could it be that at a higher level pleasure and health are mutually dependent?
- What about the request for pleasure alternatives without snags? Is that a problem to which HPERD can respond? Should it respond? Could it be that this problem is at the heart of HPERD?
- If the function of education is to create a greater sense of the possible, what ought to be the function of wellness education? Should its function be to create a greater awareness of the healthy pleasure options that are open to humans?
- How important is pleasure in our present world?
- As a nation, how well are we doing in pleasure management?
- Is pleasure likely to become more or less of a problem in the future?
- Should HPERD really focus on the role of pleasure in the modern lifstyle? Or should that be left to others?

Afterthoughts

Dreams, imaginative narrations, events that didn't really happen—perhaps they have the power to help us realize truth, at least the truth that is given us to understand. The views expressed in each of the three dreams were stated dogmatically. I leave it to you to criticize these views, to turn them inside out, to support them, to utilize them to guide your future work—anything but ignore them. Indeed, the future of HPERD depends upon your reactions to these views.

References

Abernathy, R., & Waltz, M. (1964). Toward a discipline: First steps first. *Quest, 2,* 1-7.

Adler, M.J. (1983). *Paideia problems and possibilities.* New York: Macmillan.

Alexander, H.W. (1947). The estimation of reliability when several trials are available. *Psychometrika, 43,* 533-557.

Anderson, J. (1985). Management by design. *Athletic Business, 9*(8), 28, 30-34.

Anderson, W., & Barrett, G. (Eds.) (1978). What's going on in the gym. *Motor Skills: Theory into Practice.* (Monograph 1), pp. 39-50.

Apple, M. (1983). Curriculum in the year 2000: Tensions and possibilities. *Phi Delta Kappan, 64,* 321-326.

Asimov, I. (1981). *Change! Seventy-one glimpses of the future.* Boston: Houghton Mifflin.

Atkin, J. (1981). Who will teach in high school? *Daedalus, 110,* 91-103.

Bain, L. (1983). Teacher/coach role conflict: Factors influencing role performance. In T. Templin & J. Olson (Eds.), *Teaching in physical education* (pp. 94-101). Champaign, IL: Human Kinetics.

Bentzen, M. (1974). *Changing schools: The magic feather principle.* New York: McGraw-Hill.

Berman, P., & McLaughlin, M. (1975). *Federal programs supporting educational change* (Vols. 1-8). Santa Monica, CA: Rand Corp. (R-1589/4 HEW)

Berryman, J.W. (1976). Historical roots of the collegiate dilemma. In L.L. Gedvilas (Ed.), *Proceedings of the Annual Conference of the National College Physical Education Association for Men* (pp. 141-154). Chicago: Office of Publication Services, University of Illinois at Chicago Circle.

Big business gets serious about health. (1985). *Optimal Health, 1*(6), 13-17.

Bishop, J. (1977). Organizational influences on the work orientations of elementary teachers. *Sociology of Work and Occupations, 4*(2), 171-208.

Blau, P., & Scott, W.R. (1962). *Formal organizations.* New York: Chandler.

Bohm, D. (1980). *Wholeness and the implicate order.* London: Routledge & Kegan Paul.

Bok, D. (1982). *Beyond the ivory tower: Social responsibilities of the modern university*. Cambridge, MA: Harvard University Press.

Booth, F.W. (1985). Regulation in physiological systems during exercise in trained and untrained subjects: 5 year update. *Federation Proceedings*, **44**(7), 2259-2270.

Bossert, S., Dwyer, D., Rowan, B., & Lee, G. (1982). The instructional management role of the principal. *Educational Administration Quarterly*, **18**, 34-64.

Bowen, H.R., & Schuster, J.H. (1986). *American professors: A national resource imperiled*. New York: Oxford.

Bowker, J.E., & Dickerson, K.G. (1983). Becoming university administrators: A comparison of the motivations of men and women faculty members. *Journal of Educational Equity and Leadership*, **3**, 135-147.

Boyer, E. (1983). *High school: A report on secondary education in America*. New York: Harper & Row.

Brassie, P.S. (1980). Can accreditation promote integrity without destroying creativity? *Journal of Physical Education, Recreation, and Dance*, **56**(3), 44-46, 54.

Brassie, P.S., Trimble, R.T., & Hensley, L.D. (1985). Creative financing. *Journal of Physical Education, Recreation, and Dance*, **56**(7), 44-46, 54.

Bressan, E. (1979). 2001: The profession is dead—Was it murder or suicide? *Quest*, **31**, 77-82.

Bressan, E.S. (1982). An academic discipline for physical education: What a fine mess! In L.L. Gedvilas (Ed.), *NAPEHE Proceedings* (Vol. 3) (pp. 22-27). Champaign, IL: Human Kinetics.

Bressan, E., & Weiss, M. (1982). A theory of instruction for developing competence, self confidence, and persistence in physical education. *Journal of Teaching in Physical Education*, **2**(1), 38-47.

Brewster, L., & Jacobsen, M. (1978). *The changing American diet*. Washington, DC: Center for Science in the Public Interest.

Broekhoff, J. (1982). A discipline—Who needs it? In L.L. Gedvilas (Ed.), *NAPEHE Proceedings* (Vol. 3) (pp. 28-35). Champaign, IL: Human Kinetics.

Brozek, J., & Alexander, H.W. (1947). Components of variation and the consistency of repeated measurements. *Research Quarterly*, **18**, 152-166.

Burdin, J., & Nutter, N. (1984, February). *Inventing the future: Options and strategies for educators*. Paper presented at the annual meeting of the American Association of Colleges for Teacher Education, San Antonio, TX.

Burnham, W.D. (1984). A commentary on Harry Eckstein. *Daedalus*, **113**, 147-160.

Burt, J. (1984). Metahealth: A challenge for the future. In J. Matarazzo, S. Weiss, A. Herd, N. Miller, & S. Weiss (Eds.), *Behavioral health: A handbook of health enhancement and disease prevention* (pp. 1239-1245). New York: Wiley & Sons.

Byers, M. (1983). Interview with Peter Bavacci. *Visions in Leisure and Business*, **2**(2), 32-35.

Carlyon, W. (1984). Reflections: Disease prevention/health promotion—Bridging the gap to wellness. *Health Values*, **8**, 27-30.

Carroll, D. (1984, October 16). Physical fitness businesses feeling good about growth. *USA Today*, p. 3B.

Cetron, M., & O'Toole, T. (1982). *Encounters with the future: A forecast of life into the 21st century*. New York: McGraw-Hill.

Cetron, M.J., Soriano, B., & Gayle, M. (1985). Schools of the future: Education approaches the twenty-first century. *The Futurist*, **19**, 18-23.

Clark, D. (1984). Better teachers for the year 2000: A proposal for the structural reform of teacher education. *Phi Delta Kappan*, **65**, 116-120.

Clausen, J.P. (1977). Effects of physical training on cardiovascular adjustments to exercise in man. *Physiological Reviews*, **57**(4), 779-815.

Clayton, R.D., & Clayton, J.A. (1984). Careers and professional preparation programs. *Journal of Physical Education, Recreation, and Dance*, **55**(5), 44-45.

Cox, M., Shephard, R.J., & Corey, A. (1981). Influence of an employee fitness program on fitness, productivity and absenteeism. *Ergonomics*, **24**, 759-806.

Crane, D. (1970). The academic marketplace revisited: A study of faculty mobility using the Cartter ratings. *American Journal of Sociology*, **75**, 953-964.

Cronbach, L.J. (1982). Prudent aspirations for social inquiry. In W.H. Kruskal (Ed.), *The social sciences: Their nature and uses* (pp. 61-81). Chicago: University of Chicago Press.

Dalkey, N. (1969). *The Delphi method: An experimental study of group opinion*. Santa Monica, CA: Rand Corp.

Darling-Hammond, L. (1984). *Beyond the commission reports: The coming crisis in teaching* (Report No. R-3177 RC). Santa Monica, CA: Rand Corp.

deCharms, R. (1976). *Enhancing motivation: Change in the classroom*. New York: Irvington.

de Jouvenel, B. (1967). *The art of conjecture.* New York: Basic Books.

Department of Health, Education, and Welfare (DHEW) (1979). *Healthy people: The surgeon general's report on health promotion and disease prevention.* Washington, DC: U.S. Government Printing Office.

Dewey, J. (1915). *Schools of tomorrow.* New York: E.P. Dutton.

Dodds, P., & Locke, L.F. (1984). Is physical education in American schools worth saving? In N. Struna (Ed.), *NAPEHE Proceedings* (Vol. 5) (pp. 76-90). Champaign, IL: Human Kinetics.

Douglas, J.M., & DeBona, L. (1984). *Directory of faculty contracts and bargaining agents in institutions of higher education.* The National Center for the Study of Collective Bargaining in Higher Education and the Professions.

Douglas, J.W., & Massengale, J.D. (1985). Salaries of HPERD administrators. *Journal of Physical Education, Recreation, and Dance,* **56**(3), 52-54.

Dunn, S.L. (1983). The changing university: Survival in the information society. *The Futurist,* **4**, 55-60.

Earls, N. (1981). Distinctive teachers' personal qualities, perceptions of teacher education and the realities of teaching. *Journal of Teaching in Physical Education,* **1**(1), 59-70.

Eckstein, H. (1984). Civic inclusion and its discontents. *Daedalus,* **113**, 107-145.

Ellis, M.J., & Ulrich, C.U. (1983). The Oregon story. *Journal of Physical Education, Recreation, and Dance,* **54**(5), 14-17.

Equity Action Committee (1985). The current status of equity in the School of Education. *Committee report for 1984–85* (Unpublished report). The University of Wisconsin: School of Education.

Erschow, A., Nicilosi, R., & Hayes, K.C. (1981). Separation of the dietary fat and cholesterol influence on rhesus monkeys. *American Journal of Clinical Nutrition,* **34**, 830-840.

Etzioni, A. (1961). *A comparative analysis of complex organizations.* New York: The Free Press.

Feiman-Nemser, S. (1983). Learning to teach. In L. Shulman & G. Sykes (Eds.), *Handbook of teaching and policy* (pp. 150-170). New York: Longman.

Feiman-Nemser, S., & Floden, R. (1985). The cultures of teaching. In M. Wittrock (Ed.), *Handbook of research on teaching* (pp. 505-526). New York: Macmillan.

Feldt, L.S., & McKee, M.E. (1958). Estimation of the reliability of skill tests. *Research Quarterly,* **29**, 279-293.

Flynn, M., Nolph, G.B., & Flynn, T.C. (1979). Effect of dietary egg on sperm cholesterol and triglycerides. *American Journal of Clinical Nutrition*, **32**, 1051-1057.

Frankel, M.M., & Gerald, D.E. (1982). *Projections of educational statistics to 1991, Volume 1—Analytical report*. Washington, DC: National Center for Education Statistics.

Gallup, G. (1985). *Gallup poll of teachers' attitudes toward the public schools*. Bloomington, IN: Phi Delta Kappa.

Ganstead, S.K., & Esplin-Swensen, L. (1982). Part-time employment in post-secondary physical education: Legal issues and administrative implications. *Quest*, **34**, 109-118.

Garcia, R. (1985, April). *Quality of life in the gym*. Paper presented at the annual meeting of AAHPERD, Atlanta.

Gardner, H. (1983). *Frames of mind*. New York: Basic Books.

Gerdau, R. (Producer, Director). (1984). *To save our schools: To save our children* [Videotape]. New York: American Broadcasting System.

Gingrich, N. (1985). Window of opportunity. *The Futurist*, **19**(3), 9-15.

Godbey, G.C. (1984). The ethics of marketing public leisure services. *Visions in Leisure and Business*, **3**(2), 64-68.

Goodlad, J. (1983a). The school as workplace. In G. Griffin (Ed.), *Staff development: Eighty-second yearbook of the National Society for the Study of Education* (pp. 36-61). Chicago: University of Chicago Press.

Goodlad, J. (1983b). *A place called school*. New York: McGraw-Hill.

Gordon, T.J. (1972). The current methods of futures research. In A. Toffler (Ed.), *The futurists* (pp. 164-189). New York: Random House.

Graham, G. (Ed.). (1982). Profiles in excellence: Processes and teachers in children's physical education. *Journal of Physical Education, Recreation, and Dance*, **53**(7), 37-54.

Graham, G., Faucette, N., & Ratliffe, T. (1985, April). *Elementary school principals and children's physical education*. Symposium presented at the annual meeting of AAHPERD, Atlanta.

Graham, G., & Heimerer, E. (1981). Research on teacher effectiveness: A summary with implications for teaching. *Quest*, **33**, 14-25.

Grant, W., & Snyder, T. (1983). *Digest of educational statistics: 1983–1984*. Washington, DC: U.S. Government Printing Office.

A grass-roots boost for amateur sports. (1985). *Athletic Business*, **9**(7), 10, 12, 14-16.

Gross, G.R. (1970). The organizational set: A study of sociology departments. *The American Sociologist*, **5**, 25-29.

Gross, G.R. (1971). Organizational prestige and academic career patterns (Doctoral dissertation, University of Massachusetts). *DAI, 32*, 1641A. University Microfilms No. 71-24, 843.

Haberman, M. (1971). Twenty three reasons universities can't educate teachers. *Journal of Teacher Education, 22*(2), 133-140.

Haberman, M. (1984). Teacher education in 2000: Implications of demographic and societal trends. *Education and Urban Society, 16*(4), 497-509.

Hackworth, C., Jacobs, K., & O'Neill, C. (1983). A coaches' clinic for injury management in youth sports. *The Physician and Sportsmedicine, 11*(5), 59-64.

Hage, P. (1983). Prescribing exercise: More than just a running program. *The Physician and Sportsmedicine, 11*(5), 123-127, 131.

Harris, D.V. (1983). *Involvement in sport: A somato-psychic rationale for physical activity.* Philadelphia: Lea & Febiger.

Hart, G. (1983). Investing in people for the information age. *The Futurist, 17*(1), 10-14.

Health & medicine, employee outlook. (1985, November 3). *The New York Times* (special advertising supplement), p. 16.

Hellison, D. (1978). *Beyond balls and bats: Alienated (and other) youth in the gym.* Washington, DC: AAHPERD.

Hellison, D. (1983). It only takes one case to prove a possibility . . . and beyond. In T.J. Templin & J.K. Olson (Eds.), *Teaching in physical education* (pp. 102-106). Champaign, IL: Human Kinetics.

Hellison, D. (1985). *Goals and strategies for teaching physical education.* Champaign, IL: Human Kinetics.

Hellison, D. (1986). Cause of death: Physical education. *Journal of Physical Education, Recreation, and Dance, 57*(4), 27-28.

Henry, F.M. (1984). Physical education—An academic discipline. *Proceedings of the Annual Meeting of the National College Physical Education Association for Men* (pp. 6-9). Washington, DC: AAHPERD.

Hirsch, W.Z. (1967). Educational innovations. In W.Z. Hirsch (Ed.), *Inventing education for the future* (pp. 3-37). San Francisco: Chandler.

Hoffman, S. (1971). Traditional methodology: Prospects for change, *Quest, 15*, 51-57.

Hoffman, S.J. (1985). Specialization + fragmentation = extermination: A formula for the demise of graduate education. *Journal of Physical Education, Recreation, and Dance, 56*(6), 19-22.

Howey, K. (1983). Teacher education: An overview. In K. Howey & W. Gardner (Eds.), *The education of teachers: A look ahead* (pp. 6-37). New York: Longman.

Howey, K., & Gardner, W. (Eds.). (1983). *The education of teachers: A look ahead.* New York: Longman.

Hurlburt, B.M. (1976). Status and exchange in the profession of anthropology. *American Anthropologist,* **78,** 272-284.

Husman, B.F., & Kelley, D.L. (1978). Kinesiological science: A new degree option. *Journal of Physical Education and Recreation,* **49**(3), 20-23.

Huxley, A. (1932). *Brave new world.* New York: Harper.

Hyer, P.B. (1985). Affirmative action for women faculty: Case studies of three successful institutions. *Journal of Higher Education,* **56**(1), 282-299.

Jameson, M. (1985). Keeping fit with high technology. *Corporate Fitness and Recreation,* **4**(1), 37, 39-42, 44.

Jewett, A.E., & Bain, L.L. (1985). *The curriculum process in physical education.* Dubuque, IA: Wm. C. Brown.

Jobs of the future. (1985, December 23). *U.S. News & World Report,* pp. 40-45.

John Naisbitt's Trend Letter. (1985). **4**(13), 4.

Johnson, M. (1985). Physical education fitness or fraud? *Journal of Physical Education, Recreation, and Dance,* **56**(1), 33-35.

Kahn, H. (1982). *The coming boom: Economic, political, and social.* New York: Simon & Schuster.

Kahn, H., & Weiner, A.J. (1967). *The year 2000: A framework for speculation on the next 33 years.* New York: Macmillan.

Keidel, R. (1985). *Game plans: Sports strategies for business.* New York: E.P. Dutton.

Keller, G. (1983). *Academic strategy: The management revolution in higher education.* Baltimore: Johns Hopkins University Press.

Kirby, T. (1980). Secondary risk factors related to coronary heart disease. In R.H. Cox & J.K. Nelson (Eds.), *Exercise physiology, exercise and heart disease* (pp. 10-13). Washington, DC: AAHPERD.

Kneer, M.E. (1985). *Will the parade pass us by? Claims, causes, and cures.* Paper presented at the annual meeting of the midwest district of AAHPERD, Milwaukee.

Knoblock, P., & Goldstein, A. (1971). *The lonely teacher.* Boston: Allyn & Bacon.

Kollen, P. (1983). Fragmentation and integration in human movement. In T.J. Templin & J.K. Olson (Eds.), *Teaching in physical education* (pp. 86-93). Champaign, IL: Human Kinetics.

Korfhage, B. (1985). The revolving door. *California Parks and Recreation,* **41**(3), 32-33.

Kroll, W. (1971). *Perspectives in physical education.* New York: Academic Press.

Krupsky, G. (1985). Youth baseball . . . is it all that it can be? *California Parks and Recreation,* 41(3), 16-19, 24.

Kuhn, T. (1977). *The essential tension.* Chicago: University of Chicago Press.

Lanier, J., & Little, J. (1985). Research on teacher education. In M. Wittrock (Ed.), *Handbook of research on teaching* (pp. 527-569). New York: Macmillan.

Lawson, H.A. (1985). Challenges to graduate education. *Journal of Physical Education, Recreation, and Dance,* 56(6), 23-25, 44.

Lawson, H. (1986). Occupational socialization and the design of teacher education programs. *Journal of Teaching in Physical Education,* 5, 107-116.

Learning to read. (1985, September). *Journal and Courier,* p. 1.

Lehtonen, A., & Viikari, J. (1978). Serum triglycerides and cholesterol and serum high-density lipoprotein cholesterol in physically active men. *Acta Medica Scandinavica,* 204, 111-114.

Leisure Industry Digest. (1985, July 30). p. 3.

Leisure Industry Digest. (1985, September 16). p. 6.

Leonard, G. (1974). *The ultimate athlete.* New York: Viking.

Lewis, G. (1969). Adoption of the sports program, 1906–1939: The role of accommodation in the transformation of physical education. *Quest,* 12, 34-66.

Lewis, G., & Appenzeller, H. (1985). *Successful school sport.* Charlottesville, VA: Michie Co.

Little, J. (1982). Norms of collegiality and experimentation: Workplace conditions of school success. *American Educational Research Journal,* 19, 325-340.

Locke, L.F. (1969). *Research in physical education.* New York: Teachers College Press.

Locke. L. (1974). The ecology of the gymnasium: What the tourists never see. *Proceedings of the SAPECW.* (Also available through ERIC #ED 104-823)

Locke, L., & Dodds, P. (1984). Is physical education teacher education in American colleges worth saving? Evidence, alternatives, judgment. In N. Struna (Ed.), *NAPEHE Proceedings* (Vol. 5) (pp. 91-107). Champaign, IL: Human Kinetics.

Locke, L., Griffin, P., & Templin, T. (Eds.) (1986). Profiles in struggles. *Journal of Physical Education, Recreation, and Dance,* 57(4), 32-63.

Locke, L., Mand, C., & Siedentop, D. (1981). The preparation of physical education teachers: A subject matter-centered model. In H. Lawson (Ed.), *Undergraduate physical education programs: Issues and approaches* (pp. 33-54). Reston, VA: AAHPERD.

Locke, L.F., & Massengale, J. (1978). Role conflict in teacher/coaches. *Research Quarterly*, **49**(2), 162-174.

Lombardo, J.A. (1985). Sportsmedicine: A team effort. *The Physician and Sportsmedicine*, **13**(4), 72-78, 81.

Long, J.S. (1978). Productivity and academic position in the scientific career. *American Sociological Review*, **43**, 889-908.

Lortie, D. (1975). *Schoolteacher*. Chicago: University of Chicago Press.

Loy, J.W., McPherson, B.D., & Kenyon, G. (1978). *Sport and social systems*. Reading, MA: Addison-Wesley.

Loy, J.W., & Sage, G.H. (1978). Athletic personnel in the academic marketplace: A study of the interorganizational mobility patterns of college coaches. *Sociology of Work and Occupations*, **5**, 446-449.

Malach, C. (1985). The role of sex and family variables in burnout. *Sex Roles*, **12**, 837-851.

Maloney, L.D. (1984, August 13). Sports-crazy Americans. *U.S. News & World Report*, p. 23.

Managed recreation research report. (1985, August). *Recreation, Sports, & Leisure*.

Managed recreation research report. (1986). *Recreation, Sports, & Leisure*, **6**(6) [entire issue].

Marciani, L. (1985). A new era in recreation marketing. *Athletic Business*, **9**(10), 30-34.

Marshall, S.J. (1969). *The organizational relationship between physical education and intercollegiate athletics in American colleges and universities*. Unpublished doctoral dissertation, Springfield College.

Massengale, J. (1977). Occupational role conflict and the teacher/coach. *Physical Educator*, **34**, 64-70.

Massengale, J.D., & Sage, G.H. (1982). Departmental prestige and career mobility patterns of college physical educators. *Research Quarterly for Exercise and Sport*, **53**(4), 305-312.

McBride, L.G., & Hellison, D. (1986, March-April). Toward wellness for high risk youth: A values education model. *Health Values*, pp. 37-42.

McCarthy, J. (1985). Challenges, opportunities in the club industry. *Athletic Business*, **9**(10), 38.

McInally, P. (1985). Keeping perspectives in sports. *Athletic Business*, **9**(8), 10, 12, 14-16.

McNeill, A.W. (1982). Affect as it effects fitness and total functional integrity. In C. Ulrich (Ed.), *Education in the 80s* (pp. 36-42). Washington, DC: National Education Association.

Melnick, M. (1980). Toward an applied sociology of sport. *Journal of Sport and Social Issues, 4*, 1-12.

Metz, M. (1983). Sources of constructive social relationships in an urban magnet school. *American Journal of Education, 91*, 202-245.

Milewski, J.K., & Bryant, J.G. (1984). *A survey of institutions offering sport administration, sport management, or related sport studies programs.* Unpublished manuscript, Western Carolina University, Cullowhee, NC.

Miller, J. (1984). Are you liable to be liable? *Corporate Fitness and Recreation, 3*(1), 23-24, 26-28, 30.

Miller Lite report on American attitudes toward sports. (1983). New York: Research and Forecasts, Inc.

Mills, C.W. (1959). *The sociological imagination.* New York: Oxford.

Mingle, J. (Ed.). (1981). *Challenges of retrenchment.* San Francisco: Jossey-Bass.

Minkler, M. (1983). Health promotion and elders: A critique. *Generations, 8*, 13-15.

Mood, D. (1983). Trends in accreditation in higher education. In L.L. Gedvilas (Ed.), *NAPEHE Proceedings* (Vol. 3) (pp. 74-78). Champaign, IL: Human Kinetics.

Mullins, B.J. (1984). A graduate curriculum in sport management: Considerations before taking the big plunge! In B.K. Zanger & J.B. Parks (Eds.), *Sport management curricula* (pp. 110-117). Bowling Green, OH: School of HPER, Bowling Green State University.

Naisbitt, J. (1982). *Megatrends: Ten new directions for transforming our lives.* New York: Warner Books.

National Commission on Excellence in Education (1983, May). A nation at risk: The imperative for education reform. Washington, DC: Congressional Record–Senate, S6060–S6065.

National Commission on Excellence in Education (1983). *Meeting the challenge: Recent efforts to improve education across the nation.* A report to the secretary of education. (ERIC Document Reproduction Service No. ED 240 114.)

National Education Association (1982). *Status of the American public school teacher 1980–81.* Washington, DC: Author.

1985 National Education Association Almanac of Higher Education (1985). Washington, DC: Author.

Newman, J., & Beehr, T. (1979). Personal and organizational strategies for handling job stress: A review of research and opinion. *Personnel Psychology, 32,* 1-43.

Obertueffer, D. (1963). On learning values through sport. *Quest, 1,* 23-29.

O'Donnell, P. (1984). The corporate perspective. In M.P. O'Donnell & T. Ainsworth (Eds.), *Health promotion in the workplace* (pp. 10-35). New York: Wiley.

Organization for Economic Co-operation and Development (1972). *Alternative educational failure in the United States and Europe: Methods, issues, and policy relevance.* Paris: The Organization.

Ornstein, A. (1981). Curricular innovations and trends: Recent, past, present, and future. *Peabody Journal of Education, 59,* 46-53.

Orwell, G. (1961). *1984.* New York: New American Library. (Original work published 1949)

Oxendine, J.B. (1961, September). The service program in 1960–61. *Journal of Health, Physical Education, Recreation,* pp. 37-38.

Oxendine, J.B. (1985). 100 years of basic instruction. *Journal of Physical Education, Recreation, and Dance, 56,* 32-36.

Oxendine, J.B., & Roberts, J.E. (1978). The general instruction program in physical education at four-year colleges and universities: 1977. *Journal of Physical Education and Recreation, 49*(1), 21-23.

Paludi, M.A., & Strayer, L.A. (1985). What's in an author's name? Differential evaluations of performance as a function of an author's name. *Sex Roles, 12,* 353-361.

Parkhouse, B.L. (1984). Shaping up to climb a new corporate ladder . . . sport management. *Journal of Physical Education, Recreation, and Dance, 55*(7), 12-14.

Parks, J.P., & Quain, R.J. (1986). Sport management survey: Curriculum perspectives. *Journal of Physical Education, Recreation, and Dance, 57*(4), 22-26.

Pate, R.R. (1983). A definition of youth fitness. *The Physician and Sportsmedicine, 11*(4), 77-83.

Percell, C.H. (1984). Equal opportunity for academic women. *Journal of Educational Equity and Leadership, 4,* 17-26.

Placek, J.H. (1983). Conceptions of success in teaching: Busy, happy, and good? In T.J. Templin & J.K. Olson (Eds.), *Teaching in physical education* (pp. 46-56). Champaign, IL: Human Kinetics.

Polanyi, M. (1946). *Science, faith and society*. Chicago: University of Chicago Press.

Postman, N. (1983). Engaging students in the great conversation. *Phi Delta Kappan*, **64**, 310-316.

Powell, S. (1985, December 16). Measuring impact of the "baby bust" on U.S. future. *U.S. News & World Report*, pp. 66-67.

Quain, R.J., & Parks, J.P. (1986). Sport management survey: Employment perspectives. *Journal of Physical Education, Recreation, and Dance*, **57**(4), 18-21.

Ravitch, D. (1983). On thinking about the future. *Phi Delta Kappan*, **64**, 317-320.

Ravitch, D. (1985). *The schools we deserve: Reflections on the educational crises of our times*. New York: Basic Books.

Raywid, M.A. (1983). Schools of choice: Their current nature and prospects. *Phi Delta Kappan*, **64**, 684-688.

Raywid, M.A., Tesconi, C.A., & Warren, D.R. (1984). *Pride and promise: Schools of excellence for all the people*. Westbury, NY: American Educational Studies Association.

Razor, J.E. (1983). Meeting the challenge: Physical education in the late 1980s. In K.P. DePauw (Ed.), *NAPEHE Proceedings* (Vol. 4) (pp. 68-76). Champaign, IL: Human Kinetics.

Recreation on campus: The new building boom. (1985). *Athletic Business*, **9**(4), 10, 12, 14, 16.

Recreation, Sports, & Leisure. (1985, August). Pp. 13-16.

Renfro, W.L., & Morrison, J.L. (1982). Merging two futures concepts: Issues management and policy impact management. *The Futurist*, **16**(5), 54-56.

Robin, H.S., & Robin, S.S. (1983). Women's salaries in higher education: A case study. *Journal of Educational Equity and Leadership*, **3**, 39-56.

Rosenholtz, S., & Smylie, M. (1984). Teacher compensation and career ladders. *The Elementary School Journal*, **85**, 149-166.

Ross, J., Dotson, C., Gilbert, G., & Katz, S. (1985). What are kids doing in school physical education? *Journal of Physical Education, Recreation, and Dance*, **56**(1), 73-76.

Ross, J., & Gilbert, G. (1985). The national children and youth fitness study: A summary of findings. *Journal of Physical Education, Recreation, and Dance*, **56**(1), 45-50.

Rowell, L.B. (1974). Human cardiovascular adjustment to exercise and thermal stress. *Physiological Reviews*, **54**(1), 75-159.

Rubenstein, C. (1982, October). Wellness is all. *Psychology Today*, pp. 28-37.

Rutter, M. (1979). *Fifteen thousand hours: Secondary schools and their effects on children.* Cambridge, MA: Harvard University Press.

Safrit, M.J. (1984). Women in research in physical education: A 1984 update. *Quest,* **36,** 104-114.

Sage, G.H. (1976). The collegiate dilemma of sport and leisure: A sociological perspective. In L.L. Gedvilas (Ed.), *Proceedings of the Annual Conference of the National College Physical Education Association for Men* (pp. 203-208). Chicago: Office of Publication Services, University of Illinois at Chicago Circle.

Sage, G. (1980). Sociology of physical educator/coaches: Personal attributes controversy. *Research Quarterly for Exercise and Sport,* **51**(1), 110-121.

Salaries in the industry—Gaining ground or falling behind? (1986). *Recreation, Sports, & Leisure,* **6**(6), 57, 60, 62, 64, 66.

Sanborn, M. (1985). Beyond pedagogy. In H. Hoffman & J. Rink (Eds.), *Physical education professional preparation: Insights and foresights: Proceedings of the Second National Conference on Preparing the Physical Education Specialist for Children* (pp. 58-76). Reston, VA: AAHPERD.

Sarason, S. (1982). *The culture of the school and the problem of change* (2nd ed.). Boston: Allyn & Bacon.

Savage, H.J., Bentley, W.H., McGovern, J.T., & Smiley, D. (1929). *American college athletics.* New York: Carnegie Foundation for the Advancement of Teaching.

Sawyer, T.H. (1985). The employee program director, part 2: Position and career path. *Corporate Fitness and Recreation,* **4**(6), 43-47.

Scheuer, J., & Tipton, C.M. (1977). Cardiovascular adaptations to physical training. *Annual Review of Physiology,* **39,** 221-251.

School coach hiring rules eased. (1982, June 26). *The New York Times,* p. 30.

School test: Mine passes, yours fails. (1985, September). *Journal and Courier,* p. 1.

Shane, H.G. (1973). *The educational significance of the future.* Bloomington, IN: Phi Delta Kappa.

Shaw, G.C. (1985, Spring). Debunking the myth of academe. *Thought & Action,* **1,** 5-16.

Shea, E.J. (1985). Research synthesis: A coherent view of physical education. *Journal of Physical Education, Recreation, and Dance,* **56**(9), 45-47.

Sheehan, T.J. (1968). Sport: The focal point of physical education. *Quest,* **10,** 59-67.

Shephard, R.J. (1984). Practical issues in employee fitness programming. *The Physician and Sportsmedicine,* **12,** 161-166.

Shichor, D. (1970). Prestige of sociology departments and the placing of new Ph.D.'s. *The American Sociologist*, **5**, 157-160.

Shipka, T. (1985, Spring). Bargaining and the academy: An overview. *Thought & Action*, **1**, 3-4.

Shulman, L.S. (1986). Research programs for the study of teaching: A contemporary perspective. In M.C. Wittrock (Ed.), *Handbook of research on teaching* (3rd ed.). New York: Macmillan.

Siedentop, D. (Ed.) (1976). Scholarship and research in the graduate program. *Quest*, **25**, 86-100.

Siedentop, D. (1980). *Physical education: Introductory analysis* (3rd ed.). Dubuque, IA: Wm. C. Brown.

Siedentop, D. (1981, April). Secondary physical education: An endangered species. Paper presented at the annual meeting of AAHPERD, Boston.

Simmons, A., Gibson, J., & Painoc, C. (1978). The influence of a wide range of absorbed cholesterol on plasma cholesterol levels in man. *American Journal of Clinical Nutrition*, **31**, 1334-1339.

Sinclair, G. (1983). Instructional management and the microcomputer. *Journal of Physical Education, Recreation, and Dance*, **54**, 29-30.

Snyder, E.E. (1986). Sociology of sport organizations, management and marketing. Unpublished manuscript, Bowling Green State University.

Snyder, R.A., & Scott, H.A. (1954). *Professional preparation in health, physical education, and recreation.* New York: McGraw-Hill.

Spears, B. (Ed.) (1974). *Quest*, **21**, 1-75.

A sport haven for the disabled. (1985, July). *Athletic Business*, **9**, 70, 72-74.

A sporting palace that doesn't live by sports alone. (1985, May). *Athletic Business*, **9**, 36-40.

Sports Industry News. (1985, November 6). p. 340.

Squires, W.G., Hartung, G.H., Welton, D., et al. (1979). The effects of exercise and diet modification on blood lipids in middle aged man. *Medicine and Science in Sport*, **11**, 109-117.

The State of the industry. (1985, August). *Recreation, Sports, & Leisure*, pp. 80-82, 84-86.

Statistical Abstracts of the United States. (1985). Washington, DC: U.S. Government Printing Office.

Stengel, R. (1985, September 2). Snapshot of a changing America. *Time*, pp. 16-18.

Stress: Can we cope? (1983, June 6). *Time*, pp. 48-54.

Strother, D.B. (1983). Practical applications of research: Mental health in education. *Phi Delta Kappan, **64**, 140-143.

Studer, G.L. (1977). Synthesis and coalescence. In R. Welsh (Ed.), *Physical education: A view toward the future* (pp. 22-36). St. Louis: C.V. Mosby.

Sykes, G. (1983). Contradictions, ironies, and promises unfilled: A contemporary account of the status of teaching. *Phi Delta Kappan, **64**, 87-93.

Szafran, R.F. (1984). *Universities and women faculty.* New York: Praeger.

Tabachnick, B., & Zeichner, K. (1984). The impact of the student teaching experience on the development of teacher perspectives. *Journal of Teacher Education, **35**(6), 28-36.

Taylor, J.L. (1986). Surviving the challenge. *Journal of Physical Education, Recreation, and Dance, **57**(1), 69-72.

Teachers need more respect, pollster says. (1985, September). *Journal and Courier*, pp. 1-2.

Templin, T. (1981). Teacher/coach role conflict and the high school principal. In V. Crafts (Ed.), *NAPEHE Proceedings* (Vol. 2) (pp. 70-82). Champaign, IL: Human Kinetics.

Templin, T. (Ed.) (1983). Profiles of excellence: Fourteen outstanding secondary school physical educators. *Journal of Physical Education, Recreation, and Dance, **54**(7), 15-36.

Templin, T. (1984, March). *Teacher/coach role conflict and burnout.* Paper presented at the meeting of AAHPERD, Anaheim, CA.

Templin, T. (1985). Developing commitment to teaching: The professional socialization of the pre-service physical educators. In H. Hoffman & J. Rink (Eds.), *Physical Education Professional Preparation: Insights and Foresights: Proceedings of the Second National Conference on Preparing the Physical Education Specialist for Children* (pp. 119-131). Reston, VA: AAHPERD.

Templin, T. (1986, August). *Teacher isolation and the school physical educator.* Paper presented at the annual meeting of the International Association for Physical Education in Higher Education, Heidelberg,

Templin, T., Cervak, A., & Marrs, L. (1982, April). *Teacher/coach role conflict: An overview.* Paper presented at the annual meeting of AAHPERD, Houston.

Templin, T., Woodford, R., & Mulling, C. (1982). On becoming a physical educator. *Quest, **34**, 119-133.

10 Forces reshaping America. (1984, March 19). *U.S. News & World Report*, pp. 40-52.

Thomas, C.E. (1983). *Sport in a philosophic context.* Philadelphia: Lea & Febiger.

Thomas, J.R. (1985). Physical education and paranoia—Synonyms. *Journal of Physical Education, Recreation, and Dance,* **56**(9), 20-22.

Toffler, A. (1970). *Future shock.* New York: Bantam.

Toffler, A. (1980). *The third wave.* New York: William Morrow.

Trimble, R.T., & Hensley, L.D. (1984). The general instruction program in physical education at four-year colleges and universities: 1982. *Journal of Physical Education, Recreation, and Dance,* **55**(5), 82-89.

Trimble, R.T., & Hensley, L.D. (1985). Independent study a trend in basic physical education. *Journal of Physical Education, Recreation, and Dance,* **56**(7), 37-38, 54.

Tymeson, G., & Hastad, D. (1985, April). Microcomputers in physical education and related fields. Symposium presented at the annual meeting of AAHPERD, Atlanta.

Udeleff, M. (1985). Consultant and client: Fitting for fitness. *Corporate Fitness & Recreation,* **4**(2), 35-39.

Ulrich, C. (1976). A ball of gold. In C. Ulrich (Ed.), *To seek and find* (pp. 150-160). Washington, DC: AAHPERD.

University of Michigan News and Information Services (1985, November 1). *U-M grant expands impacts of youth fitness programs.* Ann Arbor: University of Michigan.

Valentine, P. (1984, October). Leisure time. *Standard and Poor's Industry Surveys,* pp. L1-L7.

van der Smissen, B. (1984). *A process for success: Sport management curricula—An idea whose time has come.* Unpublished manuscript, Bowling Green State University.

VanderZwaag, H.J. (1983). Coming out of the maze: Sport management, dance management and exercise science—Programs with a future. *Quest,* **35**, 66-73.

Vertinsky, P. (1985). Risk benefit analysis of health promotion: Opportunities and threats for physical education. *Quest,* **37**, 71-83.

Vogt, K.J. (1984). The power of education and business. In B.K. Zanger & J.B. Parks (Eds.), *Sport management curricula* (pp. 19-25). Bowling Green, OH: School of HPER, Bowling Green State University.

Weaver, W.T. (1979). In search of quality: The need for talent in teaching. *Phi Delta Kappan,* **61**, 29-32; 46.

Welsh, R. (Ed.) (1977). *Physical education: A view toward the future.* St. Louis: C.V. Mosby.

Welsh, R. (1983). Sharpening our professional focus. *Journal of Physical Education, Recreation, and Dance,* **54**(9), 13-15.

What the next 50 years will bring. (1983, May 9). *U.S. News & World Report,* pp. A1-A42.

Wilbur, C.S. (1982). *Live for life: An epidemiological evaluation of a comprehensive health promotion program.* New Brunswick, NJ: Johnson & Johnson.

Willard, T., & Lawler, A. (1985). Megachoices: Options for tomorrow's world. *The Futurist,* **19**, 13-16.

Wolf, M.D. (1985). Injuries can cripple your fitness center. *Athletic Business,* **9**(9), 26, 28-30, 32, 34, 36.

Wong, P.T.P., Kettlewell, G., & Sproule, C.F. (1985). On the importance of being masculine: Sex role, attribution, and women's career achievement. *Sex Roles,* **12**, 757-767.

World Trends and Forecasts: Education (1984). Skill shortages threaten technological prowess. *The Futurist,* **18**(1), 79-80.

Wyatt Co. (1985, April). The darker side of wellness. *Training,* pp. 25-33.

Yeakey, C.C., & Johnston, G.S. (1985). High school reform: A critique and broader construct of social reality. *Education and Urban Society,* **17**(2), 157-170.

Zanger, B.K., & Parks, J.B. (Eds.) (1984). *Sport management curricula.* Bowling Green, OH: School of HPER, Bowling Green State University.

Zauzmer, D. (1985). Real opportunities for employee education. *Corporate Fitness & Recreation,* **4**(1), 30-34.

Zentner, R.D. (1984). Forecasting public issues. *The Futurist,* **18**(3), 25-29.

Author Index